Tree: Essence, and Teach

Simon & Sue Lilly

CAPALL BANN PUBLISHING

Tree: Essence, Spirit and Teacher

©1999 Simon & Sue Lilly

ISBN 186163 084 0

ALL RIGHTS RESERVED

Cover design by Paul Mason
Internal illustrations by Simon Lilly

Published by:

Capall Bann Publishing ng
Julia & Jon Day
Auton Farm, Milverton
Somerset, TA4 1NE
Tel 01823 401528
Fax 01823 401529
www.capallbann.co.uk

For Becky, Paul and Robyn

By the same authors, also from Capall Bann:

Crystal Doorways
Tree: Essence of Healing

Contents

Introduction   3
Tree Essences - Magic Mirrors   **9**
  The Memory of Water   19
  Flower Energy   19
  Making an Essence   22
  Using Essences   28
  How to Use Essences   29
  Meridian Massage   32
  Aura Sweep   34
  Essence Inhalation   35
  Bathing.   35
  Spraying Essences   35
  Alternate Methods of Making Essences   36
Trees of Possibilities   **41**
  The Bare Bones   41
  Presence   42
  The Hidden Presence and the Possibilities of
                                    Communication   45
  Iceberg   47
  Signature   47
  Dual Nature   47
  The Mirror Body   49
  The Landscape's Wheel   51
  Tree Cell   52
  Tree Drums   52
  Holding Vessels   53
  Time Machine   53
  Energy Generator   54
  The Elemental Tree   55
  Plant and Animal as a Planetary Symbiosis   55
  Priorities   56
  The Tastes of Light   57
  Towards Meditative States   57
  Alchemy   58
  Balance   59
  Doctrine of Signatures   59

Vessels for Deity 59
Fountain Head 59
The Tree Devas Speak 61
Spirits, Devas, Fairies or What? **63**
The Shamanic View 69
The Folk, "Pagan" View 74
The Fairy Tradition 77
The Magical View 79
The Theosophical View 82
The Celt, the Shaman and the Tree **87**
Mother of Wild Animals 88
Celts and Trees 93
The Sacred Grove 94
The Devon Grove 94
Wise Trees 97
Son of Tree 97
Tree Alphabets and Tree Calendars 98
The Forest Shaman 113
Meeting the Spirits - Methods of Communication -
The Sense Fields 119
Feeling the "Feelings" 127
Exploring the Sense Fields 128
Memory of Trees 128
Awareness of Environment 129
Identification of Trees 131
Drawing into a Tree 132
Sounding out the Trees 135
Listening as a Texture of Sound Becomes Music 139
The Sense of Touch 140
Holding Woods 143
Working With Wood 144
Wooden Bowls 145
The Senses of Taste and Smell 145
Tree Incense 146
Meeting the Spirits - Listening to Silence **149**
Basic Tree Roots Meditation 150
The Tree and Grove of Trees - Visualisation for Groups 151
Tree: Roots and Branches 154
Tree At The Earth's Core 155

Tree Roots and a Secret Chamber 156
The Fountain Tree 157
Complete Rootedness 159
The Mind 160
Quietening the Mind 162
Ground State 162
Stress and the River 165
Noisy Food 165
Silent Sitting 166
Meeting the Spirits - Shamanic Techniques **169**
Intention 173
Offering of Energy 175
Tree Dance 179
Wildfolk Dance 179
Calling the Spirits 180
Visual Doorways 183
The Doorway 183
Lower World and Upper World Doorways 185
The Underworld Visualisation 187
The Inner Guide Meditation 188
Tree Teacher Techniques **190**
Essence 191
Mantra 193
Chant 199
Sound Sequence 201
Colour Sequence 203
Trance Positions 205
Crystal Nets 208
Visual Pattern 209
Unlocking the Codes 209
Analysis of Bay 211
Analysis of Ivy 212
Analysis of Elm 214
Attunements **217**
Alder 217
Apple 218
Ash 219
Bay 220
Beech 221

Crack Willow	222
Elder	223
English Elm	224
Gean (Wild Cherry)	225
Giant Redwood	226
Great Sallow	227
Hawthorn	228
Hazel	229
Holly	230
Horse Chestnut	231
Ivy	232
Lawson Cypress	233
Lime	234
Magnolia	235
Monkey Puzzle Tree	236
Monterey Pine	237
Mulberry	238
Oak	239
Persian Ironwood	240
Plane Tree	241
Plum	242
Red Chestnut	243
Rowan	244
Sequoia (Coastal Redwood)	245
Scots Pine	246
Silver Birch	247
Silver Maple	248
Stags Horn Sumach	249
Sycamore	250
Tree Lichen	251
Tulip Tree	252
Weeping Willow	253
Whitebeam	254
White Poplar	255
Yew	256
Yew - The Root of Power	**257**
Nothing Living So Old	261
Know Thyself - Yew and You	264
Timeless Time	265

Red Tree of Death and Life	267
The Yew Initiation	272
Song of the Yew Teacher	274
The Elm - Silence Reaching to the Sky	**277**
The Ghost In the Hedgerow	277
Changes of State	278
The New Awareness	279
Uxlemitanos	281
The Elm Initiation	285
Key Qualities	286
Taking the Path of Water	287
Spinning Bowl	289
Seed Heart	289
Breathing in Light	290
The Ivy Doorway	295
Oak - Door of the Year	**309**
The Stability of Oaks	309
Thunderbolt of the Sky God	312
Rune of Day	313
Doorway	315
The Essence	316
Sutra	317
Timeless Return	319
Oak Initiation	320
Talking With Dragons	321
Dragon Dance, Dragon Trance	324
Meeting Dragons - A Guided Journey	325
Holly - Fire of Compassion	**329**
The New Sun, the Holly, the Crown	331
Green Holly Knight and Winter Initiation	333
Holly and the Goddess	337
Essence of Holly	339
The Holly Initiation	339
Lord of the Forest	342
Hazel - Tree of Knowing	**345**
Connla's Well	347
Finn	347
Hazel for Wisdom	351
The Nuts Drop, Plop!	351

Bouncing Awareness   356
Roots of Knowing   357
Among the Giants   **361**
Balancing the Elements   362
Tides of Time   363
Recognition   363
One world   363
Learning to Learn   365
To the Heart   365
Reading Guide   **368**

Dedication

From the still hub,
the silent centre
where fire and water,
earth, air and ether
are held in equipoise;

From the radiance of life
we call "tree",
I ask for the wisdom of speech
I ask for the wisdom of listening
I ask for the wisdom of understanding.

May the spirits who dwell
within the form,
May the spirits who flow
through the form,
May the spirits who dwell
behind and beyond the form
of the radiance of life

we call "tree"

feed us

sustain us
and walk with us
until we have learnt
to feed,
sustain and walk

by ourselves -
and then
may we play
together forever
in the vast joy
of this planet-mother,
Earth.

Introduction

The ideas and experiences within this book have arisen from the work I and my wife, Sue, have carried out over the last five years since the idea popped into my head to set about collecting vibrational essences made from British tree flowers, which we called "Green Man Tree Essences".

The concept of flower remedies was rediscovered in the West earlier this century by Dr. Edward Bach who, over a period of years, isolated thirty-eight flowers whose vibrational, energetic presence alone would help to ameliorate negative emotional states that underlie the majority of all disease patterns. Many people found the Bach Flower Remedies to be helpful in speeding the healing processes of the body, and from the mid Seventies onwards other investigators developed their own collections of flower essences, so that now at the end of the 1990's there are flower essences available from every continent and from every habitat imaginable.

Sue and I began making our own flower essences when we moved into the Devon countryside. There was no pattern or scheme - we just collected essences from those plants that other's research had indicated would be useful in the healing work we were occupied in, or that simply caught our eye in the hedgerow or garden. The process of making flower essences, (explained later in the text), is very simple but quite habit-forming. It is easy to get carried away - so many flowers, so many essences, so few sunny days. In the end it all boils down to SO many bottles! The piecemeal approach was a little frustrating and I was looking for a finite, coherent group of essences to work with. The local Devon hedgerow plants would constitute a huge range of new essences not prepared or analysed before. And then the lightbulb idea was popped into my head. A chance remark at the end of a lecture: "Oh,

I'd love to try hazel!" and the seed for Green Man Tree Essences was planted.

Fiona Parr, the friend who plopped in the seed, had lived for many years in the Findhorn Community, Scotland. It was there that the most well-known collaboration between Man and nature spirits occurred. So maybe it was not such a coincidence after all.

Initially we were looking at native British trees of which there are about thirty-five. This soon grew to include some naturalised and other introduced species. We reasoned that, although Edward Bach had included a smattering of trees in his selection, there should be a huge potential for exploration in the much wider range of British trees - after all, if holly and oak were found to be powerful healers then why not ash, hawthorn, hazel, alder?

A few months earlier I had read William Anderson's and Clive Hicks' book *"Green Man: The archetype of our oneness with the Earth"*, an excellent survey of this famous motif and its meaning, which coincidentally focuses quite considerably on the Green Men in Exeter Cathedral, not a spit and a tumble from where we live.

We took the Green Man as our name and logo because, as we said in our literature, "As the image of the Green Man is an interweaving of human features with leaves and tendrils, so is the interaction and interdependence of humankind with the plant kingdom. One cannot be separated from the other". Green Man Tree Essences were seen by us as a reaffirmation of the link between Man and Nature, acknowledging the healing power of life and the ancient wisdom of the peaceful trees.

Right from the beginning there was a two-fold approach to this work. The outer, exoteric side (though crazy enough to most people), was the making of essences, testing them for how they interacted with human energy systems to improve healing situations, and using them as adjuncts to other therapeutic practices. This work was given a boost when the essences were noticed by several Health Kinesiologists, notably Jane Thurnell-Read from Penzance, who found them useful in their own work. This gave us more confidence, having other experienced professionals confirming our own experiences and adding to them.

The inner, more esoteric, side of the work with Green Man is more or less described hereafter. It is not possible to easily separate healing from spiritual growth - you can't have one without the other - but in terms of practicality on everyday levels, most healers who use the essences treat them as subtle medicines, therapeutic energy substances. The content isn't so important as the positive healing effect. Only those who are travelling on a more shamanic path (whether they call it that or not), are more interested in the distinct energy-beings or spirits or consciousness behind the physical presence of the essence. In this respect, they are dealing more with Beings rather than Things and so the attitude is different.

In practice this means that we have worked with two almost completely separate groups of people. Those whose primary interest is healing and those whose primary interest is working with tree spirits. The two do intersect- particularly with kinesiologists who tend to work on the very verge of spookiness in the degree of subtlety achieved in their healing corrections. On the whole these days most complementary therapists are trying hard to gain wider recognition and acceptance of their skills, and talking to tree spirits (at least out loud!), would probably only confirm what the White Coats suspected all along!

The seed of this book, the core idea, the underlying concept running throughout, can be put succinctly thus:

5

Trees are the creators and maintainers of our reality.

From this seed idea unfurl two leaves, each of equal importance, each of which requires the other for healthy growth. The first leaf is the understanding of the fundamental, vital, life-sustaining necessity of the presence of many mature trees for the physical maintenance and well-being of the planet as a biological, ecological whole. This aspect, based on objective observation, scientifically validated, is difficult to ignore.

The second leaf is the understanding of the tree from a subjective, metaphysical and spiritual perspective - reaching beyond the physical presence to the spirit or awareness-beings connected to or related to the tree. This approach is one that tends to run counter to the Urban Western worldview of the nature of reality, even though throughout history the tree appears as one of the most widespread symbols for spiritual integration and transcendence.

These two leaves, the objective and subjective cannot of course be totally separated. They arise from the same seed -if we look at one aspect, reflections of the other will appear. For example, the biological functions of the tree can be seen in a metaphysical light, interpreted and given a meaning that few biologists would feel happy with.

What defines us as unique beings is human emotion. It is what we are best at. The poet, the storyteller and the magician are closer to our true natures than the quantity surveyor and the scientist. If you don't believe me: find a scientist and suggest the reality of a series of notions that run counter to his own dearly-held beliefs. More than likely he will react as though you have just shot his dog. Scratch a scientist and there is a raving, irrational, normal human being underneath.

6

We react to our environment. We like or dislike apparently on a whim, with equal vehemence, and given the chance, with equal rationalisation for our choice. Not only do we react continually and without surcease, but we also follow up and play with a certain category of thought we call "ideas". Not all thoughts are ideas. Most thought is as self-aware as a sheep bleating in a field - it does it to make sure it's still a sheep bleating in a field. Ideas are those cartoon lightbulb thoughts - the one's like the streaker on the cricket pitch - dashing through the mundane rumble of normal life bringing a momentary halt to the familiar, and presenting us with choice to see differently.

Ideas are not moral things - they have no code of ethics. They are not labelled right or wrong, sensible or idiotic, real or fanciful. Ideas come up because we are emotional beings and we react to our surroundings. Ideas are a response to our human curiosity. They are a sign that we are still functioning, still reacting, still feeling, still living. Ideas are the seeds of growth - the first step to develop trees of possibilities. And without possibilities we run out of choices. The situation could then arise where it seemed as though nothing could be changed because that is the way things were. This way leads to extinction.

One could argue that there have been some pretty lousy ideas in human history, but it's no use blaming the idea itself - a weed is just a seed that's grown in a place you didn't want it to. Counter to many gardeners' suspicions, weeds are not malicious. They don't grow in our flowerbeds to spite us - they are just doing what comes naturally: given the right soil they will flourish. The same is true of ideas. An idea can remain dormant for many years, centuries even, until the right conditions occur and then you find everyone is having the same idea and that idea becomes a belief, a certainty, a dogma, an institution. Or, the idea will be dismissed or suppressed as completely fanciful and wrongheaded, forgotten by all except perhaps by a few reactionaries on the fringes of consensus until one day....

This is a book of ideas. You may agree with some and you may disagree with others. The most significant ideas are the ones that you disagree with. If you can work out why you react so strongly to a certain possibility, you give yourself the opportunity to understand what goes to make up your view of reality. Whatever your reaction it is always more constructive NOT to react like a child who refuses to eat something new simply because they have never had it before and so are determined they won't like it. Enjoy the meal!

Tree Essences - Magic Mirrors

In the autumn of 1997 Sue and I were invited to the International Flower Essence Conference at Findhorn in Scotland where we were able to present some of the aspects of this work with tree essences and tree spirits. It was a good experience to meet other people making and using essences. After our return, however, I realised that no-one seems to have addressed some of the most fundamental questions regarding essences, perhaps because they do not have answers at the moment. The most basic of questions: putting aside the definitions, the stock phrases, the jargon. What is it that we believe enters into the water? What is the nature of the essence? What is the "energy"? What is the "vibration"? What turns it into "energy medicine"?

No longer are essences simply being made from flowers as they used to be. Now essences are being made of special environments, of seasonal events like solstices, of sea animals, of shells. The thought arises: if I lie in a pool of spring water in sunlight for a couple of hours is that water now imbued with "essence of me"? Does it have my energetic imprint? Is it a vibrational healing tool? And if not, why not?

The problem with flower and other essences is that their makers are looking at them as a subtle tool for alternative or complementary health, as "things to make us better", and because of this a terminology has developed that is intended to validate essences in this light.

Is there any difference between "essence", "spirit", "soul", "vibratory energy pattern", "signature"? Or are we using different words to explain the same phenomenon? Is a "spirit"

9

The wonderfully profound gaze of the Green Man foliate head in Bamberg (c. 1240) on which we based the logo for Green Man Tree Essences.

a localised semi-permanent folding of the universal field? An energy signature? Is the "spirit" in the essence or is the essence like a footprint, fingerprint or key to the spirit?

Some essence makers shared their experiences of making an essence, describing seeing lines of light, force or energy being carried from the plant to the water via the cut flowers. Others experienced the vortex of energies spiralling down into the bowl or flowing into the water as if with conscious intent.

What we are talking about here is not science as it is known today. What most essence makers and essence practitioners are doing is magic, pure and simple. Now magic is a set of processes that couldn't get more scientific if it tried but what we are dealing with here is not the actuality but the perception. From an orthodox scientific point of view all this is easily categorised as psychism, self-delusion, non-validated, non-verifiable wishful thinking. No matter how essence users agree to the terminologies of resonance, vibration, chakras, subtle bodies, electromagnetic fields and other models and paradigms, to consensus reality they are all stark staring nuts. Until, that is, someone directly experiences and benefits from the very real, potent life-changing effects that using flower essences can bring about. From a stance of cynical disbelief, the newly converted begins to learn the lingo, the jargon of rationalisation, and refers to energy patterns, learns about the chakras, the meridians and so on. All to put into a consensus context an experience beyond understanding.

We do not know what essences really are. We do not know how they work - in terms of acceptable scientific understanding. Falling outside of science, they remain magical.

There is perhaps nothing so subversive as flower essences. Easy to make by anyone. Undetectable by present technologies. Able to bring about significant healing and development for little cost, using few resources, with no adverse side

From 19th century engravings of roof bosses at York Minster. Each carving shows the intuitively realised harmony between plant growth and the movement and forms of water.

effects. Hospital trials are showing promising signs of effectiveness notably within Third World health situations. Learn how to make and use essences yourself before the paranoid pharmaceutical giants begin to take notice and influence governments to legislate, regulate and control this out of existence.

Essence is defined by the *Oxford English Dictionary* as follows:

1. Being viewed as a fact or as a property of something.
2. Something that is; an entity. Now only as a spiritual entity.
3. Specific being "what a thing is"; nature, character.
4. Substance: the substratum of phenomena; absolute being.
5. That by which anything subsists.
6. Essentiality.
7. That which constitutes the being of a thing, either a) as a conceptual, or b) as a real, entity; that by which it is what it is.
8. The specific difference of anything.
9. An extract obtained by distillation or otherwise from a plant or drug, and containing its specific properties in a reduced form. In pharmacy, an alcoholic solution of the volatile elements or essential oil.
10. A perfume, a scent.

In our work with trees and tree spirits we have found the use of tree essences invaluable. They are, for us, one of the primary keys to open awareness to the Tree Kingdoms. Through an essence we can instantly access the energy signature, the feel, the presence and the awareness-being of a particular type of tree. The whole environment can be imbued with this energy and we can immerse ourselves within it.

With the physical presence of a tree - no matter how sentient or how powerful, it is difficult for many of us to quickly go beyond the constant awareness of "selfness" that immediately creates a subject-object relationship. This can then create a divide between ourselves and the spirit worlds. We are used to our physical existence, the presence of our bodies and of being "inside" them. We are always looking out, and so we are separated from the world. What is "out there" is the realm of our five senses and if we begin to perceive or understand something not through our sense organs it is very easy to doubt the experience. It can very easily become "only our imagination".

Using tree essences we can help to remove this perceptual and intellectual barrier. Not only can we "step into" the energy of a tree, for instance when the essence is sprayed around a room, but the tree energy can directly enter into us if a few drops are taken by mouth, or rubbed onto pulse points. In other words, using the tree essence helps to amplify the experience of the characteristic feel of a tree. Not only do we perceive with our external senses the quality of a physical tree, but we activate all our internal senses as well-those feelings and body wisdom mechanisms that in everyday, externalised life we tend to ignore.

There seems to be no clear evidence from the past of the use of flower essences as we know them today, though there are similar, subtle techniques described in a wider cultural context. The most apparent seems to be the collection of morning dew, off flowers and leaves, recorded in medieval European magical traditions. Paracelsus in the 16th century is reputed to have done so to heal emotional imbalances in his patients. As he was the primary synthesiser of Classical and native (pagan) healing and spiritual techniques, it is reasonable to assume that he was borrowing from established sources. When Dr. Edward Bach first began his experiments with flower energies in the 1920's he seems to have combined

the magical dew-collecting of Paracelsus with the theoretical background of homeopathy. With direct personal intuitive insights he began by roaming the countryside at dawn collecting and drinking the dew off certain plants. For practical reasons he developed other collecting and preparation techniques that are still in use today.

Among the native peoples of the world, flowers and plants are the primary source of healing and spiritual energies. As the power of the plant comes from its spirit, many cultures will include preparations from the required plants by making broths, baths, bundles, oils, tinctures and so on, to be administered externally or internally. The chemical properties of the plant may or may not be employed in a conscious manner - the spirit is all-important. We shall see that in modern flower essence usage, subtracting all the jargon and pseudo-scientific terminology, it also comes back to the same thing: the intangible, indefinable, unmeasurable spirit of the plant. So what is a flower essence?

A flower essence is an energy signature of a plant held in water, usually preserved in brandy or another alcohol. Orthodox testing would reveal nothing other than water and brandy - there is no physical presence of the plant at all, and in this flower essences differ from that other more well-known energy medicine: homeopathy, in which at lower potencies there can still be found minute amounts of original material.

Just about the only tangible evidence of some subtle change in state can be revealed by taking a Kirlian photograph of an essence droplet and comparing them to other essences and simple water or alcohol. The energy discharge from an essence is immediately recognisable by its dynamism and corona. The most sensitive apparatus available to us is our own body, and it is on this that the essences can have immediate and profound results.

The Memory of Water

In attempting to refute the efficacy of homeopathic medical practices a French scientist, Jacques Benveniste, not only found that homeopathic principles are sound but that the primary mechanism for their function is in the nature of water itself. The bonding between hydrogen and oxygen atoms is remarkably flexible and the angles can vary more than with any other known substance. The theory goes that by this means water carries a "memory" of what it has been in contact with, carried in the atomic structure itself. This is sufficient to transfer the energy patterns to other systems like the human being, and by some resonant process alter the energy configurations by a completely non-physical means. For his startling, exact and paradigm-shifting work, Benveniste was of course immediately vilified and unceremoniously thrown out of the orthodox consensus scientific community. There is nothing scientists dislike more than a smart-ass who comes up with a new idea to upset the neat hypotheses of The Real World.

Until the last few years, when new techniques have been tried out, flower essences were largely made by the sun-water method. Flowers were collected and floated in a plain bowl of spring water for several hours in bright sunlight. The resulting charged water was then bottled with alcohol as a preservative. Nothing much could be simpler! This seems to be sufficient in nearly every case to infuse the water with some quality from the plant. The full procedure will be examined shortly, but first of all: why flowers?

Flower Energy

If it is the signature of the entire plant that becomes integrated into the structure of the water, then why are the flowers the parts so often used? It is true that nowadays essences are being made from all parts of plants from root to seed and all are effective. It may be that there are slightly

different emphases to an essence made from a root, a leaf, a seed. In general, it is the flower that is most commonly used to make an essence. If we think of our appreciation-where our attention travels to-whole businesses are built on this attraction to the shape, colour and smell of flowers. Of all the parts of a plant, the flower is the most specifically created to interact with its environment. The flower is the communication vehicle of a plant. It is there to be noticed, to be smelled, to be crawled into, to be sucked, to be pollinated by something of another realm-be that insect, bird, animal or the wind and rain. The peculiar structure of each flower acknowledges the many mechanisms of the outer world, the "not-I". It is this interaction with the "not-I" upon which the continuation of the plant and its species ultimately depends. This outwards expression of the life-force of the plants is thus perceived by us as being the powerful culmination of growth, of manifestation, of individuality, of self-awareness. Our emotions are almost automatically and immediately affected by the colour, smell and shape of a flower in a way that a leaf or stem fails to achieve. The immediate appreciation of a flower that we as humans feel, the aesthetic of the sense perceptions, shows us a biological reality. Flowers are biologically important for our survival.

The flower is like a psychic head, eye, voice and message drawing our attention and holding us in focused but free-floating contemplation. With such a deep-felt contact, carefully picking a few flower heads, placing them on water and treating them as reverential offerings from another Kingdom-the message and the messenger-is a natural ritual interaction.

From another perspective the flower is the most ephemeral expression of the energy of the whole plant and its removal will not, in most cases, permanently damage the plant.

Making an Essence

If you want to make an essence, begin by using the most straightforward sun and water method. Once familiar with this you will be more confident to modify and try other approaches.

Get a plain glass bowl that, if possible, is free of all patterns, names and numbers. Each of these will carry another vibration so it is best to avoid confusing your essence. Some better class of glassware has removable labels and inexpensive dessert bowls are often free from stamping. If you are thinking of making a few essences, you may want to have bowls of different sizes. This is because it is thought best to cover the whole surface of the water with flowers and, while some flowers are quite large, others including a lot of tree flowers, are very small.

You will need to fill this bowl with as pure a water as possible. Spring water is the best, direct from the source if possible, or else use a good quality bottled water. It is not really possible to avoid pollutants these days, even ground water may have high levels of chemical fertiliser.

It is best to make essences only of those plants that attract your attention, that draw you in some way to them. These are plants to which you have some significant link at that time so you will automatically be more in tune with their energy patterns.

Spend some time familiarising yourself with the tree or plant. This doesn't necessarily mean sitting for hours boring the spirits with doe-eyed mood-making, unless you like that sort of thing. It is best to have some heart connection with the plant's presence, but it is very unlikely that you will have no empathy or you would have no interest in this sort of thing in the first place.

If the essence is to be of a tree flower and you know the attunement techniques, you can use some to create an even flow of energy between you.

When you feel comfortable with the plant's presence (this may be almost immediate or can be a slow growth of appreciative awareness over a week or two), it is a good idea to verbally or mentally explain what you are going to do and for what reasons. Also ask permission to take flowers from the plant. The emotional intent of harmlessness and sensitivity are very obvious to plant awareness so coherent framing of thought is more important for your own clarity of purpose than to the plant. Clarity of thought may also help you to focus your emotional/feeling stance.

When you ask for permission it is important to quieten your mind and listen or feel for a response. This you might perceive as an inner voice or as a change of emotional pressure, either relaxing or tensing. If you feel resistance in some way, ask again and if the feeling remains the same move to another plant or try again some other time. If communication is good you might try ask what is the reason for the refusal. Sometimes it can be just a simple question of etiquette, or you may need to perform some small ritual act to get into a more appropriate state of mind. If it is the tree itself that is unwilling to participate, finding out why can sometimes allow you to help by offering healing. A genuine offering of assistance is never wasted-even though you might have to modulate your thought patterns to elicit a useful response. Some tree spirits can be very tetchy if they have suffered in the past from lack of care or are unwell.

When you have felt the positive response to your request for a few flowers, you can go about carefully collecting them. If possible it is a good idea to collect flowers from different parts of the tree or from different nearby trees. What you are able to reach will somewhat limit this choice as not all trees put out flowers near to the ground. Looking out for trees growing on slopes has become an automatic pastime, where more of the mature branches can be reached. How you pick the flowers is up to you and you will need to experiment with different methods until you find one that is comfortable for you. I find that different trees require different techniques simply because of the physical diversity of flowers. Some are easy to pinch off without crushing them using a pair of silver sugar tongs, others need more dextrous fingers and sharp nails to gather. Many tree flowers are very small and you will need a degree of focused patience and a relatively small bowl.

As you collect the flowers place them carefully on the surface of the water. When there are enough to cover the surface leave the bowl in full sun close to the plant. Sometimes it will not be possible to leave the bowl, so if this is the case just place the bowl on some kind of natural surface, such as wood or stone (try to avoid the strong unnatural vibration of metal, plastic or concrete).

Take care where you place the bowl. What starts off in full sun, may in a short time be in deep shade and this will lengthen the energising process. Also, if you are leaving the bowl for any length of time be aware of the possibility that it will be found by domestic animals-thirsty dogs and curious cats can demolish a days work in a flash so place the bowl high enough off the ground.

The length of time it takes to energise the water is very variable. Different essence-makers use many different rules and regulations, but what is laid down in one book may not be the most useful technique for you to use. So much depends on the conditions when the essence is being made. Classically, the optimal time for essence-making is in the early morning in spring or summer time on a cloudless, sunny day. In these conditions two or three hours is often cited as being sufficient to potentise the water. Since many books on essences are written by Americans who live on the West Coast of the USA, adverse weather conditions are rarely considered. Compared to the British Isles, southern California has no weather: when the sun is not shining, it is night-time.

Clouds, six different climates in an hour, and startlingly short flowering periods coinciding with weeks of continuous rain-this is the norm for the British essence maker. It has the tendency to create jumpy, nervous individuals who continually glance from bud to sky to bud again, but it also creates flexibility, opportunism and new ways of working. The only rule you need in essence making is: do what is appropriate at the time, according to your insight. So in conditions that are less than ideal, when there is cloud cover, or if you expect sunshine and showers between thunderstorms, allow longer exposure of the essence to sunlight. In really dull conditions you might consider putting the bowl on a mirror surface to reflect the light. On rainy days cover the bowl with a sheet of glass or a larger bowl to prevent swamping with rain water. Use your imagination and experiment. If you have been inspired to make an essence at a certain time make it then. It will be the most powerful for you whatever the conditions.

It is important whenever possible to use flowers that are in full bloom and undamaged. This very often means carefully watching your chosen tree for the best time to prepare the essence. You will find that trees of the same species will flower at different times depending on their age and where they are situated. If you find your tree has already passed its peak and is dropping petals, look around for another tree that has slightly later flowering. Remember that different parts of the same tree will often be ahead or behind the rest in its growth cycle depending whether it is in sun or shade.

If you don't have a testing skill like dowsing or muscle-testing you will have to rely more on the rules, or else quieten yourself and ask your deep mind or intuition to let you know when the essence "feels" ready to bottle.

Essences made at any time of year except very early in spring or late autumn will tend to accumulate at least a few insects, as well as wind-blown sticks and leaves. These will have to be lifted out of the water together with the flowers. What you do with these flowers is up to you, but it is important to treat them with care and consideration. They can be dried to use as a basis for incense, offerings, herb bundles; placed in another decorative bowl as an indoor display until they fade; placed back under the trees you have gathered from; put on the soil or in compost to continue the cycle of life. Whatever you do, do it with awareness and thanks. Some authors suggest a twig or leaf of the plant is used to lift the flowers off the water. Try it and see: sometimes it works, sometimes it is worse than those annoying Christmas toys with ball bearings that have to be jiggled into place simultaneously. Avoid frustration if at all possible. It is a strong projecting emotion and can interfere with the quality of your essence. A small silver spoon or silver sugar tongs are quite versatile and silver is a fairly benign, neutral metal to use.

Once the flowers and larger bugs are removed it is a good idea to filter out smaller particles of flower, pollen and creepy-crawlies. Using another clean glass vessel strain the water through a fine cheesecloth, linen or filter paper. This will help to prevent any fungal or bacterial growth in the essence bottle.

Most essence makers use a spirit like brandy or vodka for a preservative. If alcohol is a problem, a vinegar will preserve equally effectively, though the smell and taste tends to linger long after the alcohol would have evaporated. Fill the storage bottle at least half-full with the preservative and then top up with the potentised water. Give the mix a good shake to help the stabilisation of the energies. This is the mother essence.

Clearly label and date it. Most essence makers will keep the mother essence as the primary source and will use the dilution commonly called the stock bottle. Stock is made by taking a few drops, usually between three and seven, from the mother essence and putting them in another bottle containing at least fifty percent brandy and topped up with water.

Whether you use the mother essence or the stock essence (or even the next dilution down-the "dosage" level where drops are taken from the "stock" and placed in another bottle of water/brandy), will depend on how much essence was originally made and how frequently it is going to be used.

Each essence maker seems to have their own ideas concerning the efficacy of the different levels of dilution. I suspect most are adhering to a set of personal belief-systems with which they feel comfortable (and therefore effective in their own experience), rather than there being one ineffable law of nature entitled: "Essences and the Uses Thereof." We return to the original perplexity. What is it that comprises an essence? If it is essentially a physical process then it should be able to be measured in some way. If it is not a physical process then the rules of mass, weight, proportion, location in time and space, and other means of measuring the "amount" of essence present in any one bottle cannot apply. If this is so, then how can one "dilute" a vibration (with no mass etc.)? It is either there or not there . It is difficult to conceive of an energy pattern that is "not-there-very-much".

Being human, however, measurement, the process and the recipe - all the ritual of creating and passing on information and knowledge-is very important to most of us. Following instructions means that we know when we are "right" and when we have done it "wrong". Doing the same thing as someone else who has got a good result makes us happier to encourage a similar outcome, and so it will tend to happen that way. "Take three drops, four times a day and you will get better" is what the majority of us want to hear. We don't want to be reminded of self-responsibility and self-determination. Most of us haven't been trained to really understand what they mean. "Do as you're told" has been endlessly reinforced through the long years of schooling. "Do what you think is best" is only considered the precursor of avoiding or attributing blame.

Using Essences

So once we have an essence what can be done with it? How can it be used? Flower essences today are used almost exclusively in the area of healing and the various paradigms of flower essence therapy reflect and expand upon the original vision of Dr Bach. His selection of plant essences addressed what he considered to be the underlying negative emotional states that allowed disease to manifest in the physical body. By some means the energy pattern of each flower encouraged the negative state to transform to its more life-supporting and positive opposite. This view has been generally agreed and expanded upon by all recent essence makers. The specific and unique energy signature of each essence, when introduced in some way into the human auric field seems to enable positive change to come about more easily. An essence acts like a key that can unlock doors that have been shut or blocked. This is an important concept. Many believe that flower essences do not create change by themselves, but they do allow change to take place. This can be compared by analogy to a physical herbal or pharmaceutical preparation that, instead of unlocking the door leaving you free to open it or not, will carry out a full FBI raid with tanks, helicopters, hand-grenades, howitzers and CS gas blowing away anything that comes into their path be it door, wall, hostage-taker or hostage. In some situations such action is necessary, but in the main it can be avoided by carefully stimulating the body's own healing processes. This is the only thing that can heal us, and flower essences seem to be very good at doing this.

Flower essences do not work by belief or faith, nor "placebo effect", because essences work extremely well on animals, small children and plants. However, their actions can sometimes be blocked by negative attitudes or environment factors. Always when working with essences (for whatever reason, healing or otherwise), willing participation and a neutral curiosity are good attitudes to have. It is a good practice to use the essences in a conscious manner. Focus for a moment on the reason you are taking the essence, whether for healing or whatever. Give the bottle a brief shake before opening. This helps to activate and energise the properties. Visualise or otherwise acknowledge the plant's source, the spirit of the essence. Sit quietly for a moment or two as you absorb the vibrational energies into your system. Don't expect the essence to create mind-blowing altered states, instant healing, revelatory visions etc. every time you use it. All these can happen, occasionally. More often the essences will work at much more subtle levels, creating or allowing energy changes that may take weeks or months to become noticeable. This is particularly likely when you are in a state of considerable imbalance as with manifest physical illness.

Using a tree essence as a Tree Teacher Technique, the attention will already naturally be focused on a change of perception and will be looking out for subtle differences of feel. Using tree essences as a specific healing technique will be explored further in a later chapter.

How to Use Essences

The classic way of using flower essences is to take three or four drops, three times a day either placed under the tongue and held in the mouth for a little while, or placed in some water and sipped as necessary. No method is better than any other - as long as the essence comes in contact with the energy field, interaction will take place. Some people will find that certain ways of introducing the essences will work faster or more effectively for them, but it is very much down to personal predilection.

The advantage and disadvantage with the "taking by mouth" method is that it reinforces the comparison with taking medicine, with all the expectations and limitations that comes with such a view. Many people will not feel they have "done it properly" unless they stick to the old, familiar procedures. This is fine. The main disadvantage with the oral taking of essences is one of association rather than effect: it emphasises the "just-another-thing-to-make-me-better" syndrome, and this really is quite a negative, disempowering attitude, reinforcing as it does the idea that effective healing can only come from outside of oneself. It limits the use of flower essences to the role of spiritual aspirin where the name of the essence- the actual plant, gemstone or whatever-is regarded as little more than an identifying label. The stuff in the bottle becomes conceptually isolated from its real source, the plant energy, the living stuff. In this process there is the danger of becoming one-sided, of becoming a spiritual colonialist, simply taking over another part of the world and exploiting it in order to make ourselves "better" without considering reciprocity.

When taking essences by mouth was inadvisable in instances of unconsciousness or physical trauma, it was usually suggested that they could be applied topically to the forehead or to the wrist pulses. In fact this proves to be equally effective in most situations. The pulse points of the wrists and the neck and forehead, particularly the frontal eminences, (slight raised bumps on the outer edge of the forehead), are very sensitive to a change of energy and seem a natural place to rub a few drops of essence. You can even pretend it's a perfume or aftershave if you're in hostile territory.

Anywhere where there is a mirroring of the whole systems of the body in a small area is a good place to put the essence. Thus the soles of the feet, the palms of the hands, the ears will all tend to activate effectively.

If you are aware of your own strengths and weaknesses as far as the chakra system is concerned then putting a drop of essence on these points will act as a rapid enhancer and will diffuse through that system of interlinked energies. It can often be quite easy to determine our significant points: very often they are those areas that we use a lot and where we tend to get minor health problems. Where we focus our energies is where we can be vulnerable to disorders simply because depletion can more easily occur there. Thus a communicator may be prone to sore throats, thyroid imbalance or neck problems. Someone who works with the heart chakra will be very sensitive to other people's emotions and may have vague heart and lung aches from time to time. A strong solar plexus energy may be prone to food sensitivities, stomach aches and so on.

Because the seven main chakra points are in effect gateways or regulators of our energy systems, they are, in any case, important sites for essences. A drop of the right essence on the right chakra can create profound rebalancing that may otherwise take months to accomplish by other means.

The chakra system has the advantage of being fairly easy to comprehend in broad terms and easy to locate on the physical body. Some essence makers who are familiar with the meridian systems of the body have done some exciting work isolating specific meridian points as sites to apply essences for particular results. The meridian system is not easy to master quickly. Unless you have an in-depth knowledge or an accurate testing procedure that you can wholly rely on, plopping essences on acupoints may have an unsettling or even unbalancing effect on the system as a whole. However, if this method appeals to you, consider working with the end-points of each meridian (usually on the hands, feet and head), which will give a general activation to the whole of that meridian.

Meridian Massage

There is a relatively simple technique known as meridian massage that, once learned, is an excellent way to tone up the whole meridian system and if you rub a few drops of essence into your hands before you begin, will carry the essence effectively through the whole system. Meridian massage can be carried out on yourself and on others.

Working on another person: start by having them stand upright, legs shoulder-width apart and arms held palms inwards, slightly away from the body. Start with both of your hands in front of their heart in the centre of the chest. Carry out all movements in easy, flowing sweeps of your hands an inch or so away from the body. Move your hands up from the heart to the armpits and down the insides of the arms to the hands. Follow around the fingertips to the tops of the hands and then up the outside of the arms to the shoulders either side of the neck. Move up the sides of the neck and bring your hands together under the jaw so that they then travel together over the centre of the face, up towards the top of the head.

Carry this sweep on down the back of the head and right down the spine. Then follow down the outside of the legs to the feet, around the toes and then sweep up the midline back to the heart. If you follow this movement several times your hands and arms will have traced in a strengthening direction all the major meridian pathways. Complete the process by moving round to the side of the person and move your hands from a starting point at the base of the spine at the back and near the groin at the front, sweeping both hands simultaneously up the body. The hand at the front ends and lightly touches the point just below the lower lip, and the hand at the back runs over the top of the head and touches a point just above the upper lip. Repeat this "zipping up" sweep a couple of times. This helps to stabilise and secure the meridian energy.

This simple procedure by itself, even without any essence, can make a lot of difference to energy levels and feelings of well-being. Done consciously and with focus it can sometimes have a profound effect equal to any other "healing" session.

Meridian massage on yourself is the same process except you have to do it bit by bit. Start at the heart again. Take left hand from heart to front of the right shoulder down inside of the right arm to the palm and fingertips. Then repeat the movement on the left side with your right hand sweeping from heart to fingertips along the inside of the arm (hold your hand palm upwards to expose the correct bits of the arm). Return to sweeping with your left hand and now begin where you stopped before at your right fingertips, this time sweeping up the knuckles, wrist and top/outside of the arm around the shoulder and back over the chest to the heart. Repeat this on the other side of the body.

Next take both hands to the heart and sweep up your midline up the face, over the top of the head and as far down your neck or back as you can reach. Taking your hands round to your back the other way (ie. reaching back under your arms), continue to sweep down the rest of the back down the backs of your legs, around the outside edges of your feet and toes to the inside of your feet and legs moving upwards until your hands meet again at the groin, where they continue on together up the front of the body to stop at the heart. This is one circuit. You can repeat it as many times as you like, always remembering to "zip up" front and back midlines at the end of the process. Believe me, it is easier to do than to describe! Once the sequence is worked out it is well worth doing as a routine energy balance or when you are feeling disorientated or unusually strange.

The more you get used to having balanced energy the easier it is to notice when you drift out of balance, and the more awareness there is of situations that are life-enhancing and those that are potentially life-damaging.

Meridian massage with a few drops of tree essence on the palms not only restores the balance in a general way to the energy systems but helps to align to the specific energy signature of the essence. Its ritual nature, once memorised, can become a significant element of moving into balanced, altered states. Whilst it defines the physical boundaries of the body, it also resembles the donning of magical clothes, the preparation to begin moving "beyond".

Aura Sweep

A similar, less structured approach can also be used to introduce the tree essence into the energy field. Called the aura sweep, this is simply rubbing the essence into the palms of the hands and then sweeping the hands around the body through the auric field. The movements can take whatever form is comfortable, but it is a good idea to surround the head, heart and solar plexus as well as paying attention to the arms, legs and soles of the feet. Visualising the essence surrounding the body completely helps to avoid the conceptual "gaps" in the sweep. As the subtle body energies are in a dynamic flow and interaction at all times the essence signature will soon diffuse throughout the auric field. As a final part of this technique, or as an absorption method by itself, bring both the hands, cupped, to the face and breathe deeply-as if you were smelling or inhaling a wonderful scent. Despite there being no scent present this seems to help to bring the essence "inside".

Essence Inhalation

Taste and smell are the most primal of the senses, those closest to identification of physical, molecular matter and so the act of conscious inhalation is psychologically similar to eating. Smelling and tasting the precursors to ingestion. It is the identification process that allows us to recognise a thing as food or not-food. In some instinctive way inhaling an essence seems more of a commitment than putting a few drops in the mouth - we are taking the energy signature deep inside ourselves where we draw our life from the outside air. With our mouths we can spit out what we dislike, once we inhale deeply we are committed to absorbing the energy carried in the air. The act of raising our cupped hands and breathing deeply is more removed from everyday actions and so more easily slips into a ritual framework. Try it and see how you feel.

Bathing

Even more surreptitious or casual is placing a few drops of essence in bathwater. This will work more effectively if you lay off the bubble-bath, soap, essential oils and rubber ducks and treat it as simply immersion in the essence vibration. Just soak and absorb the essence for a few moments before you start washing. Or better still, (though some might find this excessive), have a bath and wash first and then have a second bath with freshly drawn water to which the essence can be added.

Spraying Essences

Finally, the method we use most often in workshop and lecture situations and which we find works very quickly and effectively in all sorts of environments: spraying the essence using a diffuser sprayer. Large sprayers can be found in garden suppliers, smaller sprays can often be found in cosmetic or bathing sections of chemist shops.

Simply put enough water in the sprayer for your needs and add a couple of drops of the tree essence. Then, remembering to adjust the nozzle to fine mist, spray the essence into the room or around yourself. Because it is such a broad, quick procedure the change in energy feel is usually very noticeable. There will, of course, be a cooling, freshening effect of the atomised droplets, but this cannot account for the rapid change of emotional mood or sense of space when different essences are sprayed around. This process can be likened to stepping into a grove of trees - one is immediately surrounded and immersed in the qualities of that tree. It feels more of an external reality, the air takes on the tangibility of a different environment, and so it often becomes easier for people to recognise and accept a change of internal perceptions and emotions.

Alternate Methods of Making Essences

It is well worth making a few tree essences for yourself, firstly to establish the ease of the process and, secondly, to experience the nuances and shifts of awareness that occur during the whole time. There is a particular state that soon descends as one goes out with the intention to make a flower essence very close to meditative states and the heightened awareness achieved during concentrated retreats. The simplicity and tried and tested efficacy of the traditional sun-water method should be used first of all.

Over the years new methods have evolved that seem to prove equally effective and provide solutions in instances where the sun-water method may be inappropriate. These new techniques slide effortlessly away from any pseudo-scientifically justifiable procedures and simply become magical invocation and evocation.

The first essence maker Edward Bach was flexible in his approach. Although the sun-water technique arose from the early dew-drinking phase, a good proportion of his flower essences were prepared by boiling. Now boiling can in no way be understood as a simple vibrational technique. The result will always be a herbal infusion or tisane of some concentration. It could be argued that the energy signature is also present in the water, but there will be quite a physical molecular presence as well. And what can be said of the remedy Rock Water? Rock Water is exactly what it says it is - water collected from mountain streams running through and over native rock. It does what it says but there is not a flower in sight. Today there are an increasing number of such "environmental essences" that have been made to capture a particular time or place. There are essences of locations, equinoxes, sacred sites, specific types of environments, sea creatures, dolphins, whales, planets and stars. All have, in some way, encapsulated the unique energy of the "target" but none can use the sun-water method as originated.

The first group of essences that we heard about using one of these new methods was a collection of Amazonian orchids. When you are dealing with rare or endangered species it might be felt that collecting a bowl full of blooms would be an environmentally unsound practice. And, considering the flowers might appear several hundred feet up in the tree canopy, dotted here and there throughout the rainforest, this would also be a logistic nightmare to undertake. The solution in this instance was to employ the energies of a quartz crystal as an intermediary, where the perfect lattice structure of the quartz surrogates for the flexible lattice of water, and in some way, receives the energy signature of the plant for a later transference back into water.

Since that time we have come across and used many different methods of essence making. The flower or flowers can be left unpicked and simply bent gently down until they contact the surface of the water in the bowl. Or, more cunningly, a container can be attached to the plant where, for a short period of time flowers can be held in water. Very recently we saw an ingenious and elegant alchemical device that carefully held the flower in a sealed chamber whilst spring water dripped over it and was collected in a lower chamber. Instead of a bowl of glass some essence makers use beautiful hollow geodes of crystal. Quartz being an extremely sensitive material, it reacts very strongly to intention and so can focus the correct or appropriate energy very accurately into the water it contains.

One of the most powerful essences we have ever tried was made by simply placing a clear quartz crystal close to a group of monterey cypresses on the California coastline. The essence maker had intended to place the crystal in a fork of the tree but was firmly persuaded by the tree itself to simply place the stone at the base of its trunk. The crystal was later placed in water and the energy pattern transferred to the liquid. It is also possible to make an essence without any process or intervention at all, except for the focused intention of the maker and the willing co-operation of the plant spirit in question. A sealed bottle already prepared with brandy and water can be left in, or close to, the plant for a specific length of time and the spirit itself infuses or imprints the water. The less human-centred the essence is, the more attention will need to be given to the exact requirements of the "target" plant whether crystal, crystal and water, open water, sealed water, sealed water with brandy, pure brandy and so on, it is best to use. Also what time of exposure will be needed, at what time of day the exact placement of the vessel and the sort of vessel to be used.

All in all, it is probably better to go with the technique that feels most comfortable. This will be the one that creates the least turbulence at subtle levels and so will tend to allow the making of a purer essence. Some essence makers enjoy picking the flowers by hand, feeling that it thus becomes a powerful shared process between human and plant kingdoms, whilst others prefer to leave the plants as untouched as possible. Depending on one's viewpoint of humanity's role and place on the planet, these viewpoints might seem either exploitative or apologetic.

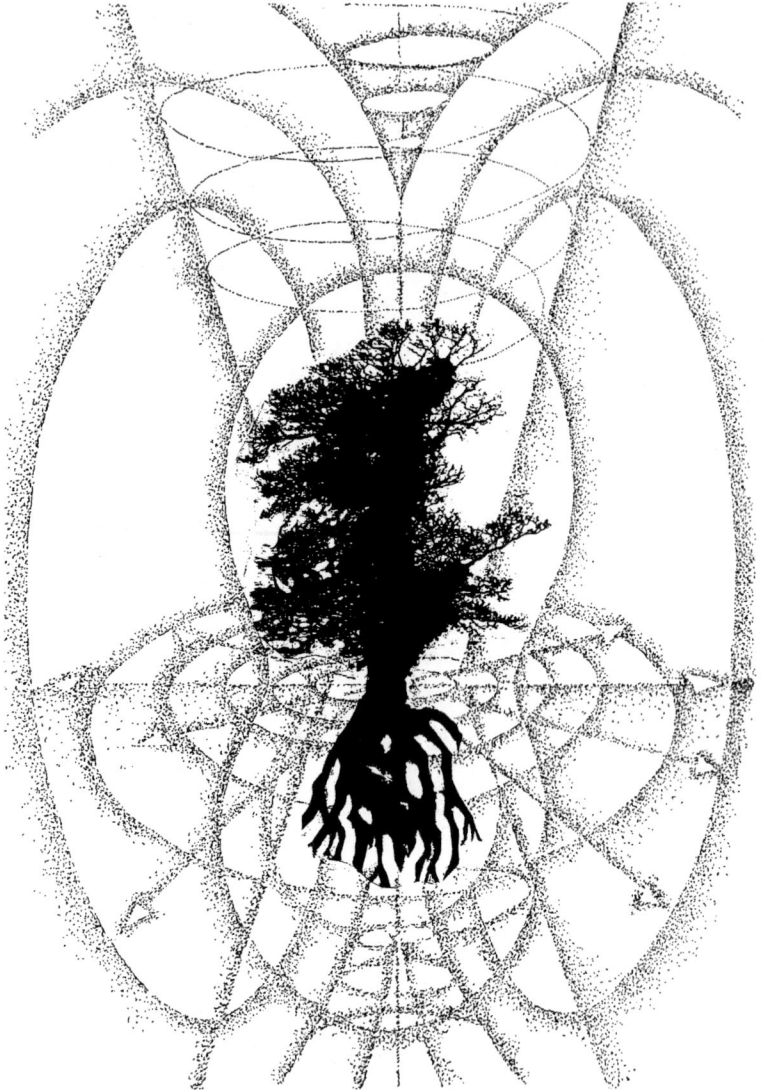

The energies of each tree extend far beyond the physical form in every plane and direction. A vortex that integrates the elements and the polarities of planetary and cosmic sources, a wheel that radiates into the landscape, a circuit of balancing and enlivening forces.

40

Trees of Possibilities

The Bare Bones

Trees are the creators and maintainers of our reality. This is so on a physical, ecological level and is also very true at a subtle, energy level.

Trees maintain climatic stability. The huge areas of forest and woodland act as a heat sink, cooling the air and regulating moisture levels, rainfall and wind speed. The Amazon rainforest "controls" the climate of the entire western hemisphere.

Trees act as locally protecting environments. Woodland is always warmer in winter than the surrounding land and it is cooler in summer. Woodland thus acts as a protective balance against climatic extremes, allowing greater survival of other species within it. Trees give effective shading from strong sunlight, a fact more evident in southerly climes than present-day Britain, though it will become increasingly important should the changes in climate and ozone layer continue. Trees shelter other species from the full force of wind and also reduce the heaviness of rainfall.

Trees create atmospheric stability by absorbing and storing CO_2 and O_2 that would otherwise alter the proportions of atmospheric gases.

The root systems of trees bind the topsoil together preventing erosion by wind and water. Deep roots create the topsoil by breaking up subsoil and rock layers, absorbing mineral nutrients not available at ground level, and releasing these nutrients during leaf decay and the rotting of fallen branches.

Without this mechanism, the only way soil could be formed and replenished is through water erosion and alluvial deposits, like the former inundation of the Nile delta, leaving all but such river valleys leached of minerals.

Tree roots control the water levels within their environment. Trees absorb tons of water through their root systems and transpire tons of water vapour back into the air. By maintaining the integrity of the topsoil and by holding huge amounts of water within their systems, trees help to ensure a constant recycling of available water. It has been suggested that the recent erratic water supply in Britain, with drought followed by flood, is in large part due to the lack of necessary tree cover to maintain the system.

So, without adequate, that is, very plentiful, tree cover: soil erodes; soil fails to receive natural fertilisation of minerals; the water table drops as rainfall simply runs off into rivers and flows to the sea; flood and drought become more frequent and increasingly damaging; sensitive and specialised species die out because of extremes of weather; wind speeds greatly increase; air temperatures increase and humidity levels drop; atmospheric gases change their relative proportions; pollutants increase.

Presence

Trees are the largest, longest- lived and most stable life-forms in most of this planet's environments. Trees provide continuity and establishment of solid, stable environments. Although some trees have lifespans of similar length to humans, like hazel and birch, many trees commonly live for several hundred years. Dating techniques and genetic testing have broadened our awareness of the lifespan of trees. In Europe, yew is the longest lived tree. Recent recalibrations have suggested that previous dates have been underestimated and that the largest yews in Britain may be well over 5,000 years old and are still growing healthily. The Fortingall Yew, at the head of Glen Lyon in the Highlands of Scotland, is probably well over 5,000 years old, and this is a fairly conservative estimate. Our local yew in Kenn churchyard, Devon, is estimated at 2,000 years whilst the yew tree at Peyhembury, which has four separate trunks around a now empty central space, has been tested by kinesiology to be at least 6,000 years.

The oldest scientifically tested trees are the bristlecone pines of California and Nevada. The oldest of these high altitude trees has been dated at 4,300 years.

Coppicing can greatly enhance a tree's lifespan. Hazel usually lives for 70-80 years, but when coppiced regularly can survive for 1,500 years. Similarly a lime tree has been found in the Cotswolds that has been regularly coppiced so that it now makes a circle of sixty trunks with a twenty foot diameter. This tree is estimated to be over 2,000 years old.

Recently, botanists in Tasmania have found a holly bush, King's Holly, that covers a section of forest floor with self-propagated clones of the original plant. Thus, all individuals are genetically identical and essentially the same plant. The existing plants were identical to fossil remains excavated from the same area, making this plant 43,000 years old!

The world's largest organism is possibly an aspen tree in Utah, USA, which has 47,000 trunks covering an area of forty- seven hectares. The original tree has reproduced by producing genetically identical suckers that remain attached to the parent tree.

The giant sequoia and coastal redwoods in the USA are the largest single-bodied organisms on the planet. The largest tree, a giant redwood, measured in 1989 was 275 feet tall with a girth of 82 feet. The coastal redwoods are less massive but

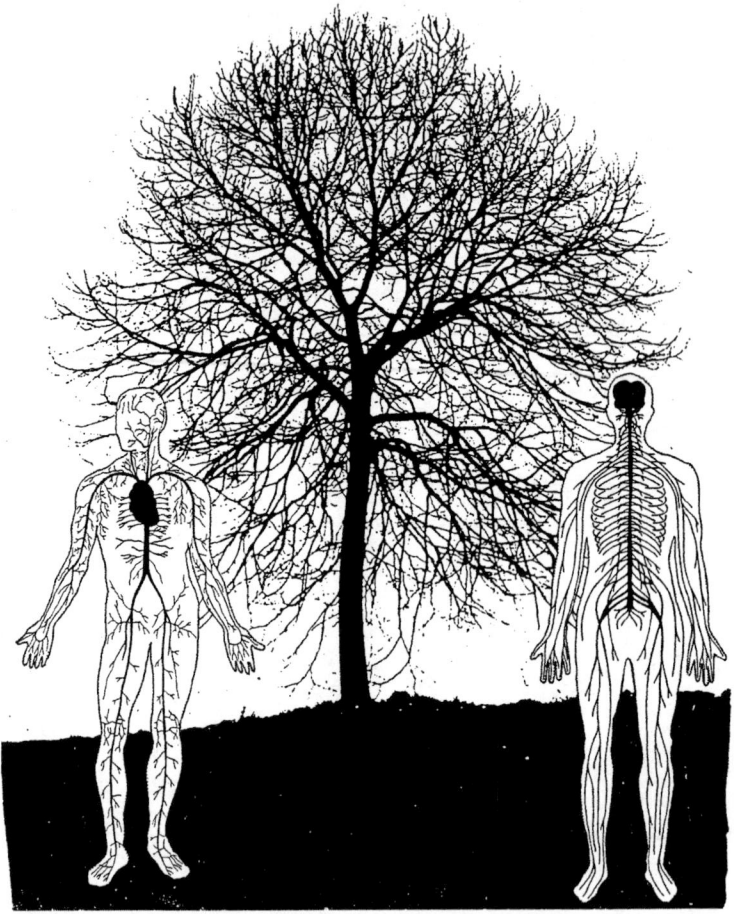

Physical form should be seen only as one aspect, one view, of the whole. Through the lens of other states of awareness, new facets will show themselves.

grow taller, the largest is at present 368 feet high. Even this is not the tallest recorded tree: a eucalyptus growing in a ravine in Victoria, Australia was found in 1872 measuring a staggering 435 feet high.

Continuing with dimensions, a fig tree in South Africa had roots extending 390 feet in to the earth, and an Indian fig tree in Calcutta Botanic Gardens is over 1,300 feet in total diameter, covering nearly three acres.

A single rye-grass plant has over thirteen million rootlets with a combined length of 380 miles. The root hairs are estimated at fourteen billion, with a total length of 6,600 miles. By these standards, how complex and extensive would a tree's root system be? Remember that when we see a tree uprooted by a strong wind it is only the toughest, largest roots that are visible, most of the structure has remained embedded in the soil.

The Hidden Presence and the Possibilities of Communication

Like a human, there is more to a tree than the physical form. Our physical bodies do not of themselves clearly indicate the presence of personality, consciousness, different levels of awareness (the conscious, unconscious and so on), nor the aspirations of the soul or spirit. Nonetheless they are within, or around, the form and can sometimes be intimated from the outward behaviour.

The spiritual nature of trees is possibly as complex as that of humans. There is the Higher Self at the angelic or "devic" level and various possible forms of consciousness or awareness such as persona, ego, conscious mind, unconscious, collective consciousness, dream awareness, body awareness and so on. All these could communicate and manifest as different entities. Each would have different degrees of knowledge and experience. Depending how one tunes in and where, one may well discover different things.

When we experience nature spirits, talk to trees, hear trees talking, as in all other more "normal" types of communication, we are translating into words, images and concepts that we can understand. Therefore just because someone experiences a certain tree as having such-and-such a spirit, doesn't invalidate a different experience of the same tree. There will probably be noticeable connections, but this is not the only validation.

Trees have a very different experience of time and space from humans. On a linear, time-based level a tree's awareness of a human being sitting underneath it, talking to it for an hour or so, would be analogous to a human noticing a fly buzzing around for a second, or a scientist tuning in to the patterns of subatomic particles. Communication just at this level would be difficult!

However, all consciousness or awareness also exists in states outside linear time. It is in these "magical" or "faery" states that communication and exchange usually takes place, that is, in non-ordinary or alternate reality.

Effective interaction with Tree Kingdoms will, therefore, more likely be successful by those who can find ways to "step out" of the normal flow of events into a timeless, potent Otherworld.

What are the reasons we would want to communicate with trees? Trees provide a stability and continuity which we lack. Trees balance and harmonise opposites. As our sustainers, we should respect their existence and pay them due attention. Their perception of time, space and energy broadens us. Because they are conscious of connectedness with all levels of creation, they can bring us to balance and restore our wholeness, that is, heal us.

Iceberg

The physical form is like the visible tip of an iceberg. In energy terms, it is the most visible in the wavelengths we commonly adopt as our means of measuring reality. It is, again, only an intimation or suggestion of what lies beyond. Like a symbol, humans and trees exist in many other realities in different forms.

Signature

Each species devises its own strategies to maintain itself in its environment. The shape, size and habit visible in each species is the outward representation of the tree's energy and "personality". The tree's signature is a reflection or echo of its greater energy function.

If this is the case, the surroundings of each tree will also vibrate with the energy function of that species.

Knowing what the signature, or energy function, of a tree is, we could seek out a particular type for a particular enhancement of our activity. Or specific trees could be planted in an environment that needed that particular input of energy combinations.

Dual Nature

The experience of trees is very different from most other life-forms on Earth. They exist simultaneously in two different environments. The root experience is completely different to the branch experience. The consciousness of root/earth and branch/air can be seen as a variation of unconscious or subconscious root and conscious awareness of the branch. If one were to contact the energy of the "root" it would probably present itself as very different from the energy and experience of "branch".

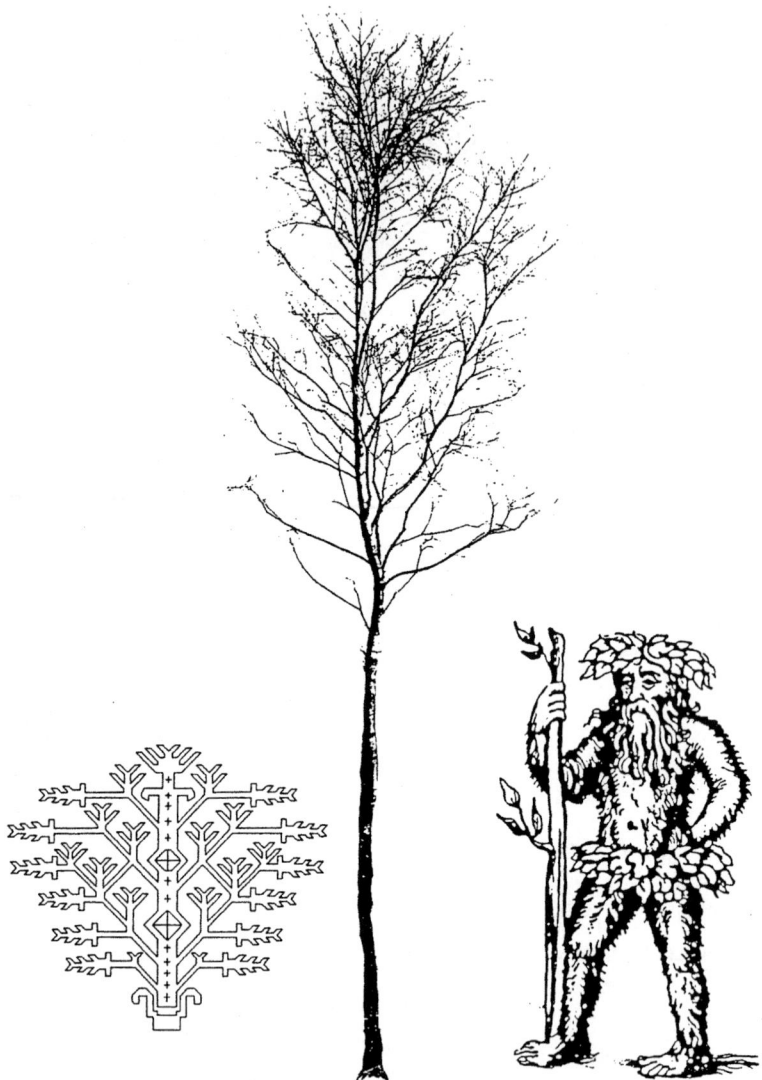

The concept of "tree" has different cultural perspectives. Each view will explore and emphasise certain characteristics that other cultures may deny entirely.

So in this way there may be at least these levels of being, or personality, or character: firstly, the physical body as a whole; secondly, the root as an inward-looking, stable unconscious; thirdly, the branch as an outward-looking, reaching, reactive conscious.

And so in terms of personality or awareness-beings, two levels may be present at very least. Due to their different functions and state, the means of contact and communication with these two types of energy may be different, and will have different information, of different usefulness to us.

The Mirror Body

We tend to think of a tree's awareness as vertical like our own - with consciousness at the top. The parallels are linguistic: the crown of the tree, the crown of the head, the trunk of the body, the tree trunk. This is far too anthropomorphic. Plants have two directional forces acting, they are pulled downwards and upwards.

Whereas we only grow upwards, trees first grow downwards and then both upwards and downwards simultaneously from the single point that is the seed. This forms a dual consciousness of different states, the "above" and the "below". They are drawn towards the fire of the sun, and to the fire deep within the earth, (the magnetic core).

In both states the tree passes between, or through, different qualities of matter - air and earth/rock. We tend to think of roots in the earth, but really they are through and between the earth.

To experience this form of tree consciousness:

> Stand or sit relaxed and become aware of the weight of your body.

Take the attention to the bottom of the feet.

Let your awareness sink below your feet on a mirror image of yourself attached to your feet.

Extend your awareness so that it simultaneously involves both your body and the mirror body.

Initially the experience will be vague but disorienting. To clarify the experience, take your attention to specific parts of the body. Start with the soles of the feet: in the physical, then in the mirror body. Next focus on the knees, in the physical, then the mirror body; the navel, the solar plexus, the hands, the shoulders, the top of the head.

Once you have become used to this swapping around, see if you can maintain simultaneous awareness in reflected spots, and then return to an overall view of yourself as both bodies.

When the exercise is completed, dissolve the image and spend a moment getting re-acquainted with the physical body.

A journey to Tree Teachers provided an interesting and powerful image of one such being. The trunk of the "tree" was composed of a single large face with large, dark eyes, reminiscent of carved Celtic heads. The hair streaming out from this head formed the branches.

At the base of the trunk was a second head, the other way up, but with identical strong features and the same fathomless eyes. The hair from this seat of awareness streamed out so as to form the tree roots. In all, the whole was a mirror image with no "up" or "down".

Celtic artworks, particularly a piece found on Anglesey, strongly suggest this same representation, though it cannot be said for sure to mean the same thing.

The Landscape's Wheel

From our perception of time, dictated by our metabolic rate, we almost ignore the presence of trees. They are immobile, constant, inanimate objects and therefore inactive, passive and rather accidental.

The tines of a wheel and the wheel's rim would no doubt feel the same about the hub. However, the wheel would cease to move, cease to function and cease to be, without this unmoving centre.

Do we fail to perceive the real significance, the true function of the tree? Apart from its obvious, physical role of creating our atmosphere, does it serve the same, sustaining, underpinning function on subtle levels of energy as well?

Why is the world axis in so many cosmologies a tree?

Why does the shaman climb a tree to the celestial worlds?

Why is Christ portrayed, as Odin is portrayed, as hanging on a tree?

Why is the Sun Dancer suspended from a tree?

Physically, the tree can be seen as a sort of extended wheel when viewed from above, spreading out, or being held fast, by the central axis of the trunk. With subtle perceptions, too, the tree is a hub or axis from which flow lines of sustaining force into the landscape around it.

Tree Cell

Trees are not an alien species. Their cellular makeup is mostly identical to animal cells. They contain the same kind of nucleus with DNA strands, the same cytoplasm, the same organelles, and so the same, or a similar consciousness of being. The main differences are, firstly, a rigid cell wall that tends to be a box-like protection, with pores for the transmission of nutrients and waste products. Secondly, plant cells contain chloroplasts, green ovoid organelles within the cell body that can move around towards the light source and that are the site of photosynthesis, the process where sunlight is transformed into energy and food. Even chlorophyll, though, has a similar structure to animal haemoglobin, the oxygen carrier within red blood cells.

Tree Drums

The presence of a rigid or semi-rigid cell wall, and in most mature cells, a hollow space inside the cell, makes plant cells particularly sensitive to resonance - they might become the receivers and even amplifiers of energy, like a drum.

Much of the solid structure, the skeleton of trees, is formed from dead cells where only the rigid cell walls remain to make a light box-girder support. Here again there is a resonant space within the tree's structure.

Think of the mature, still healthy trees, that are completely hollowed out. The excess weight of the dead tissue has been eaten by fungi, leaving the surrounding living tree much more able to withstand storms and wind damage. Many of the great redwoods have survived centuries, even though their bases have been wholly hollowed out by forest fires.

Holðing Vessels

Human experience of physicality is one of exclusion and boundaries. Even though we have many empty spaces inside our bodies they are not perceived as such. Everything inside our skins is "us", everything outside that barrier is "not us". We experience the world as always "out there". Trees, on the other hand, contain proportionately more interior space , but also envelop, or infiltrate, a huge area of surrounding space. The tree is not simply defined by its physical shape but also by the "outside" space it encloses or enfolds within its branches and roots. This would inevitably make tree awareness less dualistic - the inward looking vessel maintains a continuum with everything around it. Self becomes less solid.

Time Machine

If we understand the sun's energy, whose nature is fire energy, as "information" then each tree "translates" this into the book or library of its growing wood. As the tree matures the library, that is also the history of energy, weather, climate, seasons and so on, is stored in the very fabric of the tree's structure. In this way trees can be seen as recording, or codifying time.

If this record could be read in some way, if a way could be found to retrieve the information, then a record of the past would emerge.

When wood is burned it literally releases all the fire or sun energy that the tree has stored up in its life and growth. Perhaps the fire itself can be "read" as a history. Seers who knew how to look would have much revealed to them, perhaps.

Energy Generator
Imagine a tree beginning as a seedling.

It starts to accumulate energy and begins to transmute the elements of light, water and earth.

It accumulates power within its structure.
As it grows more energy, power, information, consciousness is concentrated and can stay stable here for many hundreds of years.

These are stable energy fields within an ever-changing environment.

Slowly, as the tree eventually ages and dies, it releases that accumulated energy slowly back into the earth where it can be accessed again.

Visualise this process as if each tree were a point of light or warmth.

Look down on the landscape alive with stable energy, small points growing bright over the centuries, spreading the light of energy into their surroundings, holding steady and then gradually becoming more diffuse and fading as other lights begin to glow bright.

Know that nothing else can infuse the world with this light.

Everything relies on this continual dance for survival and sustenance.

These are the power stations that need to be maintained.

The Elemental Tree
The form of, and the nature of, a tree:

Formed of fire (sunlight),

Held in form by water (the image of a fountain).

Both hold each other element in a stable balance - the raising of water, the cyclic fountain of water, preventing the fire from consuming the tree.

The nature of the tree is thus fire sustained by water - a balance of opposite forces.

Plant and Animal as a Planetary Symbiosis
Animals function as an apparatus for combustion and oxidation; they possess the ability of locomotion.
Plants are an apparatus for reduction or de-oxidation; they are fixed.

Animals burn carbon, hydrogen, ammonium.
Plants reduce carbon, hydrogen, ammonium.

Animals exhale or give out carbonic acid, water, oxides of ammonium and nitrogen.
Plants fix carbonic acid, water and nitrogen.

Animals consume oxygen, neutralise nitrogenous matter, starchy matter, gums and sugars.
Plants produce oxygen, nitrogenous matter, fatty matter, starches, gums and sugars.

Animals produce heat and electricity.
Plants abstract electricity and absorb heat.

Animals restore their elements to air and earth, and transform organised matter into mineral matter.
Plants derive their elements from air and earth and transform minerals into organised matter.
(based upon *"Design in Nature"*, J. Bell Pettigrew 1908).

Priorities

Plants and animals seem to have evolved from the same simple bacterial lifeforms in the warm seas of the young Earth. Those that were to become plants were able to "eat" sunlight as a source of energy with which to combine other chemicals from the environment. These simple plants contained the necessary chloroplasts that made photosynthesis possible.

Those little beings that lacked chloroplasts, (perhaps because they had been born in the volcanic plumes on the sunless seabeds and only later had swum nearer to the surface), had to make do with eating those successful ones that had managed to digest light. Animals become the eaters, the eaten become the plants.

In some respects, then, all animals are simply failed plants!

Or to look at it in another way:

> " *Consciousness has to do with energy and light.*
> *It is really very simple.*
> *Neither animals nor people have consciousness.*
> *Animals get consciousness by eating plants.*"

(From *"Pharmako/poeia"*, Dale Pendell. 1995)

The Tastes of Light

Trees have their greatest sensitivity to light either in the ultra-violet wavelengths, or in the red to infra-red end of the spectrum. That is, at either end of the human visual range. Trees reflect, that is, reject, those ranges of light energy humans recognise as green.

Green light stops the growth of plants. The human eye, on the other hand, cannot register either ultra-violet or infra-red, but it is extremely sensitive to the green wavelengths. Green is a very soothing and healing colour. It has a balancing and sedative effect on the body and mind, without which there is increased tendencies towards irritability and aggression.

Towards Meditative States

All trees and tree essences have the ability to lead us to meditative states. This is because tree awareness is always connected to the gestalt field of that species. Individual awareness is simply a part of the whole experience of "tree". The same is essentially true of humankind also, except that it is more difficult for us to experience this.

Tree awareness probably exists in cyclical, or spiral time. Human awareness, at the conscious level, exists in a linearity of past-present-future. All conscious thought is active on this linearity: we are either re-evaluating past memory or projecting into future activity. The present doesn't carry thought in the same way. Perception of the present becomes memory or speculation by habit rather than necessity.

Tree awareness is held in the present and so requires no thought process - or not a human sort of thought process. When we use an essence we absorb some quality of tree consciousness and so find it easier to release the habitual linearity of thought. This is the first step to the establishing of a state we can call meditative. The different quality of

57

meditative states will depend upon the "flavour" of the tree and upon the user's personal energy predilections.

Tree awareness is concentric and 360 degrees. Individual awareness is the centre of a circle of energetic liveliness that is inclusive of many other circles of awareness. The central, individual awareness is not experienced as separate from the circle around it - merely as a denser focus of peculiar factors of view and form. "I" does not have the same meaning where each individual experiences no spatial movement or change of view. As humans, we are always in a state of physically changing relationships with our environment. We need to be constantly self-referring at quite a superficial, surface level of awareness. Existing in the same place with less differentiated physicality, such as organs of digestion, senses and so on, there is no need for a tree to be constantly self-conscious. More of the awareness can be directed outwards towards the circle's circumference. It is inclusive awareness rather than exclusive awareness.

Some common experiences of meditators can clarify this form of awareness. At a certain level of consciousness sensation of the body disappears ("I wonder where my hands are?"). Body position in relation to the surroundings alters - one feels that one is facing in another direction, or cannot recall where one is. The sense of time disappears so that a short period seems long or a long time, short. Thought continues at a surface level but there exists awareness of an underlying, non-verbal vibration of energy - often experienced as bliss, light or sound. All these sensations are the products of the relaxation of the sense of self-identity - or, if you will, entering into tree spirit awareness.

Alchemy
"Trees are the only means by which sunlight can be turned into matter and energy."

Balance

A tree cannot choose its place of growth. It can only survive and flourish by adjusting its form to harmonise with the prevailing conditions. The very fact that a tree grows up, matures, flowers and bears fruit means that it has succeeded in maintaining that balance for hundreds, even thousands of years. It is this ability to remain balanced and flexible, to absorb and let go, to just remain harmless, that is often transferred to the tree essences.

Doctrine of Signatures

Each species shows different habits and characteristics which are the outward visible manifestation of the energy with which they are formed. This is why the ancient Doctrine of Signatures can still be relevant in identifying the properties of a particular tree. The Doctrine simply recognises that the outward form reflects the inner energies and that a symbolic link, whether it be shape, or colour or habit is a link nonetheless and will create a resonance in a similar structure of pattern within us. Many organs in plants and animals are shaped by the vortex energies of moving matter. For example, whatever the function of the organ, the formulating energies are often identical - a heart-shaped flower will resonate with the physical heart.

Vessels for Deity

In one shamanic journey, there was an impression that the very characteristic of still balance allows trees to be the temporary hosts to vast, spiritual beings, or "gods", when they wish to experience the reality of the physical world.

Fountain Head

One journeying was to a peculiar landscape inhabited by swans. For as far as the eye could see there arose fountains of

From its very first growth a tree is moulded by the interaction between its genetic makeup (the spiritual or 'devic' blueprint), and the changing factors of its environment. Symmetry, pattern of growth and Ideal form are modified by the dynamic interplay of the elements.

water, like geysers, coming straight up into the sky from the ground. Strange sights often meet the traveller to the Otherworlds but it was only later that I was able to make sense of this place, and its significance. The landscape was simply reflecting the qualities of the water element, interpreting life in terms of its relationship with water. The fountains were trees as they would appear to a consciousness tuning into the water element. The physical body of which we are usually aware is, from this perspective, merely the mechanism by which the water is moved. In fact, trees are so important from this view because they are the only significant places where water in liquid form escapes from gravity and moves from a lower to a higher level. Every other manifestation of water is flowing downwards towards the centre of gravity, or along the surface of the ground, horizontally.

The Tree Devas Speak

Quotes from the channelled communications of Dorothy MacLean in *"To Hear The Angels Sing"* are among the most powerful and evocative statements of the need for large trees.

" We are the guardians of the Earth in many ways, and humans should be a part of what we guard..."

"...Trees are vital to man and to life on this planet, and some of us are eager to experience this contact with some humans before others destroy what we have built up..."

" We would emphasise the absolute necessity for large trees for the well-being of the land. This is not merely because we partly control rainfall, but we also draw forth inner radiances which are as necessary to the land as rain (is)."

"...the planet needs more than ever just what is being denied it: the forces which come through the large and stately trees."

" *Trees act as a protective skin to the Earth and in that skin bring about necessary changes. We devas are outer sentinels of that change, able to do our work where others could not.* "

" *Vast areas need us, and by us I mean large trees in general. We simply cannot emphasise this enough. We are the skin of this world; take us away and the complete planet, no longer able to function, dries up and dies. Let us be, and the whole creature purrs with contentment, and life goes on in natural sequence, becoming ever more aware of unity.* "

" *What is important now is consciousness. Our nature worlds are essential; much of man's worlds, created with a sense of separation, is not essential. Together we can create a better Earth.* "

" *Great forests must flourish, and man must see this if he wishes to continue to live on this planet...Nothing could be more vital to life as a whole than trees, trees and more trees.* "

" *We channel a type of force that has a steadying influence on life... Man does not realise that, among other things, his natural environment is full of forces that correspond to, and therefore can bring out, some part of his own makeup, and that he is influenced by his environment in many subtle ways...you are bereft of some part of yourself and of your heritage when you denude the land of large trees.* "

" *We devas would like to dance around in the consciousness of every human being to wake up to what you are. We would have you know that you are light beings and not confined to your physical presence. Simply because you think you are so confined, you'll remain so, but when you are aware of us and come to our level, you are part of a larger world which is also home to you... so join us often to be educated about yourself, and do it in the love of the One.* "

Spirits, Devas, Fairies or What?

There was an episode of *"The Twilight Zone"* (or was it *"The Outer Limits"*?), whose plot revolved around someone mistakenly entering a place between dimensions where their subjective experience of time is so rapid that the "real" world appears to have stopped completely: the only perceivable change is the normally invisible flickering of a lightbulb. The idea was reworked in numerous *"Star Trek"* stories where the hero's presence is only felt as the briefest movement of air or an unintelligible whisper. They have become "ghosts" or "spirits" to their fellow humans, but to themselves they are as real and solid as ever they were.

Belief in spirits is not encouraged in our modern world. One of the fundamental elements of human cosmology has been largely dismissed or discredited as superstitious simply because personal experience is held to be less valid than the measurements of man-made machines that prove incapable of measuring other worlds.

However, it is still (just about) acceptable to believe in one or two supreme spirits, as long as they are metaphorically dressed in the clothes of a State religion. There seems to be a rather large avoidance of logic and common sense here! If you allow one great, big superphysical supreme spirit, (plus a handful of card-carrying bona fide helpers), how can there not be any place for spirits of other kinds as well?

For most of humanity's existence, as far as we can tell from remaining evidence, there has been a universal belief in other planes of existence inhabited by all sorts of spirits and beings. Huge exertions by the individual and the nation have been

Tree spirits talking. Woodcarving from choirstalls, Cathedral of St Bernard de Comminge, French Pyrenees 1535.

carried out to worship, subdue, placate, communicate with, work alongside such beings. Then, in the last few blips of time, during a couple of hundred years (not even the average lifetime of an oak tree), one group of industrialised, urban humanity decides that everyone else before them, their own forbears and ancestors, were simple-minded and delusional and that the beliefs in spirits (except the One Big Exclusion), were simply superstition fed by uneducated reaction to natural phenomena.

At one level this is perfectly understandable. Look around. Where have all the spirits gone? There is little objective evidence available: no machine that can measure spirit activity, no respectable double-blind experiments that can be laboratory tested and confirmed. The language of science can define most types of phenomena in terms of physical reaction or energetic interaction. Mystery is named and put into an equation and so is no longer a mystery. What cannot be measured and named, no matter how often it may have been experienced, falls outside of scientific procedure and so in terms of science doesn't exist. But the mistake here is to believe that a method of human investigation (one among many), namely scientific method, is the only means to get to know reality.

Objectivity is one of the battle cries of the scientific belief system, and yet we perceive reality through our own individual sense fields, and we create machines with which our senses can interact. Real objectivity is impossible for any subjective observer. As Jim DeKorne puts it in *"Psychedelic Shamanism"*: *"...if such a state of perception were possible, there would be no question about what is "true", since the truth would be obvious to all observers. Therefore, since we cannot be objective, except in a relative sense, "objectivity" must be a function of the imagination. That is, I can imagine what objectivity is, but I cannot be objective in any true or ultimate sense except...in accordance with socially imagined* rules, such as the scientific method. This consensus objectivity is indispensable for daily living but we must not forget that it is only an abstraction (like money) created to facilitate social intercourse."

Life is always and only can be a subjective experience. If there is an objective reality at all we would only be able to experience it through our own sense filters. So what then is the basis of our perceived reality?

It is easy for us to imagine a point of no dimensions. So too can we experience a line which has one single dimension of length. Two dimensions - a surface with length and breadth - is a simple, familiar concept for us, and a form with length, breadth and height, we identify as a solid object: what our physical world is made of. Because our senses have developed to work with three- dimensional reality it is incredibly difficult to imagine where a fourth or fifth dimension would fit in. Everything already seems to be full up with three! Yet, if we existed in a two-dimensional world of length and breadth we would find it equally impossible to conceptualise a third dimension. In order to be able to perceive other possible dimensions we need to go beyond our senses and the perceptive beliefs based on those senses.

Jim DeKorne suggests we can do this by understanding that we perceive everything from the same centre or "point", which we identify with our own subjective self or psyche and that our familiar three external dimensions appear to radiate outwards from us. In this way we are always at the centre of the space/time surrounding us. As there is no room for more dimensions to be perceived "outside", dimensions higher than three can be perceived only "inside", or at the subjective centre. Thus a fourth (or more) dimensional being would be experienced as an interior phenomenon - as an inner voice or hallucination.

Now because our thought patterns and language are determined by three-dimensional living, we cannot easily use ordinary language to define our experiences of higher dimensional states. We are familiar with the non-verbal symbolic language of dreams and other messages from our unconscious, but even then, in present society we pay little heed, dismissing them as "just imagination", "all in the mind", by which we infer "not real". Just because our experiences of higher dimensional states are similar to dream images, and do not follow the rules of three-dimensional reality, it doesn't mean that the entities of those realms are any less real in their own space . We are filtering and interpreting the experience via our own central point of personal consciousness.

With this model of reality in mind the cosmologies of those technicians of tribal consciousness, the medicine men, shamans and priests, seem scientific and objective. Knowing how to shift their awareness inwards they could focus on their "central point", the zero-point of no dimension , and from there access whichever higher dimensional level they required. Suddenly the world is full of spirits. Robert Monroe pioneered teaching the technique of Out Of the Body Experiences. His researchers roamed the entire physical universe Out of Body and found no signs of any other beings. But once they learnt to shift levels to a finer dimension the variety of non-human sentient beings was staggering and all-pervasive.

Perhaps the spirits haven't gone anywhere. We have just forgotten how they can be seen and heard. By putting all our attention on getting to grips with the nitty-gritty of three-dimensional existence we have mislaid the skills that would enable us to see things from other levels.

The next chapter "Meeting the Spirits" will give suggestions for beginning to learn this process again. The remainder of

The horned one: deity, spirit or shaman? Stag's horns or tree branches?

This section will consider who or what we may be contacting in Tree Spirit work. For convenience we can divide the points of view under several headings. Each presents a fairly coherent picture of belief, though there are obvious mixing of ideas from one area to another. When it comes to working practically with Tree Spirit energies it may not matter which system is adopted as a working model. However, it is usually better to use only one model at a time - parallels can always be found between any two systems, but the point with parallels is that they never meet (except at infinity).

The Shamanic View

The shamanic view of the reality of spirits has the longest history and so influences and feeds into many other, later systems of thought. Each culture has developed its own shamanic constructs, but generally speaking the world is seen as existing on three main energy levels: the Lower World, the Middle World and the Upper World. Everyday reality, the world perceived by the senses, exists as part of the Middle World. Any three-dimensional thing is understood as a fragment of the real object which co-exists on many different levels of being - much as a tip of an iceberg indicates a huge reality beneath the waters. Everything thus becomes symbolic. Every object, being and event creates a complex system of interactions or dimensional ripples and it is the skill of those shamanically trained to identify and interpret significant interactions and, if necessary, modify them for maximum benefit to all. All of existence is seen as a living, egalitarian flux of energy and power. From the shamanic viewpoint, nothing exists that is dead matter. The existence of a perceivable "thing" automatically means that there is a spiritual reality behind and beyond that "thing".

To perceive the spirit counterpart of a physical object the shamanically trained shift consciousness just slightly. Three-dimensional reality still appears but, depending on the degree

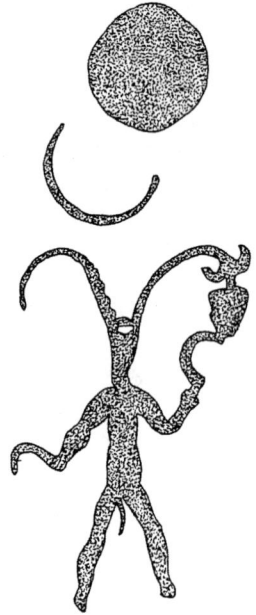

The shaman's visions and experiences with spirits in the imaginal worlds have been recorded for many thousands of years on petroglyphs, carefully chipped from exposed rock faces at sacred sites. The spirits of trees or other plants are recorded alongside recognisable forms and animals.

of awareness-shift, it either becomes pervaded with sentient life-force, energy flows seen as auras, glows and so on, or the spirit beings, the spirit principle of each object can be seen and interacted with. The form the spirit takes is often very specific to each culture, particularly where strong traditions are important. This is exploration within the Middle World.

The Lower World always deals with power. It is the dark, rich fertiliser of the past that sustains and fuels the other worlds. Whatever form it takes, and it has limitless appearances, it deals with the roots and causes, the cthonic ancestral tides of energy.

The Upper World differs in the quality of its energy from the Lower World, though it too takes all physical landscapes into itself. It tends to be the realm of teachers and gods and is often associated with star people and other extraterrestrial energies. Clarity and understanding, new ways of doing things and getting an overview of the world are some characteristics of the Upper Worlds. Whereas the Lower World holds the past and concretises energy like a power of gravity, the Upper World is expansive and contemplative.

It is usual for all members of a shamanic-based society to have links to a Middle World three-dimensional object, animal or tree, with which a personal bond is recognised or developed. This symbiotic link between the human and another spirit acts as a guiding force in life and can act as a guardian and teacher in all Worlds. The spirit healer, shaman or priest establishes closer bonds with many more spirits or with more powerful spirits to enable them to act as intermediaries between all levels of awareness and the shaman "journeys" to the Worlds with the help of his spirit helpers. Spirit helpers can either be guides or allies. Once integrated, guides are ever-present and wholly reliable, the equivalent of our "guardian angel". Allies, on the other hand, tend to be for specific purposes and are asked to help only when required. A

Enigmatic yet powerful images, reminiscent of those found in the mysterious crop circle phenomenon, suggestive of sentient spirit energies.

powerful healer, for example, might have many spirit allies for helping diagnose and heal different kinds of disease. Contact with guides and allies is often established or maintained by keeping a fragment of the physical object, be it stone, animal part or plant. These "power objects" act as a focus for the spirit energy to manifest.

A shamanic based society would treat all beings as sentient and would tend to respect the integrity of everything around them. Talking to trees, animals, clouds, rocks would be a natural, spontaneous activity. Awareness, at least to some degree, of subtle energies would be a prerequisite in most activities whether it be hunting or preparing herbs, making a pot or crafting a song. Depending on the religious and cultural context of the tribe or society, such a world view can be either prohibitively fear-filled or creatively harmonious.

The main technology of the shamanic world-view is the trance state. We now tend to see trance as an unproductive or vulnerable condition, as "being under the control of" or "not being aware". Using the word "dream" might be more appropriate because the qualities of dreaming in sleep are somewhat similar to trance, except that one is generally aware of the self and the body in a way not usually experienced in sleep. Often referred to as non-ordinary reality, the trance state is a particular functioning mode of the brain and body and is as simple to move in and out of as any other state of consciousness. Traditionally trance is achieved by several means: physical exhaustion, fasting, dancing, sense deprivation, pain, repetitive singing or chanting, drumming to specific rhythms and speeds, and ingestion of sacred psychoactive plants. But for the essential ritual and spiritual context, the average rave provides all the stimuli for entering trance! In what is called "core shamanism" that is, basic shamanic technique removed from any cultural context or belief system, the usual way of entering trance is through dance and drumming or rattling. Many people would doubt such a seemingly simple thing as an inherently boring and monotonous drumbeat could profoundly change our perspective on reality, but thousands of years of experience prove that there is a scientifically repeatable way of altering physiological function in a few moments.

So, to recap, the shamanic viewpoint of spirits is that: everything is alive; everything has one or more spirits; it is possible and indeed desirable to know the nature and the wishes of the spirits; a trained individual can communicate with the spirits at will and can enlist their help; there will be particular spirits that can attune more closely to each individual and these can become guides and allies; all manifest activity, weather, food sources, disease, healing and so on are the result of spirit activity reflected back into Middle World three-dimensionality and requires action at subtle spirit levels to effect physical change.

In some respects, Plato's image of The Cave is a shamanic view. The phenomenal world is merely a shadow of activity in the supra-physical or spiritual world which is the Real World. The vast majority of human perception is limited to seeing only the smallest fragments simply because of habit patterns and predilections. This point of view passed along to the Neo-Platonists such as Plotinus, who in turn influenced the more metaphysical thinkers of the Early Christian Church, particularly its heretical side-shoots, and later fed into the metaphysics and magical thought of the Middle Ages.

The Folk, "Pagan" View

In many respects the folk view - which is the view of the peasant, the land-worker, the farmer - is a continuation of the native shamanic view, or at least the stubborn clinging to a pre-historic, pre-literate, pre-State-owned structure that has been diluted or re-translated in the terms of the current popular religion and mixed with superstition. (Superstition being those beliefs still in common currency where the reasons for those beliefs are no longer known, that is, non-rational belief.)

Invaders may come, liberators may go, but on the whole, invaders and liberators are interested in political or religious power - not in growing vegetables and rearing animals! Commoners may be slaughtered and exploited but there's always someone needed to grow the food and clear up the mess. A tangled thread of continuity remains in every rural community, until such time as increasing pressure from outside causes it to break down and collapse.

The folk view is land-based. It is fundamentally about specific landscapes: this river, this rock, this tree and the history, legends and tales related to the topography of a small area. The knowledge is a mnemonic amalgamation of different times and different beliefs fitted together into a jigsaw of rich significance. Spirits may now become saints, local deities may now be fairies or elves, but overall the view is one of knowing the history, respecting the spirits and acting in traditional ways on festival days. Because the very continuation of a folk tradition is often determined by the degree it is kept secret, it is naturally an undercover, private, word of mouth trans-mission not easy for any outsider to get a full or accurate picture.

The modern pagan worldview is a consciously determined rebuilding of an assumed past within its own belief structures. Both views, however, essentially maintain the same premise that an understanding of the need to harmonise with the land and its inhabitants is vital for material and spiritual well-being. The subtle entities -spirits, fairies, gods etc. are caretakers for that well-being and fertility and at those locally known sacred places they are propitiated and acknowledged.

Tree spirit carved in wood at Bishops Lydeard Church

There may be a huge wealth of knowledge hidden in folk and fairy tales concerning the nature and characteristics of tree spirits, but so much would depend on the accuracy of transmission and translation. It is so easy to change the name of one tree for another, and over time to edit out important details. What we can say fairly certainly is that within this tradition the spirits are linked directly to places, rocks, trees, and that they rarely seem able to move far away from their homes. They are the spirits of place, the spirits of nature, the consciousness and personality of the landscape.

The Fairy Tradition

There is a huge variety of description and definition in fairy lore - so much so that it often appears to be the repository of every psychic and paranormal encounter worthy enough to be remembered and retold. As though it were the subtly manifesting memory of the land itself, the fairy experience is nearly always within a mythic timeframe. They are perceived as beings from olden times, in antiquated dress, following ancient custom in their behaviour. Whether they are benevolent, malevolent or disinterested, due care and respect must be paid to them when they appear.

Many types of tree and specific natural sites have fairy connections but, on the whole, the traditional view of the fairy kingdoms suggests that these sites are gateways to their world: interfaces between dimensions. Although some fairies, or fairy-type encounters, indicate them inhabiting a tree, for example, and by their behaviour caring for or nurturing the tree, they are not of the tree itself. Fairies do not appear to be the same as tree spirits (ie. the Classical Dryads for example), or a tree soul as perceived in the shamanic view. Some records of fairy encounters do seem to be with nature spirits as such, but the majority seem otherwise.

There are many theories as to the true origin and nature of fairies. Some suggest that they are connected with the dead, either as unbaptised or heathen souls, and their association with burial mounds would naturally lead to this conclusion, especially by those Christians wanting to place fairies within their own familiar spiritual hierarchical cosmology. In a similar way fairies are said to be fallen angels who either failed to reach Hell before it was sealed or who were not quite so rebellious and so only fell as far as Earth. Other views present them as the remnants of, (or the memory of the remnants of) ancient aboriginal races and in a similar vein the slowly dwindling remains of forgotten deities. From the 17th century onwards, particularly in the Classically influenced literature, fairies are increasingly portrayed as diminutive beings closely linked to the processes of nature - that is, they are absorbed into the magical tradition as astral or elemental spirits.

A strong tradition is that the fairy kingdoms are a real race of invisible or spiritual beings living in a generally invisible world of their own that in some way is parallel and has a relationship to our own. This is the view presented very fully by R. J. Stewart in his books dealing with the Underworld Tradition and he presents a powerful, coherent picture of a parallel yet reachable world. That dimension has its own ambience and we ourselves have found it a useful adjunct to our other work with trees. However, in his more recent books on the subject he does tend to, rather crudely, deny the reality of other people's experiences of subtle beings that they have interpreted, or labelled, as fairy. Although he may be technically correct in limiting his definition of Faery, it ill behooves a promoter of one imaginal realm to denounce other's imaginal experiences as delusional or naive. As we continue this survey of worldviews it may become apparent why some of this confusion has arisen.

The Magical View

The magical or Hermetic view of spirits is important to us because it is this view more than any other that has influenced the direction of metaphysical thought in Europe that carries within it many hidden assumptions of our present worldview. This view is an amalgamation of the esoteric teachings found within the main religions of the West. It is a vast area of imagery and system and is, historically, the approach of the medieval intellectual and philosopher ("lover of wisdom").

Whereas the shamanic view has a tendency towards integration and holism, the magical view very definitely creates a polarity between spirit and matter, light and darkness, good and evil. One of the core Hermetic concepts, which perhaps originated from, or was promulgated by, many separate heretical and gnostic groups, is that the matter of the physical world can only become animated by the soul, which is seen as a spark of the Original Creator. This fragment of the Whole is always, therefore, striving to return to its Source, to become fulfilled and whole once again. Such a view immediately creates an antagonism between the manifestation of the world of matter and the world of spirit, which is seen as trapped, beguiled or disguised within it. This antagonism is often implicit in the mainstream religious dogma but in the magical view it becomes explicit and the motivating force for evolutionary action.

Whilst the shamanic view is essentially cyclical, the Hermetic is linear and evolutionary. In this cosmology there is a clear hierarchical chain of beings that are ascending towards the Creator or descending towards matter. Mankind is generally seen as midway on this ladder of existence, able through the gift of Free Will to climb higher than the angels or sink into the darkest regions of Hell.

The key to the magical view is the acquisition of knowledge. The universe of external reality, the macrocosm, is seen as a reflection of internal reality, the microcosm, and vice versa. "Outside" and "inside" are aspects of the same reality. The modern phenomenon of the hologram, each part of which contains the whole, would be perfectly understandable to this view. The magical activities of talking to spirits, summoning angels, conjuring demons is seen as a practical means to gain wisdom from other planes of existence. And alchemy is a transmutation of matter that parallels an interior transmutation of physical to spiritual. A multiplicity of non-human spiritual entities derive from a huge range of ancient and apocryphal sources: gods and demons from Egypt and the Middle East; Classical Nature spirits, especially the elemental spirits of Earth, Air, Fire and Water; Arabic demon kings and Qabbalistic Orders of Angels. The magician's world is seen as an endless chain of spirit falling into or clambering out of matter.

Magical procedures, then as now, were based on the principles of resonance, sympathy and vibration. All the senses were focussed on the intended conjuration by means of name, invocation, talismanic diagram, incense, astrological timing, ritual gesture and so on to create a strong enough bond with the spirit to allow it to manifest. Although the precise nature of these focussing devices are culturally specific, the principals behind them are universal and can be found any-

---

Opposite: A crossroads on Dartmoor. The sense or presence and the numinous is a natural part of living close to the world. In undisturbed places thoroughout Britain there can still be found a harmonious blending of symbol and belief that enhances the spirit of a place. This small crossroads, an Otherworld doorway of Celtic and folk tradition, consists of a small hummock of grass, an ancient hollow oak pollard and a rough-hewn granite cross. Both cross and tree seem to echo each other's quality of permanence and sanctity.

where in the world where there is a need or desire to communicate with the invisible realms.

Within the Hermetic view there is a pervading idea of supernatural teachers, hidden Adepts, who watch over and initiate worthy disciples into their own branch of the Mysteries, and who give a helping hand up the rungs of the ladder towards the ineffable knowledge of the Creator.

Because of its closeness to many heretical beliefs the magical tradition always had to keep its head well down, but even so, many fell foul of the Church and suffered its penalties. Through the upheaval of the European Reformation the magical view transformed into the scientific view, stripping itself of any serious consideration of the supernatural and spirit worlds yet maintaining the concepts of orderly progress, hierarchical development (though now seen in terms of increasing complexity of form rather than spirituality), and the thirst for knowledge.

Only during the 20th century were the powerful Hermetic symbolism and the various strands of the magical hierarchy to re-emerge, little changed. C. G. Jung revitalised interest in the interior reality of Hermetic symbolism, whilst the Theosophists combined Hermetic with Classical Indian views to create a whole new terminology of spiritual reality. They too reinvigorated the concept of Inner Plane Teachers that still develops in the channellings of various Ascended Masters and their disciples today.

The Theosophical View

Theosophy remained a vital movement for a comparatively short time before it fragmented under pressure from within. However it drew together intellectuals, mystics, psychics and magicians and presented a coherent, though complex, cosmology that still underlies many of the assumptions of

New Age thinking. Brought to the West by a Russian emigre, Madame Blavatsky, Theosophy was an amalgamation of inspirational (channelled) material with newly translated Classical Indian texts on the subtle anatomy of man and the spiritual structure of existence, together with Qabbalistic and Hermetic ideas. Of particular relevance to us here is their concept of devas and nature spirits. The term "deva" was borrowed directly from the Sanskrit. Meaning "shining one", and used loosely to describe any god or spirit, it quickly came to refer to any large, conscious, overwatching spiritual being of Nature.

The Theosophists view the devic realms as a parallel evolutionary hierarchy to our own, though with its focus on different aspects of creation. Whereas physically embodied creation is focused on evolutionary activity, devic creation is focussed on stabilised Being. The stream of physical evolution is seen as a Hermetic ladder of striving towards understanding greater consciousness - the spark rejoining the fire, the drop flowing to the ocean, whilst the devic evolution already exists within unlimited, boundless conscious Awareness and strives towards understanding the nature of bounded form through directing the processes of manifestation.

The language used to describe devic beings is drawn from many esoteric traditions. Use of terms like gnome, elf, fairy, deva, are ways of labelling a perceived and perceivable awareness-being and this does cause some confusion with those people who use the same words to define different types of being altogether, as we have already seen.

Every level of manifest creation is understood as having a parallel guiding or activating devic energy. So the largest devic beings are those of planetary and solar systems who channel and mould the raw energy of consciousness towards matter and direct the tendency towards manifestation. Devic beings can be seen as the vessels that hold the shape of the contents of the vessel. They are not necessarily of the same substance as the vessel but they "inform" or "enfold" the matter and energy within. In some ways the concept of the devic realms is similar to the Platonic Idea or Prototype, the Jungian Archetype, and Sheldrake's Morphogenetic Fields - where some subtle shaping tendency establishes the boundaries of form into which the physical matter flows to take shape according to its nature.

So the highest devic orders hold the thought, pattern and sound of the vibration of an entire system, whether that be a planet, a landscape or a species. Holding the pattern steady is the devic means of achieving focus and purpose. We may be aware sometimes that a certain area of landscape has a very individual "feel" to it, a character of its own. Looking from this Theosophical perspective it is the "feel" of the devic thought-pattern that moulds the landscape into its distinctive form: the landscape falls into shape around the devic pattern.

When perceived by sensitives, devas of this magnitude are often described as huge beings of light, or spinning vortices of energy, that enclose and permeate the entire area under their care. They are often compared to great angels - as the planetary devas are compared to archangelic or god forms.

The next level of devic manifestation has a smaller range of consciousness and align themselves to the patterns of a particular devic "oversoul". They become the spirits or guardians of the subdivisions of the devic whole. So the deva of Willow will hold the Idea of "willowness" in all its manifestations, and to this Idea will be drawn other devic spirits who will attach to a particular group of willows or a particular tree and become its spirit or guardian.

The smallest, most specialised members of devic evolution are those awareness-energies who guide, enhance or encourage the physical functions of their chosen host. They are the elementals or fairies, usually psychically perceived as tiny bright lights dancing around, through and between the physical structures, and who seem the most adaptable in their outward form, often mimicking or reflecting the belief systems of human observers.

The elementals are divided into four main groupings as in Hermetic tradition from the Classical original. Those elementals concerned with fire itself and all fiery, energetic processes are known as salamanders; water elementals concerned with liquid movement and watery environments are called undines; those of the air and atmosphere are sylphs; and those of earth, soil and the crystallisation of matter are the gnomes. As each branch of elemental has well-known traditional forms, that is how they often appear to those with subtle sight.

To picture this system a little more clearly we can parallel the devic entity with the human being. The "body" of the deva is composed of all the independent discrete entities within its care, as our own human body is composed of individually functioning cells and organs. The main distinctions are that, firstly, a deva "oversoul" is always aware of all parts of its "body" whereas we more or less let our bodies get on with it with little conscious control or interest. Our attention tends to be directed outwards to the world beyond our body's boundaries. Secondly, a deva's "body" may be located in many different physical locations - wherever a part exists it is encompassed by the consciousness of the deva. That is, the deva focuses its awareness inwards.

The Theosophical view has been explored by many sensitives this century, notably Geoffrey Hodson, and more recently by the Findhorn Community in general and by Dorothy Maclean in particular. Personally, I find the latter's channelled and inspired writings from devas to be amongst the most useful.

They seem to carry the different flavours of each being well and contain much specific information. Probably because of the difficulty of translating from one state of being to another, much that purports to be from devic sources is vague, woolly and overly saccharine and very often bears more of the imprint of the channeller's own agenda than the character of the devic source.

Working in conscious partnership with devic awareness, "co-creating", has a growing number of advocates, and cynical critics of this worldview need to consider the horticultural and environmental benefits that often seem to result from this cooperation, and to parallel the ambience of this view with that held by "traditional" peoples such as the Hopi and Kogi, who also consider themselves as guardians and gardeners in close rapport with the spirit beings of Nature.

The Celt, the Shaman and the Tree

There are many excellent books cataloguing the place of the tree in mythology, religion and culture. Throughout the world in nearly every period of history and prehistory the tree emerges as a symbol of primary cosmological importance. A symbol is an object or thing in its own right that, by its very characteristics serves as a metaphor for concepts that may not have very much to do with the thing itself or with objective fact. A symbol is psychologically more powerful than a simple thing just because it can bring together in the mind a constellation of concept and imagery. A symbol is a gestalt, an overview, a shorthand expression for a particular quality of human existence. The rational and scientific duality that creates subject and object, denies the power of symbol which in traditional societies, unites the outer and inner worlds.

The Inuit of the northern polar regions and the subarctic tundra are perhaps one of the few peoples who live in a completely treeless environment and so have few references to trees in their cosmology. The indigenous peoples of Northern Europe, on the other hand, dwelt on the fringes of vast, nearly impenetrable forests with cultivable meadows and thinly wooded downs. Trees were the raw materials for a large proportion of their technologies. They were a source of nourishment and also of numinosity. The forest was the provider of food and a world where humanity was at best a temporary visitor, at worst a trespasser in the territory of spirits and hungry predators.

These forests are long gone, but contemporary documentaries, diaries and journals of Westerners entering the remaining jungles of South America clearly remind us of the need for a deep knowledge of the environment if we are to survive there. In such tree-encompassed worlds the relationship between tree and human is direct and potent, as we shall see a little later when we examine a contemporary shaman's experiences in the Amazon.

Mother of Wild Animals

There is a frequent ambiguity in human relationship with the forest. For those from outside its borders it is an alien world, full of the power of both life and death. Sometimes the forest is a magical, benign place but more often it is the dwelling of demons and spirits. There is a hymn, a shamanic song, from the tenth mandala of *Rig Veda* that, even in translation, gives a view of the Indo- European experience of the wild forest. Here it is benign and mysterious, but there is also a frisson of Otherness, and perhaps a yearning for the boundlessness of the greater world whilst looking back to the comfortable security of human society.

The song is addressed to a goddess energy, Aranyani, the tutelary goddess of the forest and the mother of wild animals:

"Aranyani, Aranyani, who art, as it were, perishing there, why dost thou not inquire of the village, does not fear assail thee?

When the chichchika replies to the crying vrisharava, Aranyani is exalted, resonant, as with cymbals.

It is as if rays of light were playing about, and it looks like a dwelling, and Aranyani at eventide, as it were dismissed the waggons.

This man calls his cow, another cuts down the timber; tarrying in the forest at eventide, one thinks there is a cry.

But Aranyani injures no one unless some other assail him; feeding upon the sweet fruit, he penetrates at will.

I praise the musk-scented, fragrant, fertile, uncultivated Aranyani, the mother of wild animals."

(*Rig Veda* 10.10.18)

The Celts have become, mythologically, if not in reality, the benchmark of indigenous native European spirituality for many people. The Celts seem to be our very own "Red Indians". They are a potent projection of our psyches in which historical and archaeological evidence whimpers in the background of a stage-hogging, melodramatic diva. Like the Native Americans, the tribal groupings of Celtic peoples were generally mutually belligerent and incapable of mounting a unified, concerted effort at resisting imperial colonisation.

They are the heroic vanquished, the Beauty and Truth of the Glorious Past erased by an unthinking, pragmatic, work-a-day present. The Celts, who bravely stood up to the Romans, the Anglo-Saxons, the English, the French, the Normans and whoever - the spiritual defending against imperial materialism. For a culture that at one time spread from beyond the Black Sea in the east to the Atlantic coasts in the west we know precious little about them. Relying on oral transmission rather than the written language, we can only get to grips with these ancestors of ours through the clues they left in stories and archaeological remains, and from the reports of other contemporary observers who had dealings with the Celts.

People may have been speaking a form of Celtic language as early as 2000BC, and the art of Bronze Age Europe and early Celtic culture shows a distinct continuity, which probably also indicates a continuity of religious beliefs. It was the collapse

90

of the Hittite Empire in central Turkey in the 12th and 13th centuries BC that fed cultural and technological change. Ironworking had been a secret monopoly of this kingdom and with its demise, skilled craftsmen began to roam through Europe trading their knowledge. The earliest known, clearly definable Celtic culture is called the Hallstadt period, which significantly covers a mineral-rich area of Switzerland and Austria, where mining had been a familiar skill for many centuries.

What seems to be clear is that the Celtic expansion is one of culture rather than peoples - though movement of tribal groupings was an endless parade throughout the prehistory of Europe. Celtic language and culture is one of several branches of the Indo-European tree whose roots were in the barren wildernesses between the Caspian Sea and the Hindu Kush and whose other branches grew eastwards into India, as well as westwards to establish the Mediterranean cultures of the Classical world. Modern scholars are beginning to see remarkable and fundamental parallels between the best preserved Celtic cultures of Ireland and Vedic India, not only in language but also in religious terminology, science and the structure of society.

Opposite: Decorated copper sheaths about six inches long from Tal-y-Llyn, Merionethshire, Wales. The central image of this foliate design is a typically enigmatic Celtic head with large almond-shaped, prominent eyes. The mirrored design on each sheath uncannily resembles the appearance of tree spirits as seen in contemporary shamanic journeys. The benign and simultaneously threatening faces, the disorientation ("which way is up?"), and the leaflike and spiral flows all reinforce this impression. The two large leaves or ears are frequently found in Celtic figurative art. Their significance is unclear but they seem to indicate deity, or at least spiritual power - emanations from the place of power, the head. From the Early La Tene Style, c. 300BC.

91

Celts and Trees

One thing is clear: trees played a major part in Celtic belief systems. Their sacred groves, the "nemeton", is mentioned by fairly reliable Roman historians. Clearly of more significance is the fact that the Roman armies made sure that sacred groves were their first targets when subduing unruly Celtic areas. The motivation for the invasion of the British Isles came largely from the fact that the continental Celts, under continued pressure during the 1st century BC from Roman aggression, regarded these islands as the home of druidic learning and so the source of Celtic resistance to Latin acculturisation. The holiest place in Britain was Mona, the Island of Anglesey, where druidic training was centred. The Roman destruction of its sacred groves and all who attempted to protect them ended the last hope of independence.

Not to be outdone, the Celts themselves were not averse to destroying each others' sacred groves and holy trees during inter-tribal warfare. Like the taking of warrior's heads and the bonding of the defeated in servitude, destroying the source of tribal identity and its spiritual focus transferred its power to the victors.

Opposite: An Early Celtic flagon handle decorated with spiral, foliage and spirit head. These three themes linking the world of man and plant continue throughout the Celtic period and well into the medieval period. Though individual motifs derive from other cultures - particularly the Classical Mediterranean - the continuity and prevalence, and the unique development, of Celtic art shows what a deep power such images retained long after the original meanings had been forgotten. The Celts were particularly fond of Roman and Greek wine, a powerful intoxicant derived from a single type of plant, the grape vine. Sacred brews are a recurring theme in Celtic mythology, and the fact that they derive from plant sources would suggest a conscious awareness of the spiritual nature of trees and other plants.

Carrying on this noble tradition, Christian missionaries, both from Rome and from the Celtic lands themselves, chopped and burned their way through many of the remaining groves when other means of dialogue or persuasion failed. One of the worse culprits was St. Boniface, an English monk from Crediton in mid-Devon, who swept through Europe tirelessly destroying sacred sites not of his own religion. Ironically, an upland area of central Devon, midway between the Dart and Exe moors, not far from Boniface's home, is recognised from its place names as constituting a sacred Celtic landscape.

The Sacred Grove

One thing that is known for certain about the Celts was their religious and spiritual character, (excessive from the Roman's pragmatic point of view), and that their spiritual life was focused around the sacred grove - the "nemeton". Every tribe was focused around a sacred grove, tree or stone and place names derived from "nemeton" are still found throughout Europe. It is recorded that in 280 BC a great Celtic convocation was held at Drunemeton, "the chief sacred place", in Galetea, a Celtic enclave in central Asia Minor (present day Turkey).

Tacitus, one of the more trustworthy Roman chroniclers, wrote in *"Germania"*:

> *"The grove is the centre of their whole religion. It is regarded as the cradle of the race and the dwelling place of the supreme god to whom all things are subject and obedient."*

The Devon Grove

Place names containing the word nymet, nimet, or nymph and nympton are related to the Gallic (continental Celtic) word nemeton - holy place. The same word can be found in Welsh where it is nyfed; Old Welsh where it is nimet, meaning a shrine or holy place; in Old Saxon a forest sanctuary or holy grove is nimed; and in Celtic the root is nemeto-nemetis, a sacred grove.

In mid Devon there are two areas where these names are clustered. Between Crediton and Okehampton there are at least nine placenames with nymet. A little farther north, along the River Taw, in the high hills midway between the moors there is a group of four nymptons.

At Broadnymet, just east of North Tawton, the remains of a neolithic henge has been rediscovered which consists of an eye-shaped enclosure with two entrances and an internal "pupil" of pits. Barrows and ring ditches are also at this site. The area had obviously been regarded as sacred for many centuries before the Celtic Iron Age. It has been suggested that this sacred forest may have been as large as 1200 square miles in area.

There are a large number of churches and chapels clustering here, a further indication of the adoption or takeover of a pre-eminent sacred area. There are quite a few dedicated to St. Martin of Tours. This is yet another pointer to strong pre-Christian worship as the man was never happy unless he was tearing down and destroying pagan altars in wild and remote corners of Europe. Broadnymet derives from "brode nymet", meaning: very sacred grove, suggesting that here was possibly the most sacred centre of the entire sacred landscape.

The northerly area is still well-wooded in its valleys and does have the quality of an island outside of time. There is one special area here, not visually spectacular, but by all appearances a haven for the spiritual entities who once perhaps roamed more extensively in this region. The human guardian lives there in her wooden bungalow inherited from a female relative. Visitors, especially those who stay overnight, are very often disturbed or unable to sleep because of all the

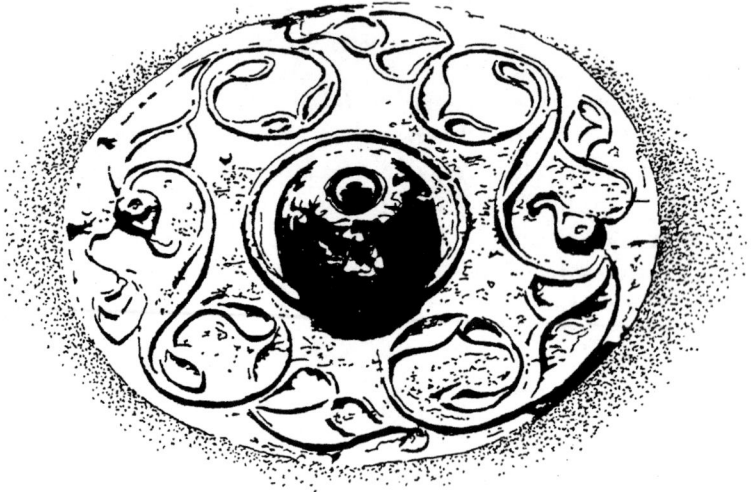

A shield boss, approx 38cm(15 inches) across recovered from Wandsworth, London. Dating from the 1'" century BC. This design shows the characteristic perceptual play within British Celtic art. Strict symmetry is avoided, plant becomes animal and animal, plant. Such fluidity suggests an understanding of the awareness present in all life, whether plant or animal. The fact that such designs appear frequently on battle gear may carry a magical significance. Tribal art worldwide has symbolic meaning. There is rarely "pure decoration" to be found anywhere. In this context it could be assumed that the designs are either protective or an enhancement of power, and therefore indicate that trees and plants were held to contain this same power.

inter-dimensional comings and goings. Many are aware of a large being that inhabits the garden and is known as the Green Man. Even amateur video has sometimes unexpectedly revealed some unidentified presences, and in some areas of the grounds it is unwise to leave your car as the electrics have a habit of failing. There are places like this throughout Britain, places where the old energies still hover and where the people live quietly in the old way of things.

Wise Trees

Throughout the existing documentation of the Celtic tradition, mainly as it was written down in Ireland, and to some extent in Wales and as it is buried throughout in local folklore and tradition, trees continually appear linked to wisdom, learning and poetry. The connection can be found in the modern Welsh words: "*gwydd*" - trees; "*gwyddon*" - a magician; "*gwyddor*" - science; "Yr *Wyddor*" - the alphabet, all somehow linked with that archetypal mystic and magician, Gwydion.

Son of Tree

Trees became linked to the ogham alphabet of the far West and later, to the Welsh coelbran. There have also been suggestions that some techniques of communication used arrangements of leaves and twigs to convey secret messages. It seems that trees became associated with specific lineages of traditions and mystery schools though it is not clear whether this is a purely geographical link or of spiritual significance. The latter is quite feasible particularly considering the frequent appearance of names that translate as trees: son of oak - MacDara; son of rowan - MacCairthin; son of blackthorn - MacDregin; son of yew - MacI, MacIbair; son of holly - MacCuillinn; son of hazel - MacColl. It is possible that these relate to tribal guardians or totems, or perhaps to types of personal initiation the individuals had undergone in their training. In Ireland there existed a type of poet named "dos" who, apparently, was so called "from his similitude to a tree....that is, it is through (or under) the name of a tree they "learn their art"..."

Irish law also stated categorically that the felling of specific trees would incur set fines. For a chieftain tree, that is, an oak, hazel, holly, yew, ash, pine or apple, a heifer would be forfeit for cutting the limbs or branches and a cow for cutting the trunk. For commoner trees - alder, willow, hawthorn, rowan, birch and elm, a cow for the tree, a heifer for the branches. For shrub trees, blackthorn, elder, spindle, white hazel, aspen, strawberry tree and test tree, a heifer. For the bramble trees: fern, bog myrtle, furze, briar, heather, ivy, broom and gooseberry, there was a fine of a sheep.

Tree Alphabets and Tree Calendars

One of the best known associations between the Celts and trees is in the ogham alphabets and the tree calendars that derive from them. It is ironic that this system has probably done more to upgrade the spiritual significance of trees than any other set of imagery, and yet, in all likelihood, the system is entirely spurious as far as authentic Celtic tradition is concerned.

The sequence of trees associated with lunar months - seems to have little internal logic as to which tree should appear where in the yearly cycle. The whole shabang was begun by Robert Graves in "*The White Goddess*".Graves drew on dubious scholasticism to further his hypothesis by moulding an inaccurate ogham sequence and bending linguistics to give them all tree names. Graves did have some sense of responsibility, for he asked a revered Celtic scholar for an opinion on the thesis. He was advised not to pursue the matter as it lacked all scholastic credibility, yet he persevered regardless and the rest is history (or not). Had Mr. Graves bothered to consult the works of his grandfather, Charles Graves, a leading authority on ogham at the beginning of the century, he may have avoided some of his most blatant errors.

The naming of ogham characters does vary from text to text, but most mention twenty-five letters, not the eighteen of Graves and his dubious source O'Flaherty. Some texts do say the ogham letters were named from trees, but they were also linked to places, animals, colours, directions and so on. It is now considered that the original ogham script contained twenty characters in four groups of five with a later five added to accommodate Greek and Latin characters not already included. "The characters were probably given names in the fourteenth century AD (no earlier) for teaching purposes, so that children could recognise them" (a quote from Celtic scholar and linguist, Peter Berresford Ellis, in an article: *"The Fabrication of "Celtic" Astrology"*, Astrological Association Journal, 1997).

If this is indeed the case, it would be as if a stranger had come across and then read an entire spiritual tradition into "A is for Apple, B is for Bear, C is for Cat, D is for Door..." and so on....!Rejecting Robert Graves and the hoards of tree calendars in no way diminishes the close spiritual relationship between tree and Celt, but it does remove some of the dogmatic straightjacket of meanings that have become set in neo-Celtic doctrinal concrete over the last few decades. Popular attributions tend to inhibit the desire for personal exploration into what energy characteristics the trees actually seem to possess.

It is not impossible that a coherent system of correspondences between ogham and trees did exist. Ogham seems to have been linked poetically to many concepts, allowing the skilled poet to juxtapose and riddle his way to any number of magical meanings, but as far as the Celtic scholars are concerned, there is no evidence for a tree calendar, or tree zodiac or a

complete tree ogham. To again quote from Peter Berresford Ellis:

"L = luis (claimed as a rowan) either comes from luise (flame, blaze) or lus (plant, herb). It is not placed in a context that makes either derivation reliable. N = nion or nin (claimed as ash) is a fork or loft. H = uath (claimed as hawthorn) means horror or fear. T = tinne (claimed as ash and sometimes holly) means a bar, rod of metal, ingot etc. M = muin (claimed as vine) means neck or throat. G = gort (claimed as ivy) means a field. R = ruis (claimed as elder) is from the word for red...".

Some commentators have drawn poetic parallels between the usual linguistic interpretation and the tree names. A skilled poet can likewise create significant links between the disparate. Poetic kenning and poetic truth is not quite the

---

Opposite: Among the most enigmatic of Celtic artwork are the many coins cast by each tribal region. Many designs can be traced to Classical originals but there is an obvious shift away from literal figuration to symbol. As emblems of tribal wealth and power it is likely that the chosen symbols are of particular significance to each tribe - like the tartans and badges of the Scottish clans. Trees do not appear very often, but there are examples, sometimes identifiable like ash and ivy leaves. Above: depending on which way it is viewed this coin seems to show either a deer browsing on a tree a potent symbol of life-force within the primal forest - or, turning the coin around, antlers become the feet of a bird displaying coxcomb and decorative tail feathers. It may also be significant that there are thirteen circles linking the imagery to the lunar year. As well as a dweller and guardian of the wood, the deer has tree-like qualities, with antlers like branches that are able to be shed and regrow. Below: A fierce beast, possibly a dog, is guarding a fruit- bearing tree. Below its feet are what could be tree roots or perhaps a cut branch, a sickle and another tree with sickle-moon like protrusion.

same as historical veracity. Such parallels may provide significant spiritual insights but they should not therefore simply be accepted as what was originally meant in the original texts.

There is an obvious discrepancy here between the linguists who have in-depth knowledge of the old languages in the original manuscripts and the contemporary disciples of Celtia, who, despite a fabricated system, seem to be able to extract meaning and valuable insight. This shows us that it is wise to check the sources of information as carefully as we can, to validate received wisdom with personal practical experience at all times - but not to dismiss something simply because it is not ancient ("authentic").

Working with tree spirits directly is the most important process, but we have found that gleanings from folk information and Celtic references to specific trees have given valuable avenues for exploration. Personal experiences in the imaginal realms of tree spirits do seem to reiterate and validate some of this traditional imagery. It is difficult to determine here which is chicken and which is egg, but what

---

Opposite: The Romanesque, between the 10th and 13'th centuries was the first great cathedral building period. From a simple unadorned beginning vegetative decoration and allusion took over, until at the height of cathedral building the Christian Church was doing nothing so much as reconstructing sacred groves in stone. From the earliest cave-like simplicity the power of the tree took hold. First column capitals, then vaults and ceilings became the image of plants in stone. This vegetation became inhabited by figures from Christian and pre-Christian times. None is more ubiquitous than the elusive and often carefully concealed figures of the Green Man. He appears as the spirit from which many of the vegetative dreams arise, as if it were the very image of the numinous intelligence of the natural world.

can be said is that surrounding each tree energy and each tree spirit there is a certain identifiable constellation of image and meaning. This acts as a language of symbol whereby tree and human kingdoms can interact. Like all language, the vocabulary is continuing to expand.

This book contains many images drawn from our Celtic heritage. No matter what survives as far as authentic literature is concerned, the surviving art and artefacts clearly demonstrate the importance of the plant form to the Celts. This is absent in the Anglo-Saxon period where animal forms predominate, and it was merely from the space-fillers in Greek and Etruscan art that the Celts derived many of their original motifs.

Opposite: A detail from the Milan Candlestick made around the beginning of the 13th century, perhaps in England, portraying one of the Rivers of Paradise personified. In much medieval art the relationship between the human world and the world of nature, the World Tree, is ambiguous. Depending on one' s own frame of reference the figures can be seen as benignly living within the tree or they can appear to be struggling to control or master the abundant and wild growth. This dichotomy, essentially the pagan view and the Christian view, was perhaps more important to the medieval mind than we would guess. After all, even as late as the middle of the 15th century pagan priests were still being brought to trial and executed in London. The "pagan", right from the first Roman use of the term, was the country dweller at home within nature. The Church was at home in its urban centres, the towns and cities surrounded by walls to keep out the wild world of nature. The fundamental concept of duality, of dark and light, matter and spirit, evil and good that existed in many of the preChristian religions of urban Western Asia became entrenched also in the Church. The world was seen as a lascivious temptation, a trap preventing souls from reaching God. It is ironic that the most beautiful expressions of belief take the form of the tree and the forest in the great cathedrals of Europe.

The Celts chose the patterns they used for a purpose, like all cultures do. They chose what was aesthetically satisfying, technologically feasible and spiritually relevant. Whether this also carried culturally specific, widely understood religious iconography is not so easy to say. It is very difficult to know the psychological stance of a people at such a distance in time - even their words are interpreted and given meaning from our own view of the world. As more becomes understood about shamanic world-views in tribal contexts, primary Celtic source materials are re-evaluated from this point of view. However, because Shamanic Studies is a popular area among both scholars and seekers at the moment, the evidence will inevitably be selected to uphold these current theories.

Opposite: The "inhabited scroll" is the most prevalent motif of medieval art. It derives from Celtic spiral patterns, Tree of life imagery from the Mediterranean world, and animal interlace from Northern Europe. Animals and humans scramble, climb and merge with the branches and leaves of the all- pervasive tree of life. As well as being a flexible artistic device able to fill any space with a limitless variation, the inhabited scroll becomes the symbol for the container of life, (that is, the World Tree). It also is the tree as sustainer and symbol for Christ who is the "True Vine" and who inhabited the tree (hung on the Cross), as many pre-Christian deities had before him. The image of the tree thus becomes synonymous with Christ and his teachings - surely no accident of iconography.
In the Arabic world the tree becomes the main motif for Paradise. Islam as it developed into an iconoclastic religion unwilling to portray humans, took the tree as symbol for all that is abundant and perfect - a natural thing to do among desert-dwellers who are acutely aware that the trees of the cases mean water, life and much needed shade.
There was also a cross-fertilisation of imagery from the Celtic monastic communities of Ireland and the North African and Egyptian Coptic Christians which helped to create the "carpet" pages of the famous illuminated manuscripts, that, in their turn, helped to re-introduce this later Celtic art back into Continental Europe with Irish missionaries.

Those who examine the existing material of the Celtic heritage, which has for centuries remained untranslated and unread in dusty corners of libraries, are becoming increasingly aware of the close ties to Indo-European heritage, notably with the Vedic cultures of northern India. The language of names, concepts, even astrological and cosmological systems, show a common origin. There is, as we have already seen, some tree imagery in classic Vedic literature but the Celtic flowering of individuality must owe as much to the lands they dwelt in and passed through, as well as the structures of the Neolithic mind.

The shamanic view of the world is important to understand as it seems to encompass those primordial techniques of altering perception that allow glimpses of other sorts of reality apart from the consensus. Whatever the cultural context the

---

Opposite: Exeter Cathedral has many examples of the Green Man hidden amongst the stone foliage. This intricately carved corbel-stone that supports one of the nave vaults has a complex symbolism. At its lowest point there is a Green Man head from which arises all the surrounding vegetation. This seems to be a representation of the World of nature. This spirit is supporting the Virgin and Child, Redeemer of the World. Above Mary's crown two angels hover with censers. From one perspective of iconography the Green Man can be equated with the Serpent within the Tree of Knowledge upon whose head Eve's seed has been prophesied to step - Nature as tempter vanquished by the manifesting Deity as He redeems the Original Fall of Man. Alternately, the Spirit of the World, the Green Man, is the true support for the Mother (Goddess) and Her reborn Son. Victory over Nature or victory with Nature - this carving illustrates a human problem yet to be solved. Perhaps there is a solution, too, within the imagery. The Mother and Child are in the middle. Mother Mary (as Goddess) specifically mediates between Heaven (the angels) and Earth (the Green Man), spirit and matter are harmonised. Or is the whole carving simply a disguise for an older cosmology - the Goddess manifesting from within Her world as a spirit would emerge from its tree?

human brain has remained the same for hundreds and thousands of years - the same tricks, the same techniques, will bring about ecstasy because they have proved to consistently create changes in the brain. It isn't necessary to believe in the objective reality of spirits to be able to enter a trance state. It isn't necessary to believe in religious dogma to enter meditative states. With a human mind, given the opportunity, it will simply happen as a natural function of being. It is the interpretation of these experiences is what fuels the development of cosmologies and religions.

As shamanic techniques seem to be near universal in tribal society structures (and still existent though given stricter control and religious trappings in urban communities), it is valid to look for shamanic-type experience and techniques in

---

Opposite: There's no getting away from the fact that in Judeo-Christian tradition, as in so many others, the beginning of mankind' s history involves trees. Within the Garden of Eden the two trees, the Tree of Life and the Tree of Knowledge, are central to the story. Within Mesopotamian religious imagery the tree is the place of immanence within which the deity lives. The Jewish exile in Babylonia clearly influenced much of the Genesis material. Throughout the Old Testament and into the New Testament books trees continue to play a transformative role: the Tree of Knowledge; Moses' Burning Bush speaking with the voice of God; the royal line of David seen as a branching tree; the wooden cross upon which Christ redeems the whole of mankind for that original little incident with a tree and an apple.
The vehemence with which the Church restricted the place of women in society was largely due to the millennia-old traditions of the Mediterranean lands where priestesses were the main religious practitioners. It is·Eve, the woman as first priestess, who gets the knowledge first. She initiates via the tree. Ecstatic priestesses led all seasonal and ritual celebrations with drums and rattles. The Church first forbade these musical instruments inside church, then forbade women to speak in church and then excluded them completely.

Celtic culture. Despite re-interpretation and censorship by later Christian commentators, enough remains to indicate plenty of parallels with shamanic cultures worldwide. It is thus possible to consider the Celts' relationship with trees in the light of other cultural examples.

The Forest Shaman

This is the story of a contemporary shaman in Peru. It shows the relationship between humans, spirits and plants that may have existed among the Neolithic and Celtic peoples of Britain long ago. (Putting the geographical distances aside for one moment it is as well to recall that the native peoples of the Americas were basically Neolithic up until the last century, and that a common Central Asian origin has been posited for the spread of peoples into that continent as well as for indigenous Europeans).

In these societies many sorts of shamans exist, some with broad skills in healing and divination, others who will work only with a certain illness or skill like weather control. In some forest communities the most highly regarded shaman is not one taught by apprenticing to another shaman or

---

Stone Calvary Cross, St. Thegonnec, Britanny. Here the crucifix is clearly transformed into a tree with its lower branches pruned. The Cross became the Tree very early in the spread of Christianity through Northern Europe. The Passion fitted so neatly into the Northern traditions of Woden the Father god of inspiration, magic and warriors, who hung himself on the World Tree for nine nights and days in order to gain the wisdom of the runes. The tree became the offering alter of all those sacrificed to Odin. A tree is a convenient object upon which to hang oneself, but it is more than this. The tree is a worldwide symbol of transcendence - the means to go beyond the normal state of consciousness, the means to grow outwards.

inheriting the power from a family member, but from learning to work directly from the trees.

Don Agustin Rivas-Vasquez has lived along the River Amazon all his life. He worked as a sculptor and when he was thirty-five he was visited by a shaman for healing and began his own training. After about a year he was able to heal children but his teacher said that if he wanted to heal adults and become a shaman he would need to spend some time alone and use special diets in order to learn about plants and roots.

He visited a place by a river that he was fond of and there found a very large tree that had a large hollowed out interior where he decided to live as he dieted. He lived within this tree for the best part of a year eating only rice and plantains. Here Don Agustin worked with different plants - first of all with trees and then with smaller plants. His primary teacher was the ayahuasca spirit, that would show him in visions which plants he was to work with. A spirit would appear to him in human form and tell him to drink from a certain tree and how long to stay on that diet. In this way he would learn the

---

Opposite: As Eve transformed humanity with the help of a tree, as Christ and Odin achieved victory and power through a tree, so the Buddha finally achieved enlightenment under a tree. Trees seem to give authority and authenticity to spiritual experience. Trees are an obvious source of shade and protection but their constant appearance as places of revelation goes beyond the purely utilitarian. In both Western and Eastern art trees are often included in compositions where none are required within the narrative. They are clearly a useful artistic devise for balancing a composition - but do they also provide balance at another level of awareness too? Why is the figure of a saint or holy man so much more effective when placed next to a tree? Does the artistic perception of "rightness" in a composition simply reiterate the energetic reality of trees: that tree equals spiritual force? (Bronze shrine of the Buddha preaching under trees, Sui Period, China).

"icaros", the tunes of the tree. Every night he would sing the "icaros", the tunes that came to him, tunes without words. At a later stage Don Agustin would find the "mariras", the words, applicable to the plants he was drinking.

> " *The shaman must know the "icaros" and "mariras" of many spirits, because they are the magic that attracts the spirits. If one spirit is not enough or is not able to do a healing, the shaman must invoke another. The shaman is a conductor who knows the "icaros" of the spirits.*"

The discipline of isolation and special diets enables the shaman to rid his body of toxins so that he can begin to see real, worthwhile visions of spirits. In his own experience and that of his teacher, until the body is cleansed and one's personal fears are dealt with it is only they that will manifest as spirits and demons in visionary experiences - bad trips of personified neuroses.

> " *When one follows a diet and drinks a plant, one can see the spirit of the plant. One can talk to the spirits. They will tell you what you want to know. They will take your hand and show you their world.*"

(From "*Ayahuasca Shamanism: An interview with Don Agustin Rivas-Vasquez*" by Jaya Bear, "*Shaman's Drum*" no. 44, 1997).

This description of a contemporary practice has much value when considering the role and methodology of tree and other flower essences in both the contexts of healing and travelling in spirit realms.

Evidence for a Celtic analogue for ayahuasca, or for another entheogen, is now being looked for by those interested in the spiritual use of plants in shamanic contexts. Not all cultures employed plant substances as the main methods of achieving altered states, but there are certain clues in the literature and later traditions that may suggest that the Celts combined this method alongside others. Apart from secrecy and suppression of information other difficulties in this search are the correct identification of plant names and the method of preparation. Without the knowledge of a living tradition it is very difficult to learn processes that may render inactive plants active or render harmless those that are fatal when taken on their own. The recurring motif of the magic cauldron of illumination and various descriptions of divination methods are presently a rich source for speculation.

Hawthorn tree spirit, with feeding birds. All Saints Church, Sutton Benger, Wiltshire (14th c.)

Meeting the Spirits

Methods of Communication - The Sense Fields

We have already seen that there can be many definitions of what spirits are. Although not many people consider the existence of independently existing, non-physical awareness as an objective, verifiable reality we all use the word "spirit" today within the same context that our distant ancestors might have used and that they would have understood. Expressions like " spirit of the place" and "lack of spirit" have the same meaning, though the interpretation nowadays is different.

The world-view has changed. As science became the consensus belief system, it gradually excluded spirits from every aspect of the outside real world. Now the only place a spirit can reside is inside us. So when we talk of "spiritless streets" or "raising one's spirits" we are referring to internal, emotional responses to external stimuli. The view of the traditionalist in the identical situation might be expressed in exactly the same words, but they would be meant objectivity; so the first phrase comes to mean there are no spirits here and so I feel bereft within myself, and the second: there is a strong spirit presence here that uplifts me emotionally or: my own spirit or spirits are empowered and strengthened.

Whether we accept the existence of external awareness and intelligent spirits or whether we believe we are alone in a complex mechanical biology, we all still tend to react on a feeling level in the same way. These feelings we interpret according to our favourite models of reality. Perhaps the main difference is that, in general, we see ourselves as isolated individuals receiving signals from an exterior real world of which we partake and from which in some way we feel alienated and separated. The traditional, tribal view sees us as fully inter-acting as an equal part of the world, seeing from within. Traditional peoples live within the world, urbanised Westerners live upon it.

There is a fundamental and far reaching effect on our comprehension of what is inside and what is outside. When we exist "inside" the world our emotions, thoughts and feelings take on a significant, independent existence-we move amongst them as we move amongst the plants and animals around us. Like the rocks and plants, feelings and thoughts may tell us the quality and energy of every location. From "inside the world" everything is viewed as a part of the whole-a rock, a feeling, a plant, a word are parts of the landscape. Inside our heads feelings and thoughts do not belong to us any more than the butterflies and birds passing through a hedged field "belongs" within those boundaries.

From an existence "outside" the world we need more closely defined boundaries. We need to know where we are, what is ours, what is possible, and what it means. Feeling alone, we need certainties and clearly marked possessions to define us as different from "out there". A more linear view of time and space emerges, cause and effect, past, present and future all arrive to establish structure and a controlling pattern of meaning is put onto everything. In this world-view thoughts and feelings define us rather than help to define what is all around us. They are our thoughts, our feelings and they have no business outside our own heads. The chat-tering streams of thought dwelling in the past or endlessly weighing up the future are the only ghosts we allow.

When we live within the world, as a part of continuously interactive elements, mind exists everywhere, consciousness and awareness can exist everywhere and talk to us, and we to it. When we are living against the world, mind is seen as small and tightly locked up inside us. It becomes what distinguishes "us" from "that". It becomes the noble torchlight that strives to penetrate through the stupid happiness of physical things. We deny the possibility of communication because we believe only that we are the possessors of mind.

A psychologist might feel increasingly uncomfortable with such notions recognising what he believes are the signs of dissociative states, delusions and projections associated with schizophrenia and the non-functioning states of mental illness. Such errors were also made by early Western anthropologists confronted with shamanic practitioners. What can safely be said is that, although there may be a perceived similarity of states of mind and behaviour, one group of activities and views leads to a greater sense of integration, health and knowledge, whilst the other leads to increasing fragmentation of self and inability to function in any world effectively. As I hope you will soon see, the techniques explored in this chapter all work, one way or another, to help us to relax into the world and to meet the energies that live there.

Until we have had the experiences of spirit reality we can only take someone else's definition or explanation of what spirits are. If we start off with a new broad definition that is fairly free from cultural attributes it will allow us to continue working towards our own definition and will suggest ways and means of exploring the area.

It is always easy to see when a word has become unable to cope with the volume of concepts loaded onto it. The *Shorter Oxford English Dictionary* has two full columns on meanings and uses of the word "Spirit". Taking a brief survey we have:

Finding an unobstructed view of a tree and quietly observing is an excellent way of feeling the presence of its spirit. Oak tree, Exeter, Devon.

122

1) breathing. (Literally from the Latin *spiritus*)

2) animating, vital principle-the breath of life.

3) incorporeal, or immaterial being or intelligence conceived as opposite to body or matter, or intelligence conceived as distinct from, or independent of, anything physical or material.

4) the soul of a person.

5) a supernatural,incorporeal, rational being or personality, usually regarded as imperceptible at ordinary times.

6) the active essence or essential power of the deity.

7) the active or essential principle or power of some emotion, frame of mind etc.

8) a tendency, inclination or impulse.

9) a particular character existing in or animating a person or set of persons. A special attitude of mind.

10) the broad intent or meaning of a statement etc.

11) Courage, mettle, vigour, vivacity.

12) a movement of the air, a wind.

13) subtle, highly refined substances or fluids

14) a liquid of the nature of an essence or extract from some substance.

15) strong alcoholic liquor for drinking obtained by distillation.

Among these definitions and uses there are some key central concepts. They are: core intelligence; activating energy; effective, concentrated distillation of itself; its immaterial, subtle and volatile nature i.e., not easily defined. Thus we can come to a broad understanding of "Spirit" as "discrete energy intelligence". "Discrete" because although immaterial and subtle it tends to be focused as the core or centre. "Energy" because its presence is assumed to vitalise, vivify and animate the physical or emotional aspects of things. "Intelligence" because without it life, or significance, or meaning, or movement ceases to exist-it has inherent orderliness (in order to remain a discrete point of awareness some orderliness is needed else random outside events would tend to break it down.). Orderliness implies flow of information back to a centre of control-a point of awareness or consciousness.

Now, as everything of a physical nature continues to remain in the physical world for a length of time we must assume, by the previous definition, that everything has one or more spirits. Even if you were only to allow the most rudimentary of definitions, everything, to be a "Thing" with boundaries (where it starts and stops), needs somewhere, somehow to be aware of those edges of itself and maintain them in some way. It could be argued that it is the "laws of nature" or of physics that prescribes what interaction atoms might have with each other-but a "Law of nature" could simply be a different definition of "Spirit", or "Discrete energy intelligence"!

Because of their central, activating presence we have always been interacting with the spirits of things. We do it all the time, naturally and spontaneously. Perhaps we have not realised what we are doing when we find, for example, a tree or a particular place to be very harmonious and beautiful. But when we are drawn to a special spot or an object the emotions we feel of comfort, relaxation, joy and appreciation are the indication that some part of us is resonating or vibrating or attuning in a life-supporting and life-enhancing way (assuming that our energy structures as a whole are fairly well balanced). Nothing develops or is maintained in life/ evolution/ creation that serves no function. Appreciation of beauty and aesthetics are merely the refined, and usually culturally modified, natural biological, sense-derived, reactions to the world around us. We like, notice, appreciate, recognise, and enjoy those things that we perceive as life enhancing; we avoid, dislike or ignore those things we perceive as life damaging.

If it were not important for us as a species why should one tree attract us more than another, one smell more than another, one view more than another? Assuming that the trees, smells and views were all equally or apparently benign and not threatening to us. Watching our feelings of like and dislike helps us to stop, often inappropriate, behaviour patterns. One of the most significant effects of training in art is watching feelings and reactions that arise and learning to manipulate those feelings in others. Recognising sense data when it arises from an object or image that is distinct from the world in which some reaction is necessary.

Our likes and dislikes, our leanings and predilections should, biologically-speaking, serve as the maintainers of our health and security. This ideal situation obviously breaks down through the imposition of other beliefs and ideas about the world acting through the conscious everyday mind. Our sense information about the world is interpreted through the model we have ourselves constructed to work out how the world works. What we sense, the raw information, is interpreted and perceived-fitted into our own idea of how things are and understood within this personal framework. At this point what the body knows, that is, the gut reaction, the intuition, the sub-vocal feeling level of communication, can differ radically from what the conscious awareness wishes to understand.

126

Feeling the "Feelings"

Becoming aware of this feeling level is vital in order to
with spirits. Feelings and emotions are perhaps the
fundamental defining characteristics of being human.
may explain why so much science is incomplete ιⅇu
ineffective.

Science works to reduce or deny the most vital element of
humanity. It usually fails miserably but still maintains the
myth of objectivity. Feeling is as important as thought. For
feeling is the body's response to the world, whilst thought is
the conscious awareness's response to the patterns received
via those feelings-the running commentary, interpretation,
analysis and associated juggling that we ironically call "the
rational mind".

It is very important in this work to be aware of feelings as
they arise before we try to rationalise them away. And one of
the easiest ways to learn to listen to this level of awareness is
to focus on the physical senses. This helps to hold our
attention in the present and prevents, or at least slows down,
the streams of thought.

Unless we learn to understand the other forms of
communication possible within us, we shall forever be
expecting spirits to pop up and declaim perennial wisdom at
us. Unless we learn that "discrete energy intelligences" can
communicate via any or all of the senses we will be expecting
full technicolor visions and will ignore anything less
spectacular.

Unless we can learn to quiet the conscious mind-chatter and
become actually aware of deeper levels of awareness and of
underlying currents of energy, we will believe "no one is out
there" though they may all be shouting as loud as they are
able.

The techniques and ideas in this section are chosen to help develop those qualities needed to become aware of tree spirits in a conscious way.

Exploring the Sense Fields

If we start off with what we know, it is easier to begin aligning the whole of our awareness to that of the Tree Kingdoms. What we know best are our senses: sight, hearing, touch, taste and smell. When we experience things via our senses we tend to believe them. If we pay real attention to what information our senses are giving us it is the best way to integrate ourselves more fully with our surroundings and this, in turn, enables us to become aware of the continuous information and energy flow of which we are a part.

It doesn't necessarily take gigantic feats of concentrated effort to achieve a great deal of insight from our sense data. When we are interested and excited by something we naturally focus in with our attentive powers. It is an effortless, natural process. In fact, the worst thing that can probably be done in any of this work is the use of forced will and expending great effort. Relaxation and awareness allows great focus, effort and strain tends only to distract us from any other sensation or experience.

Memory of Trees

A remarkably potent exercise as a starting off point is to recall and write down all significant and memorable times and places where trees played a part in our lives. There will be very few of us who will not have had a favourite tree during childhood, and even if your own tree tale is not rich and detailed, your own memories will trigger interesting patterns of experience and emotion. If your childhood home had a garden, what trees were there? Did you have a favourite? Were there trees lining the street? Trees at school in the playground? Do you remember visiting or walking in different sorts of wood or forest, and how did you feel? Think of the important or precious things made of wood in your life. Remember the look and feel of them, and how you felt about them. Take time to remember such things. Over a period of days or weeks you may be surprised how much of your life has been interwoven with the presence of trees and the quality of wood. If at this point there are some trees you can't identify just make as good a description as you can-you'll probably come across them again.

Awareness of Environment

As you travel around from home to work, walking in the town or in parks or gardens, become more aware of trees and how their presence or absence effects the feel of a place. Also be aware of how your own feelings may alter in the presence of certain trees. It is such a common experience that a walk in the park or the woods can change our moods and outlook, that many people do it instinctively, without consciously deciding to. When we are pressured, unhappy, or have lost our sense of personal power in some other way, it is natural that we should seek a place of power where we can feed our own spirit. And when we visit these places, this is exactly what we are doing. We are communicating with spirits. All the time there is a flow and interaction between "discrete energy intelligences". This interaction may be on a level way underneath the awareness of most people or it may be at the level of appreciation and emotion.

Certainly emotion, being a strong human characteristic, seems to cross the species barrier where language-based intellect fails nearly every time. It is very difficult to mask or disguise an emotional response-its out before we know it. Therefore if we feel truly appreciative and engaged in any surroundings this is what will draw from the spirits a response. Marko Pogacnik in his book "Nature Spirits and

Elemental Beings: Working with the Intelligence in Nature"
(Findhorn, 1997) stresses this point continually: it is the non-verbal forms of communication like emotion, image-making and sound that the spirits recognise and to which they respond, and by which they can be energised. Conscious verbal thought is a thin watery soup, a mosquito buzz that is little more than a meaningless annoyance. Emotion with all its tastes and colours is the real food that spirits appreciate. The skill in using language is to direct and hone the emotional energy. This can then act as a feedback system so that we can see where we are and how we can further shape and define our feeling-into-the-world. It is perhaps for this reason that so much traditional work with spirits comprises techniques to express and heighten emotional involvement and subdue the intellectual assessment, so emphasising the feeling of the moment whilst suppressing the qualities of logic, linearity, analysis, categorising and definition. Use of rhythm, movement, songs and soundmaking, learnt ritual procedures and ritual behaviour all help to reinforce those qualities needed to "slip between the worlds".

Because our mind works by patternmaking it is really important to develop our abilities to recognise what our senses receive. There is a tendency to fail to notice things which we cannot adequately label. An unnamed thing becomes a general category and this is then placed into the general background rather than standing out as a strong pattern.

Identification and recognition of as many elements in our natural surroundings as possible is a primary survival skill that increasing urbanisation and economic interdependence is rapidly degrading. "You don't miss it till its gone" is the motto of the environmentally comatose. Education in each country's ecosystem and learning to recognise species on sight is one of the only ways to prevent that system's destruction. If you don't know what was there in the first place, how are you going to see destructive changes when they begin to occur? If you can't remember the types of birds that once came into your garden how are you going to realise that they are no longer there?

If trees are understood merely as convenient ways to store future furniture there will be little chance of coming to any other experience except "It's there until it's needed for something else".

Identification of Trees

Learning to identify trees means having to look at them closely, to see them as they change throughout the seasons, to notice the growth patterns at different stages of development. To recognise trees in their flowering period can the relatively simple, but in midwinter with no leaves or fruit a whole range of other clues need to be found, such as - bark structure, twig shape, bud placement and so on. The physical form of a tree echoes the whole species' strategies for integrating all the available cosmic and terrestrial energies and intertwining them with the peculiar characteristics of the local environment. The physical tree is what anchors the other dimensions of "Tree-ness" to the three-dimensional world, in the same way that our physical body holds or focuses our personality, psyche, spirit, soul and other non-corporeal elements, such as belief and memory. When we can see a tree and get a broad feel for how its energies are working we will automatically begin to slip into that awareness where conscious communication with the tree spirit can occur.

The following suggestions are made to help begin this process of recognition.

Find a tree identification book that you can work with and begin to see how many trees you already know. Check the identification book whenever you see a tree you can't name.

You may need several books. We find some useful to carry in the car, others have better illustrations or photographs, some show bark patterns clearly, or silhouette, others have better background information.

Some trees are easier to identify than others. For example, in the willow family cross-hybridisation occurs very readily making precise identification sometimes tricky-but don't worry if you can only say "well, it's a sort of sallow hybrid". Most people wouldn't be able to get that far. Personally, I still haven't got to grips with the many varieties of conifers growing in this country. But gradually, each year, new markers can be learned that will help to identify a few more trees.

Identification by sight at all seasons of the year, both close up and in the distance is a gradual learning process that will take several years looking at the seasonal characteristics and habits of each tree. Eventually, a certain nuance of spring or autumn colour will be enough for you to pick one species from another.

Drawing into a Tree

Another excellent way of seeing trees is to draw them. Drawing is one of the best ways to narrow the focus of the attention on a subject in an effortless, spontaneous way. Unfortunately the greatest proportion of the population has been brainwashed into believing that they can't draw or "aren't any good at art", and freeze immediately a pencil is placed in their hand because of the misguided fear of "not doing it right". There are ways to bypass, or at least alleviate, this terror-and it is well worth working on. Most people doodle quite happily. If you are a doodler but panic at a "proper" blank piece of paper, try to get into a doodling state of mind. The end product is not at all important. What you are left with after the process of drawing is simply a by-product. The value has been in the quality of attention and connection that happens between you and the tree, as you co-ordinate eye, mind and movement of hand to understand more of what you are seeing than you usually would. Accuracy and lifelike images are not important. If you freak about a blank piece of paper (thoughts of spoiling the nice clean sheet etc), then use newspaper, or notepaper already scribbled on, the back of an envelope, your cheque book cover-anything that doesn't say "art", "neat", "realistic", "recognisable". Don't be timid. You have to let the energy between your emotional feel and the tree's form flow easily. This doesn't mean nice, flowing lines or any such preconceived effect. If you are nervous, whatever you do don't use a pencil and rubber. Get a big felt tipped pen or marker pen, something thick and indelible. You can't make a mistake because the only rule is to look and then make a mark. It is perfectly OK to end up enjoying yourself-it is not a sin. If you find that after a certain point you just enjoy the marks or doodles then forget the tree and carry on.

Trees, you will certainly discover after drawing a few, are very large, very complex shapes so don't feel you need to faithfully reproduce every twig and leaf. Work with general shapes or small details, or whatever bits draw your attention most. The drawing isn't the reason why you're doing the exercise-it simply provides the focus of attention for your own awareness. Gazing dreamily at a tree will provide much the same energy contact at a feeling level, but you might not be consciously aware of any thought patterns or change of state. Drawing helps to integrate feeling and conscious awareness so that we know what is going on.

Photography can also help to tune our sight into tree forms, but it can be even more frustrating than quickly sketching. When we look at a tree we filter out all the background clutter and can easily pick out the shape and detail. It takes a lot of patience and well-sited trees to be able to get as clear a

Becoming a tree: all the senses are fully involved in the qualities of plant consciousness so that the human being is simply a quiet vessel within which the tree spirit is experienced as fully as possible. (Green Man from Crediton, Devon).

photograph as you would like. But again, just looking through a view-finder focuses the awareness of the object of our perceptions, and this is the main aim here.

Sight, understanding and mind all are closely associated together in our perception of the world, do you see what I mean? Hearing is also inextricably linked with the understanding of language, but also has much stronger feeling associations with non-verbal music and other sounds. Touch, taste and smell are firmly in the realm of feeling. Conceived of as primitive senses, they have startling abilities to create instant "gut-reactions" and deeper emotional responses that are much less controllable than sight and hearing. To fully appreciate the tree we need to use our senses.

Sounding out the Trees

We can use the sense of hearing both with single trees and in copses and woods. It is simply a matter of turning our attention to what we can hear-the quality of sound-both internally and externally. We may be hearing those physical sounds that the tree is making as it moves in the air, and the birds and other creatures inhabiting the same space. But we can also very easily become aware of the quality of sound that could be equated with the degree of atmospheric or subtle stillness, peace and resonance that is really a human interpretation of non-physical awareness. So a profound silence or stillness may seem to descend with no alteration in the volume or nature of the sound. It can be more like the conscious mind-chatter reduces, or that quite suddenly a new quality of space appears to us where normal sights and sounds seem to be surrounded or encapsulated in a vibrant, invisible vessel or medium: a truly non-ordinary state of reality. Such a state occurs especially that the liminal times of transition at dusk, dawn and midnight and in the presence of ancient trees. This quality of sound, or of space, can be disorientating and even threatening. With a reduced thought-stream it is possible to become aware of other perhaps more potent sources of consciousness and power emanating from the world around us. The ability to settle with, and stay with, this growing feeling of unease and the sudden conviction that you are maybe in the wrong place at the wrong time, is a useful test for clarity of awareness, grounding and insight. The tendency is to suddenly increase the activity of rational thought processes-to begin again to talk or think loudly to oneself in the hope of drowning out the fears that seem to well up. Whistling in the dark. If we maintain a neutral stance both emotionally and mentally, it may be that there can arise some understanding of why the emotions have emerged in the first place, and why the quality of listening, of space, has shifted.

Unless there is a definite memory trigger from a past event it is likely that such shifts and the accompanying feelings of unease are due to a peripheral awareness of a spirit or spirits that have likewise become aware of our presence. This effect, similar to the hairs on the back of the neck standing up, or the feeling that someone is behind you, may be valid indicators of a spirit awareness turned in our direction, whether embodied or incorporeal. Fear arises in these instances because there is a lack of information regarding the nature of that attention. Is it hostile or benevolent? Are we to be dinner-guests or dinner? Fear here is a sense of loss of personal control. Fear also arises when there is a more powerful presence than ourselves, that approaches near to our own energy field. The desire is often to run, to get away as quickly as possible, to return to a situation where we (erroneously) believe that we are in control once again. It takes considerable will-power, but to hold back and become more aware of the quality of the energy change can lead to a constructive flow of information in both directions. In such circumstances it is important to:

- acknowledge the presence and be attentive to all sense data,

- stand your ground as a legitimate Earth creature, but without losing sense of humility in equality

- ask if there is any specific message to receive

- ask if there is any specific action needed to be performed.

If you do find you have run away before you could respond in a more balanced way see if you can return some other time.

Visiting Ebbor Gorge, near Wookey Hole in Somerset, many years ago, on a hot afternoon the rocks and trees were simply experienced as benign and cooling. Returning with a friend just before sunset, we rambled along the paths for a while, sitting on the high cliffs looking out over the ring of low hills surrounding Glastonbury Tor and watching vapour trails of distant spark-like aircraft pass close to the new crescent moon floating in the cloudless deepening blue sky. At a certain point, as the path turned deeper into the woods and dusk fell, that particular quality of hearing came upon us both. Like the air becoming taut, every rustle in the undergrowth and every leaf-fall was crystal clear. The woods suddenly ceased being benignly neutral. As if a presence had woken up, we were sure of the sensation of being surrounded by attention. In this world we no longer belonged. Rationality began to waver, sounds became magnified, rustling in the brambles became potentially threatening. Our sense of self, the boundaries of our minds, could be felt melting away and there was a distinct sense of an overwatching female form-the spirit of the gorge perhaps.

On this occasion, we left as hurriedly as was possible in the deepening gloom. Both of us had interpreted this strong, silent attention as if we were trespassing where we did not belong. This may have been the case, but it is far too easy with the continual influence of Judeo-Christian belief systems to slip into the human v. Nature, Spirit v. Matter, guilt trips. Such assumptions are completely erroneous and purely a fantasy of human construction. Right, wrong, guilt, innocence, holiness and evil are all human value judgements of little relevance to other kingdoms. It is our own desire to categorise and label everything according to our own world-view so that we can decide how to behave in an appropriate way towards everything. Most of us have so few experiences of coming face to face with the raw, uncompromising, unjudging power of a spirit awareness that we yearn for familiar labels and to know where we stand. Instant judgements and inappropriate actions seem more solid than staying centred, aware, humble and attentive. Yet it is only when we stop fear and shut up that the fears will melt away and a more compassionate active relationship with spirits can emerge.

Of all trees, listening to the qualities of space under ancient yews can unnerve many people. Like the experience in the woods at dusk, but even more devastatingly immediate, the presence of yews seems to drain all coherent thought-stories out through the feet into the ground, leaving one wondering in a vague, empty-headed way whether it will be possible to maintain self consciousness at all with such a heavy weight of silence descending through the deep green darkness. Other trees too, at times, may bring about this fear of dissolution - especially when we are employing the sense of hearing. Most of us are so accustomed to our continual, rambling thought-stories that they are mistakenly identified with "self", "mind", "soul" or some other term for our personality or uniqueness. When this verbal self-diagnostic, self-verification quietens down or even stops momentarily as that full, silent, listening silence descends, we panic and grasp at any irrelevancy rather than disappear into the Universe.

Habit, and some of the exercises covered later, will help to bring familiarity with this quieter, more receptive state, enabling us to feel quite at ease in a variety of non-self-defining states of awareness. Once the mind has experienced silence and can effortlessly return to happy chatter a few times, it is less resistant to new experiences, knowing that it can re-emerge as unchanged as before.

Listening as a Texture of Sound Becomes Music

Sitting under a single tree and focussing on the sounds that can be heard is another good way to begin active listening. In this case it is not listening in a focused, analysing manner - which is how most of our listening is done. If the attention can be relaxed yet still "turned towards" the sense of hearing without homing in on particular sounds, it is possible to begin hearing the complete web of sound as a single complex tide. In most instances this is fairly difficult to accomplish in normal waking states because the mind has the tendency to flit from individual sounds, identifying each one and then moving to the next. What is needed is a random, complex noise upon which the mind finds it difficult to focus precisely, yet has a sufficient range of frequencies to prevent boredom. It is this type of sound that quickly induces a light trance state where sense experiences can be registered by the mind without falling out of its neutral state. Such a sound is easily found under trees. In autumn, a breeze will rustle and create sonic cascades amongst the drying leaves; find a stand of aspen or black poplars; in winter pine trees roar like the sea in even a light breeze; in spring and summer there is the added drone of insects, a lime tree in flower has the unbelievable richness of millions of honey bees collecting nectar. Explore the possibilities.

All that is needed is to settle down comfortably - preferably under or close to a tree - and turn the attention to the quality of sound. It may feel comfortable to close the eyes or maybe lower them to the ground so that the focus is on hearing rather than sight. Notice the qualities of sound under different trees in various weather conditions and the corresponding thoughts and feelings that arise. Under some trees it may well be easier to enter a listening trance than under others. In a successful trance state all sounds will be heard simultaneously without excluding any. A definitely musical experience will appear - rhythms and counterpoint will begin to interweave. Voices and tunes may be heard. All this will happen when the neutral mind collects and gently moulds the sounds into patterns. How the mind organises the sounds will be a blending of its own inner tendencies and immediate requirements with the environmental energies of the particular tree and its spirits. It is for this reason that "tree listening" is a useful attunement and communication technique. For even if there is no audible or apparent sound emanating from the tree, we are within the atmosphere of the tree and whether we are aware of it or not, our energy field becomes coloured by the tree's own energy field or spirit. Thus with practice what we hear can be a clear communication from the tree's awareness using some aspect of sound, be that song, chant, melody, conversation, silence, space or resonance.

The Sense of Touch

Our primary sense of sight could be defined as "touch at a distance", for whatever is seen is understood in terms of surface, texture, direction and colour. We translate what is seen in physical terms, and this is a kinesthetic, or "feeling" experience. It is such a continuous experience, and one that is so familiar, that it might require extra attention to notice processes other than the ordinary identification or labelling procedures. Before the development of language a baby experiences sight in terms of texture and colour that carry strong physical and emotional qualities. That this subjective personalisation of sight continues throughout life can be demonstrated in adults using muscle-testing techniques. Looking at different objects, colours, photographs, can be seen to constantly challenge and alter the balance of energies flowing through the meridian system. What enhances and what weakens is unique to each individual, but what can be demonstrated is that looking at a photograph of another person who is known to have had an energy imbalance of some kind at the time of photography will reflect temporarily in the energy of the viewer. There is an intimate and immediate, unavoidable transformation of information at a body ("feeling") level when the eyes rest on objects "out there".

Seeing is therefore not just registering light and interpreting pattern. Seeing is "seeing" - that is, understanding, something of the physical state of the object as it is translated by our own personal experience of being a solid object. This gives some validity to the seemingly random anthropomorphism that we can hardly escape from. It suggests why a tree might look happy or sad, relaxed or tense and so on, and why looking or drawing a tree can really, at very deep levels of energy exchange, help us to integrate and communicate with another being - essence to essence.

So when we place our attention on a tree we have already opened the communication channels. Getting closer to the tree - entering its space - allows us to hear the qualities of sound and silence that its own energies modify and emphasise. Touching the tree itself, body to body, creates a physical, mutual experience of solidity. The contact is direct and unequivocal and the appreciation of form, texture, temperature is at the level of the physical. With touch, a powerful, conscious link is made between tree and human through which a wide range of information can flow.

Lawson Cypress.

142

Holding Woods

One of our initial demonstrations at talks and workshops involves holding samples of different woods. Most people, unless they work with wood in some way, do not realise that holding wood from different trees creates completely different feelings and experiences - its not something that most people would think of doing. It demonstrates within a minute or two the clear evidence that we can all feel something different from different wood - that the energy experienced is real and quite apparent.

To try out this experiment, and to have them around for other purposes, collect small lengths of branch of the same diameter and about four inches long. Two lengths are needed, one for each hand. It doesn't seem to matter much whether the wood is freshly cut or old dead wood, both are keys to the energy of the tree. Going out after a high wind or storm can furnish quite a store of useable branches and others can be collected from hedgerows, particularly after they have been cut back in spring and autumn. If the short lengths are lightly sanded to take off any identifiable texturing of bark, there will be less physical clues as to their identity.

Begin by standing in a relaxed, easy position and take a short time just to register how you feel - your physical state of comfort and your emotional mood. Take a few slow, deep breaths and establish your own solidity and weight. Then simply pick up one pair of woods and hold one in each hand. Initially this exercise is simply a recognition of difference, so it is not necessary to hold the woods for more than half a minute - just long enough to get the feel for what it is like. Has your sense of body shifted? Is your balance the same? Are there new sensations, emotions or thought patterns? Register any changes and then quickly put the woods down and pick up another pair. Repeat with all your samples. This is a process of interaction between wood and human, so although there are a characteristic range of experiences we have noticed for each wood, not everyone will describe the same feelings or emotions. It is possible to hold the woods whilst sitting down, but to begin with standing adds to the strength of altered awareness - the attention is more focussed on the body together with the usual sensations of gravity so that any changes from the normal become more obvious.

Working With Wood

Working with wood itself, holding it, recognising the grain and colour of different trees, is a good way of familiarisation. It can involve all the senses and actively increases the appreciation of the physical and subtle energy characteristics of a tree. We live in a world of chipboard and plastic and are losing sight of the fact that until fifty years ago wood and trees, of all sorts and in numerous ways, were our most important natural resource.

One of the reasons it is not that way today is, of course, the over-exploitation and failure to sensibly manage and look after reforestation. However if we lose sight of the benefits and aesthetics as well as the subtle energy enhancement that wood puts in our human environments, one of the closest historical and mutually beneficial relationships between man and trees will disappear, along with the last of the trees, speedily followed by our own demise.

In the past, trees were planted to give timber. Wood was technologically essential, so trees were planted. Woodland and forest were managed to ensure the best growth of trees for a continuing provision of wood into the future. Harvesting useable timber doesn't necessarily mean the death of trees. Many species can withstand or even benefit from selective removal of branches. At the moment, however, we are so in need of trees that great care and new methods of using wood are required together with well-organised and massive replanting. Even the simplest whittling of wind-felled sticks will help to establish a practical bond between the spirit and the human.

Wooðen Bowls

We have found a very useful tool for working with woods and tree spirits in simple, turned wood bowls. The ones we prefer to use are the simple beaker shape between four to six inches in diameter and deep enough so that they can be comfortably cupped in both hands keeping full contact with the wood. These bowls can be used for attunement in the same way as the sticks, but the quality of energy is more focused within the hollow interior and the grain structures of the wood. Attention can be focused into the bowl and this makes it possible to engage the sense of smell by putting the face close to the rim and breathing deeply.

The Senses of Taste and Smell

Taste and smell are the most primal of the human senses. Scent evokes powerful memory and emotion, yet we are verbally inadequate when it comes to describing a smell precisely - it is usually necessary to fall back on analogies borrowed from the other senses. Remember to smell the trees you visit. Learn to recognise the species from the scent - both of their environment and of their leaves, bark, flowers or fruit. Some trees' scents are clearly recognisable, whilst others are much more subtle and will only become apparent in certain conditions or seasons.

Remember which trees you played on or near when you were a child, there you will come across the evocative quality of scent. Descriptions of scents in books are usually very subjective and pretty unhelpful. What might be cloying and sickly to one nose will seem subtle and musky to another. Work out your own definitions and descriptions - pay attention to where the smell activates in your body: both in your mouth and at other sites. Can you summon up the memory of: fresh green buds and early leaves of elder? (perhaps the top of the list for British plant pungency!); the scent of privet flowers on a hot sunny day in June; the smell of oak bark; the deep green scent of yew trees; beech woods in autumn; hedges of Leyland Cypress after rain; the scent of cedarwood, apple and linden?

Taste is so closely related to smell that without the latter, only the simplest of differences can be identified. It is well worth establishing the taste of trees, though more caution is needed in this exploration than with the other senses. It is very important that you learn to identify those parts of a tree and those trees that are toxic. Even if a species is not known to be toxic there is still the possibility of an allergic reaction.

Becoming clear on the issue of toxicity can be a frustrating business because terminology and definition are so often loosely employed. Some herbals do not clearly differentiate between those that will cause temporary mild discomfort and those that will cause irreversible, nasty death. Or those that, when fed in stupendous amounts to laboratory rats will induce cancer, and those that will destroy your liver with a few mouthfuls. The rule with taste is to know what you are putting in your mouth, and if it is not clearly and well known for its edibility, such as hazelnuts, DO NOT CHEW OR SWALLOW. Holding a leaf or flower in your mouth will be sufficient to get an energy feel, a link with the plant spirit. If you want to do any more, then research your subject fully both in traditional and modern herbals, (you will find significantly different usage often appears in older texts).

Tree Incense

Leaves and bark have been the basis for making incense since flint first struck flint, and is a great way to familiarise yourself with tree smells. Again it is wise to check on toxicity levels, but being sensible and not inhaling lungfuls of, for instance, yew smoke in a hermetically sealed room, should cause few serious problems. The nose is very sensitive to minute amounts of scent so even holding a lighted match to a dried leaf will give enough puff of smoke to experience quite clearly. A whiff even of aromatic yew smoke has to be weighed comparatively against other environmental inhalant toxins such as diesel exhaust, dioxin emissions, carbon monoxide, formaldehyde, plutonium......and then a personal decision has to be taken.

Other tree products that can be sensually explored are essential oils and resins, as well as alcoholic distillations and tree wines. Recipes and ideas can be found in old country herbals and many recently published pagan and wiccan sourcebooks.

Sacred tree and sacred stone, Varanesi, India.

Meeting the Spirits

Listening to Silence

The beauty of working with the sense fields is that it effectively takes the mind away from itself for a while. The focus is primarily upon the non-verbal centres of consciousness. In order to listen to the voices of the spirits we need to make a silent space within the mind that is free from incessant chatter and labelling. It isn't necessary to create a void of echoing stillness. We just need to clear a small space and set it aside from the casual clutter of everyday thought streams.

The processes known as grounding and centreing are essential prerequisites for easily sliding into the state of watchful internal stillness. There are many different ways to become alert, secure and focused in the present. Some, like the work with the senses, are founded in body awareness. Others use the qualities of the mind, patterns of thought and imagining skills to turn the attention towards a new range of subtle experiences. The millennia-old, tried and tested methods of attaining shamanic consciousness will be discussed in a separate chapter, though in truth they use they same predispositions and preferences of the human mind that are discussed here.

Different minds will balk at different instructions and easily acquiesce to others. It will take some personal experimentation to discover which sorts of techniques work effectively for you, though even then it is wise not to completely ignore the more slippery and aggravating ones. Learning to handle the mind is the most valuable of skills (a pity, then, it is not taught in schools), and any practice and

149

unforced discipline will bring rewards eventually far exceeding the effort expended. We shall be looking at simple breathing exercises and other meditations as well as visualisation exercises.

First, there are a sequence of guided visualisations based upon the tree that will help to ground and centre your energies, naturally bringing stability and a reduction of physical and mental activity. Once learned, the "feel" of this exercise can be recaptured very quickly - even as you are walking or travelling in a vehicle.

Basic Tree Roots Meditation

Begin by settling down in your seat so you are comfortable. Make sure your feet are uncrossed and firmly placed on the floor. Take a few slow, deep breaths and relax further into your seat.

Take your attention to the body. Feel its solidity and weight. Become aware of the pull of gravity downwards. Focus on the feel of that pull.

Allow your awareness to follow that sense of weight down to your feet. Focus on the weight the soles of your feet. Focus on the feel of that pull.

Now allow your awareness to continue downwards beyond your feet and begin to feel or see the energy as growing roots extending downwards into the earth and outwards in a widening circle around you. Feel those roots of energy as they search deeper and deeper, establishing you firmly and securely upon the surface of the planet.

Allow gravity and the magnetic attraction of the Earth's heart to draw your roots deeper and wider with each breath you release.

When you feel secure and well-rooted begin on your inbreath to draw sustaining energy back along your root paths into your body. Feel the nutritious and life-giving energy of the Earth slowly fill your whole body as it travels upwards from the very root tips of your earthed awareness.

Continue to draw the energy in with your inbreath and on the outbreath allow that root system to strengthen and spread deeper and farther outwards from your place.

Remain in this pattern of feeding and growing for as long as you like and when you are ready, slowly allow the imagining to fade. Become aware of the edges of your physical body - your hands, feet, how you are sitting, what is going on around you in the room. Move your fingers and toes slightly, take a few deep breaths. And when you feel ready, with eyes downcast, slowly open your eyes. Take a minute or two to fully return.

The Tree and Grove of Trees - A Visualisation for Groups

Extend your body energies down through your feet and deep into the Earth as if they were tree roots.

Feel the energy spreading and finding a place of the most stability and security. You are completely rooted and firm, and you can reach for nutrition and draw up sustenance from the Earth's own energy.

When you feel that your roots are established, extend the energy through the centre of the body and the spine reaching outwards and upwards. Draw down into your centre, into your midline, the energy of the sun and stars.

Continue drawing the energy downwards into your body whilst you simultaneously draw the Earth's energy upwards.

Green Man meditating. Lichfield Cathedral, Staffordshire.

At first you will probably have to alternate between the "roots" and the "branches", but when the visualisation is clearer maintain the two together so that you are drawing both earth and solar energy into your centreline.

Now join in a circle and, keeping your image as a tree clear in your mind, imagine a ring of trees with topmost branches and deepest roots touching each other. Communication and energy passes between every tree in this grove. Reach out with your hands and join with those on either side. Feel the free flow of harmonious energies passing through you.

Now see above the topmost branches, in the centre of the circle of trees, a brilliant sun radiating golden light and warmth. With the energy you feel, draw that globe downwards towards you. It increases in brilliance and power as you draw it down into your being. Now it surrounds the whole grove of trees and, ever increasing in power, it spreads outwards to surround and protect the entire space.

With the energy that continues to feed you from the sun and the earth, concentrate it, pull it together into a small, bright sphere. When you have full control of that energy and it has become the size of a football, a tennis ball, a ping-pong ball, place it in the centre of your body just below your navel - as if resting on the top of your pelvis. Here it will stay energising you and harmonising all your energies.

Now focus again on your "roots" and your "branches", with each inbreath draw the energies from above and below along your spine, and focus that energy in that small sphere below your navel.

After a few moments, become aware of your surroundings and when you are ready open your eyes.

Tree: Roots and Branches

This is a visualisation exercise that allows grounding and centreing and then opens access to more universal types of energy. It is important to be entirely secure with the rooting procedure before adding branches. To be able to maintain both ends of the visualisation simultaneously will take practice but once established really helps to focus all types of energies within the physical system.

Begin in the same way as the "roots" meditation. Relax your body whether seated or standing and allow your awareness to sink downwards to your contact with the ground.

Extend your awareness beyond your physical body in searching roots that spread deeper and wider with each exhalation. Continue until you feel really secure and well-rooted.

Now, with the intent that your sense of rootedness will remain as you take your attention elsewhere, focus on the area of your upper body. Become conscious of the space above the top of your head. Feel the energy of the sun and the vast spaciousness of the universe gently drawing up your energy. Mould that expanding energy into the form of boughs and branches growing in an ever-widening dome upwards and outwards.

Once you have a clear sense of these spreading branches see if you can maintain in your awareness both the root system below your feet and the branches above your head. If it helps, you can visualise your physical body as the tree's trunk holding in place, and focusing, the energy of root and branch.

When this image is comfortable and stable begin to sense and integrate the energies that each outgrowth of your awareness is receiving and releasing into its surroundings.

This imagemaking of the interaction of energies can take many different forms. Try different ones and settle with those that work best for you:

a) with the inbreath, breath in energy from the earth through your roots; with the outbreath extend those roots deeper and more securely. Alternate this with breathing in energy from the universe through your branches, and breathing out your energy to extend farther out amongst the sun and stars.

b) inbreath through roots filling the body with energy; outbreath up through the branches into the cosmos.

c) inbreath through the roots ; out into cosmos; in from cosmos; out into earth.

d) inbreath from branches and cosmos; outbreath into earth.

e) on the inbreath, simultaneously breathing in through both roots and branches filling your central point, hara, heart or a particular energy centre that needs extra energy, and them breathing out through both roots and branches.

Choose beforehand which visualisation to follow or begin with one and see if another sequence occurs naturally or seems more appropriate. It is a good idea to experiment between freedom and discipline. The most important point is not to create areas of strain or tension in any practice.

Tree At The Earth's Core
Begin as usual by settling into a comfortable position and relaxing into the weight and gravity of your physical body.

Allow the awareness to sink downwards into the ground and to extend as searching roots.

As well as allowing a general downward and outwards growth, intend a vigorous taproot of consciousness to dive strongly straight down towards the very centre of the earth. Once your root system has become a strong, secure image, really focus on the deep thrusting taproot.

It dives through soil, subsoil and rock. It is strong and sure of the pull to the earth's core. You may perceive many different levels of possible scenes, landscapes and matter as your awareness dives towards the heart of the planet.

When you reach that central point of energy allow as much as you require to flow into your body. You are of the earth's body, made of its energy. Be aware of this unbreakable bond with the planet. Allow your awareness to settle and take comfort from belonging.

When ready, allow the imagery to fade and return to here and now.

Tree Roots and a Secret Chamber

Settle down, breath deeply, relax. Become aware of your relaxed and heavy physical form. Allow your awareness to sink down below your feet into the ground.

Imagine your energy awareness growing and spreading out as if they are roots - searching for a secure hold, reaching and finding all the sources of nutrition and energy that you require to grow and thrive.

Breathe in that nutrition from the earth and on the outbreath relax and allow yourself to settle firmer and deeper into the supporting energies of the earth.

After a few minutes of focusing on your awareness roots, begin to gently look for a special place hidden deep within the heart of your rooted awareness.

It may appear as a small, bright space, or a room or chamber, cave or some other clearing surrounded and protected by your root energies.

Carefully explore and investigate this space. It may be inhabited by some beings or it may contain some objects. Whatever is there represents some aspect of your relationship with the world - an offering of yourself, a gift, some advice, some help, to allow you to integrate further towards your full potential. Feel the quality of the space. If you are offered a gift of some kind you will also have something that you can exchange as a parting gift.

You can reach for and enter this secret space whenever you feel a need to retreat into yourself for healing or rest. It is a safe, secure and healing environment where teaching can also be received. If a particular tree is your current focus of work, following this pattern of imagery will be a way of communicating to some spirit forms of that tree.

The Fountain Tree

Quieten your energy, sit comfortably and take a couple of slow, deep breaths.

Take your attention to your contact with the ground and allow your awareness to travel downwards and out as if it were forming roots.

Allow these roots of energy to find a strong and secure hold within the soil and rock. With each inbreath draw in the sustenance from their surroundings.

Beechwood in spring, Little Haldon, Devon.

Feel your body filling with powerful surges of life-giving energy at each breath. With each release of breath your root system extends further downwards and in a wider circle, gathering in strength and power.

Each time you breathe in, the power builds in your body until it reaches a point where you feel you can absorb no more.

At this stage, allow the force of energy to column up through your body in a continuous stream and up above the top of your head.

See that stream of energy forcefully flowing through all your body and somewhere, way above your head, see that column of energy spread out and fountain down, back to the ground in a continuous rain of gentle energy.

The fountain falls to earth around and upon you. It is absorbed into the ground where your roots draw it in once more and creates a cycle of cleansing and feeding energy up through your body, columning up above your head, fountaining back down to the ground in a protective, rejuvenating, enlivening cycle of rising and falling, absorbing and releasing, filling and emptying, breathing in and releasing the breath.

When the process has come to a close, just focus again for a short time on the strength and endurance of the root system you have established in the earth, and then gradually bring yourself back to normal awareness.

Complete Rootedness
Begin as usual with relaxing breath and body.

Allow awareness to move towards the pull of gravity.

This time allow the roots of your awareness to extend not just from the soles of your feet but from all parts of your body - toes, feet, base of spine, fingers, arms, back, chest, ears, eyes, mouth and top of the head.

Awareness from the whole of your body extends and reaches down and around to create a total rootedness and groundedness in the earth.

Focus on those parts where it seems more difficult to visualise the roots extending outwards.

The Mind

Because the world of spirits is largely other-dimensional (otherwise it would be obvious in our three dimensions), we need to be able to travel outside those familiar three dimensions in order to experience or to interpret that data we receive. This is where the mind comes into its own. As has already been suggested, the mind, as our personal central point or focus of awareness, being a point, has no dimensions as such and so can access other realities of which we are not normally aware. In order to do this the normal conscious functioning and processes of the mind, and its three-dimensional home - the brain, needs to be quietened or modified. Rather than always looking out of the windows of our perceptions we can simply decide to turn and look somewhere we have forgotten all about : the room from which we gaze out on to the world of form, one room of many in the great house of dimensional possibilities.

Several skills need to be learned that will give the ability to turn away from, or view differently, our habitual interpretations of sense reality. This involves stopping the mind from interpreting the world in its own familiar patterns of categorisation and labelling. Essentially this necessitates stopping or modifying the language stream of the awareness,

160

or by re-interpreting and re-defining meaning in ways other than linguistic, such as the use of pure sound or symbolic image. Also, there needs to develop a way to move from our habitual viewpoint and explore, in a controlled and useful way, other rooms and corridors of "chez realite".

The first skill helps temporarily to break the grip of fascination the mind has for the world of form. The second skill channels and directs the mind in ways that allows awareness to explore non-ordinary reality. Essentially, these two processes can be crudely likened to: bringing to a skidding halt the runaway horse upon which we have been riding for as long as we can remember and, having stopped its uncontrolled headlong dash, learning how to gently coax it along those paths that we ourselves now would like to travel upon.

To continue with this analogy a little further: the horse can be stopped by force - tripping it up or bashing it senseless - or it can be stopped by drawing its attention to something more interesting and enjoyable than its present state. Likewise the mind can be stopped by harsh means or subtle. Each individual mind will react differently to every method and some may be more productive and appropriate than others. All spiritual techniques known to humankind work to achieve these two aims. Remember that it is not possible to isolate mind, brain and body from each other, so often the techniques will seem to be physical or behavioural rather than purely mental in character.

Shamanic, ritual and trance techniques all clearly work because they succeed in shutting off, or diverting, the everyday streams of thought. This gap in normal reality is then exploited in order to slip down a new corridor of consciousness achieving results not possible through ordinary means. Whatever the method, the first process is to bore, bamboozle, confuse or silence the mind, and once this is achieved, to reactivate the mental processes in very specific, controllable ways. This reactivation generally consists of the use of directed imagining or symbolic image or sound. These prevent the return of the conscious thinking process at the surface of the mind which work on everyday labelling and defining of form (such as: me-not me; real-not real; possible-not possible). The use of image and symbol is the natural way our deep mind communicates with us and the world, and it is also how other awareness-beings can communicate. At these levels the mind is still needed to interpret experience, but it will draw off experience from within deep consciousness and the dream-mind where distinctions of body and mind, real and unreal, past and future are either understood as irrelevant or are non existent.

Quietening the Mind

So the first important step in this work to meet with spirits is to quieten the mind. Quietening our mind is not necessarily an imposition of total silence or a gagging of consciousness. Often the preliminary stages that create a re-focusing of the attention are sufficient to settle us into a new state of mind where there is at least a little space for new thought patterns or perceptions to develop. As most modern Westerners are not taught to examine sense data in detail, unless they have been trained well in the arts, focusing on a single interesting object such as a tree or piece of wood for more than a cursory glance, say for ten or fifteen minutes, can in itself bring about a new freshness of mind.

Ground State

In order to know whether any technique has been effective or a communication link opened, there must be a clear experience and memory of what was the normal state of functioning beforehand-otherwise there is no point of comparison that can be subjectively relied upon. This is an individual' s base line of awareness, what has been called the "ground state". Unless we know our ground-state we are really unable to satisfactorily define any new experiences or states of awareness. In order to establish our ground-state we need both to step back from experience and examine how we are sensing, feeling and thinking, whilst at the same time engaging completely openly and fully in the present moment.

Most of us dwell within a linear-thought stream of mental chatter and monologue which concerns itself to a very large degree either with past memories or with future consideration. The rest of the time, between brief glances at sense data to make sure we are where we think we are, the mental processes largely freewheel in thought-stories and daydream sequences. Reducing or turning the attention away from this continual burbling stream of language and not engaging in any other focused thought patterns (like concentrating on the work in front of you), is essential for developing a clarity of awareness in the present moment, Now, where we are.

We do not need to do much, or go anywhere else, or attain monumental discipline after years of asceticism, to achieve quietness of mind. Quietness of mind isn't thought-free silence, necessarily. Because we experience the presence of mind as thought/language this is what we are most aware of. This is the characteristic of mind that we are most familiar with. For an increase in quietness, to allow space and attention away from our internal chatter, we simply turn our attention somewhere else. It is not productive to try to drown out thought-stories with commands to "shut up and be peaceful!" Sufferers of tinnitus, have been given relief by learning to move their attention away from the noise which then seems to reduce and finally disappear. The noise, thought in many cases to be the amplified sounds within the head, doesn't actually diminish but the focus of attention has learned to move away from it. The same process can be accomplished with the thought patterns of conscious

awareness. The skill is to identify those techniques that work best for each individual.

Stress and the River

Quietening the body quietens the mind and vice versa. In order to quieten body and mind think of the human energy system as a stream. To remain a stream the water must continue to flow along its pathways. The body is maintained by interactions of flowing energy both at physical and subtle levels - blood, lymph, electricity, meridian ch'i, pranas, subtle bodies, chakras and so on. A stream that contains many rocks, pebbles, drifts of wood and debris makes a lot more noise than one that has a smooth sandy floor. A body where the energies are diverted by blocks and stresses also makes more "noise". If the energy blocks and stress build-ups can be reduced there is automatically a reduction in unnecessary thought.

Noisy Food

Many traditional preparations for meeting spirits use processes of purification and purging to clean out toxins and waste products from the body. Fasting and special diets quieten down the normal body activities whilst often exhausting the participant so that altered awareness states are much easier to accomplish.

Anyone who teaches dreads the "graveyard watch". This is the period in the early afternoon after lunchtime where it is the most difficult to keep the attention of students. With the body busy processing food, the mind is naturally less active and feels sleepy. Nearly any mental focusing process will be much more difficult immediately after eating a meal. In contemporary western urban society many people live their lives in a state of perpetual food digestion. Is it any wonder that there seems to be a lack of awareness with regards to the realms of the spirits? No sooner has one lot of food been digested than another meal is shovelled in to take its place. Becoming a food faddist is simply a neurosis borne of over-supply, but it is worth observing how different foods affect individual consciousness and perhaps modifying our eating habits occasionally to allow optimum conditions for meeting spirits.

Silent Sitting

One of the easiest methods of turning the attention away from mind-chatter is to become aware of another natural, effortless process. Breathing is perfect for this. It is always going on, it's easy and natural, and we don't have to learn how to do it . Many meditation systems use the breath as a basis for practice. Silent sitting or "shi-ne" is a core technique for Tibetan practitioners. There can be many variations on a theme, and it is worth experimenting a little to find one that feels most suitable. An exercise very close to these sitting meditations can be found as a tree-taught technique called "Breathing in Light" (see the chapter: Elm - Silence reaching to the Sky).

Here we shall look at the basic processes of "shi-ne". As a technique it is designed to relax the whole consciousness of body and mind whilst retaining full awareness. It is not necessarily a comfortable experience in itself, but once a degree of stillness is acceptable to the body/mind the practice becomes easier to do, and ten or fifteen minutes of regular practice soon pays off.

First it is necessary to get into a comfortable seated position. What is needed is an upright but relaxed spine. This means that the base of the spine needs to be higher than the knees, so tilting the pelvis forwards to a position where the spine naturally remains upright when relaxed. The simplest way of doing this is to put a small, firm cushion beneath the base of the spine, whether you are sitting in a chair or cross-legged on the floor. If in a chair, another small cushion in the small of the back prevents lolling into the chair and keeps the lungs free to move naturally.

Place the hands in the lap, right resting upon left, and pull the chin in slightly just so that there is a slight stretch at the back of the neck easing the bloodflow to the brain. Close the eyes enough so that light still enters, but no clear images can be seen, and with the mouth slightly open, rest the tip of the tongue on the roof of the mouth just behind the teeth. This placement of the tongue naturally maintains an energy flow into the head and the relaxed mouth prevents unconscious tensing of the jaw. Any or all of these positions may feel awkward for a few times but will soon feel quite natural.

Now to begin the practice itself simply turn your attention to the movement of the breath. Don't think about the breath, or control the breath, just put the attention on it. When you become aware that the last five minutes have been spent thinking about something else, simply return to the awareness of the movement of the breath. Within this particular form of shi-ne there are different variations that either increase or decrease the content of the practice. The most "formal" shi-ne counts each outbreath up to a certain number, say twenty-one , and then counts from there back down to zero. Wherever the count is lost it is begun again at one. This version is useful in quietening the mind when it is so full of thought that it seems impossible to rest with the breath.

The second, slightly less "formal" version places the awareness on both the inbreath and the outbreath. Slightly more subtle is to focus awareness only on the outbreath. During each of these types of practice all sense information - hearing, touch, taste and thought itself, is experienced as being within the movement of the breath, becoming part of the practice rather than a distraction from it. Thus the finest version of this shi-ne is simply to sit with presence of awareness of anything that is going on within the sense fields - not necessarily focusing on the breath but including that with any body sensation, sound, smell, thought, emotion or whatever.

All of these techniques thus let us relax into our surroundings, to be comfortable where we are, to stop analysing and simply to exist within the world. This is what has been called "the simple goodness of being". When the practice is successful false boundaries diminish and dissolve - and this is essential if we wish to move effortlessly and safely within and between dimensional states. Relaxing into "what is" rather than "what we think should be" immediately opens awareness to a multitude of possibilities, and having established a personal experience of mind without object (or at least able to be slightly more detached than usual), it is easier to maintain stability and integrity in the face of unknown energy -awarenesses.

Shi-ne as a practice in itself can be revealing as to the nature and predisposed patterns of the individual mind. It can be quite astounding what is thrown up in terms of imagery or emotion. Simply returning to the awareness of the movement of breath whatever mental environment you may find yourself in is the only way to continue.

Meeting the Spirits

Shamanic Techniques

A close definition of "shamanic techniques" is not an easy one to make. Only a very broad statement would allow all the wide variety of methods to be included. They are, as Mercia Eliade named them, techniques of ecstasy - means by which the soul or spirit temporarily leaves the body to travel to some sort of spirit world. They are, as the contemporary shaman Michael Harner says, ways of entering non-ordinary reality. The degrees of immersion can vary from the merest shift of awareness, through phases of conscious dreaming and altered perceptions to fully dissociated hallucination. Truly in the traditional context every other state of consciousness except the normal waking state really is a shift into spirit worlds. Thus, dreaming is as much a doorway into non-ordinary reality as trance inducing ritual or ingestion of sub-lethal doses of psychotropic plants. What methods are used depends upon the cultural context.

Contemporary shamanism is heavily influenced by the core shamanism of Michael Harner, an anthropologist who, after experiencing many different shamanic trance techniques, selected the least life-threatening, but effective methods. Despite the increasing anthropological evidence of the near-ubiquitous use of psychotropic plants in ritual context in every culture except monotheistic, urban societies, the present paranoia over plant misuse has made it very difficult to objectively look at this area without a colouring of moralistic prejudice.

Urban society has developed as an organism that only functions when its constituent individual participants adhere

Two Green Men with what has been identified as wormwood or mugwort growing from theier mouths. Roof boss, Exeter Cathedral, 14th c.

to fairly rigid behavioural rules. Few urban cultures have allowed for the flexibility that non-ordinary reality requires except within a tightly controlled, elite priesthood. The Eleusian Mysteries of Classical Greece was perhaps the most successful blending where, on a regular basis, the entire population was able to partake in a transcendent psychotropic experience. The value of such shared spiritual journeying has been shown to be one of the most powerful, cohesive and integrating experiences that a cultural group can achieve. Formal ritual within hierarchical religions attempts to recreate the same unity of vision , but the very fact that most religion becomes state-owned can easily water down any apotheosis to banality.

Core shamanism wisely steers clear of this can of worms by focusing on more socially acceptable, and admittedly safer, techniques of trance induction. The pan-cultural similarities and parallels simply stem from the fact that human biology requires identical stimuli to shift into trance: many beliefs, many cultures - one nervous system.

Trance is born when awareness moves away from everyday consciousness. Traditional means use not only plants, but any form of sense deprivation like darkness; disorientation; exhaustion, such as that brought on by sleeplessness, fasting or dance; repetition of rhythm: chant, drumming, rattling. All these processes alter normal body chemistry and move the mind away from normal thinking patterns. Ritual context, the "set and setting" of trancework, is the map that directs the shaman to the desired spirit realm. The drum and chant is the vehicle.

Sonic driving, the repetitive, monotonous beat of a drum or rattle, has been found to cause entrainment of the brainwaves when certain speeds of beat are used. Any constant, unchanging sound will cause the brain eventually to become disoriented or entrained, but those most used in shamanic trance are speeds between 120 and 240 beats per minute. In practice, each person will tend to have a certain frequency most conducive to slipping into a trance state, and often it is not so much the speed of the beat as the resonance that is set up. A drum that builds up overtones and begins to "sing" will carry the journeyer away much more effectively than a dull, mechanical thud. It is the slower beats that can build up long, complex overtones. With the faster beats, we find that it is the sound of the drumbeat itself, rather than the overtones, that act as the doorway to the ecstatic experience.

Whatever the beat chosen, it usually needs to be at least two beats per second. If you have a drum play it yourself until you find the natural beat. It is usually necessary to have another drummer or a tape of shamanic drumming as, unless very practised, the trance state will disrupt your playing, immediately bringing the awareness back to the body.

Here is not the appropriate place to investigate all the techniques of shamanic and neo-shamanic journeying as there are many other books that cover the subject exhaustively, but perhaps a few pointers will be useful.

Once the mind has become familiar with the techniques of sonic driving and allowing the awareness to move into the dreamlike states of the imaginal worlds, it becomes possible to journey to any sound that provides constancy and fluidity - that is, continuing without pause or variation. A stream, wind in trees, a didgeridoo, a jaw's harp, a drum, a gong, the sound of the blood pumping through the ears, all can be used when necessary. With practice entering non-ordinary reality is as easy as turning away from ordinary reality, and the transition can be immediate.

The classical cosmological model of Lower World, Middle World and Upper World with power animals, allies and guides may or may not be useful in your tree spirit work. Sometimes the contexts are useful, sometimes not. However, it is a good idea to become familiar with these simple maps as they will help to locate your experience and supply a safety net of categorisation should you find yourself in a little deeper than intended.

Many rules of shamanic journeying are culturally specific. The most important rules are the most basic. Always say "please" and "thank you", don't assume you know the rules of the country you find yourself in, don't judge events by the standards of ordinary reality. The experience of non-ordinary reality can be frustrating and confusing unless it is constantly remembered that what is happening is being interpreted by the conscious mind in terms of known imagery. What is occurring is an interaction of energy fields, a non-brain-based experience translated into familiar language.

Poetry and song are the most suitable vessels to contain these journeying experiences. Translating into a linear story, a cause and effect sequence of events, can distort the actual significance of the experience. A shamanic journey is not a guided meditation, nor a visualisation, but it does have elements of both. It is less important to be purist about the methods employed than to find methods that are effective and significant for you. Lacking our own coherent metaphysical cosmology it is easier for Westerners to accept non-traditional systems and make them work. Those societies with strong cultural models of reality of what does and does not occur in non-ordinary reality, (for example, what spirits are met where and when), are automatically, and simultaneously, in a stronger yet more inflexible position.

Intention

A successful journey requires several things to make it work. Firstly a clear intention as to the goal is necessary. This can be very specific, like seeking the answer to a question, or more

Scots Pine, Kenn churchyard, Devon.

174

general, such as meeting a teacher or visiting a place. Without an intention clearly fixed in mind an experience can be unclear or confusing. Usually the greater the need for an answer, the more impetus that experience will have. This doesn't necessarily mean, though, that the journey will be any more elaborate. Sometimes the answer required may be just a short phrase or a simple, symbolic image. When there is a clear intent such experiences can be easier to understand, but they may still need time to interpret correctly. Anyone can dream, see visions and hear voices, only a shaman has learnt the meaning of what the spirits bring to awareness and can thus use it for the benefit of the community.

To the shamanic consciousness no event or experience lacks significance. This is not something that just happens, nor can it be learned from much else except personal experience and clarity of awareness. However, as we are not pretending to be shamans, just using shamanic techniques and principles, even the most impenetrable symbol or gnomic utterance, once brought to the conscious mind, has an energetic effect on the subtle systems of the body and this can be enough to trigger the necessary responses. Shamanic vision works primarily through the heart, the feeling-body-consciousness, rather than the analytical mind. It is magic rather than science, and this is why shamanic techniques focus on the senses and employ techniques that silence the analytical, separating parts of the mind.

Offering of Energy

Simple, steady drumming, without rhythm or change is an excellent way to build up energy for working with the spirits. And this is the second prerequisite for a successful journey - the expending of energy as an offering or sacrifice, an exchange, a gift to the spirit world.

Very often, when instruments are used, the higher pitched sounds like bells, rattles and cymbals are thought to summon, or attract, the spirits. The particular piercing quality of these sounds, together with the omni-directional quality they have, seems to cut through normal dimensional barriers, creating in the listener a confusion of time and space as though one were entering into a timeless place. The brain certainly recognises such signals as a signature of dimensional shifts - these types of sound frequencies are used habitually by the writers of film scores where otherworldly, ethereal encounters are indicated.

Across numerous cultures dancers wear bells on their limbs or attached to clothing so that every movement, every offering of physical energy, is accompanied by this spirit-summoning sound. The cacophony of high-frequency vibrations disorientates or disengages the normal analytical consciousness whilst the low frequencies of drums and drone instruments builds up a grounding, energising, motivating charge that provides the necessary boost for awareness to travel elsewhere, to journey. The high frequency disengages us from ordinary life but leaves us lost in a void of vibration. The pulse of the drum has a direct, stimulating effect on heart and brainwaves making us act once more, but with an awareness of that other place, non-ordinary reality. Small bells attached to a string or tied to a stick, or worn when dancing are well-worth investigating. We have found that, once some excitement and anticipation has been built up, multiple bell tinkling over and around participants lying or sitting with eyes closed, is the fastest way to get them to enter non-ordinary states.

The simple exertion of drumming without pause for half an hour or more is a great clearing and cleansing process in itself. Accompanied by dance it can lead to deep trance. Dance in this shamanic context is not necessarily what an observer would recognise as dancing. It is more a body-initiated movement that may be both subtle and slight, or frenzied and energetic. The death to shamanic, or power dancing, is self-consciousness. Power dancing is essentially an internalised process of establishing a flow of body-consciousness, allowing the body to move, or not move, as it wishes. This, of course, can be highly therapeutic in its own right. From such diverse fields as Ch'I Kung and biodynamics it has been recognised that breaking down the physical tensions and psycho-spiritual blocks in the muscle tissues can free up enormous amounts of physical and emotional energy of use in healing. The !Kung and other bushman tribes of southern Africa have developed this into a fine art, dancing to free up and stimulate a vast reservoir of energy , "n'um", which , if controlled, can be directed to others who need healing. There are close parallels in this type of work with the psycho-spiritual exercises that draws earth energy and kundalini, (dragon or serpent energy), into the conscious control of the yogi's subtle energy channels.

Dance, seidr (shaking or swaying in the northern European traditions), movement, exercise: any un-self-conscious building up of body heat and loosening of tense muscles can be classed as power dancing - the offering of energy to the spirit - a demonstration of the force of life within the context of a living world, an exultation of simple, uncomplicated existence. Moving to a constant shamanic drumming, letting the body move as it wishes with the resonances and echoes, quietens the mind and allows that all-important interior spaciousness to begin to be perceived. Once the body itself begins to feel the quality of non-ordinary states within this spaciousness, the internal senses can guide the journeyer far better than a questioning, head-based consciousness.

Dance by standing still with eyes closed, or covered by a scarf or tasselled headband, or even brush long hair forward over the eyes, so that you can free yourself from the surroundings. Use subdued lighting to create a private, safe ambience. If you are working with others make sure there is enough room so

Red oak leaves in spring.

that you don't accidentally bump into, or touch others. Unless you are dancing on the spot make sure there is a safe, clear space to move in. Shamanic dance can't be judged by others. It is an internal process. If one were to watch those fully involved there would be a certain power or beauty to each movement, even though in any other context it might appear foolish or gauche.

Tree Dance

Because disinhibited movement is not all that usual, even inside the rave or disco, we usually begin with a very simple, effective dance known as the Tree Dance. Having become familiar with a specific tree each participant finds a space to stand with enough room to move freely around that area should they wish. Movement is optional with this dance. Time and space are also optional, and usually distort or disappear quite rapidly. With eyes closed or covered the dancers simply listen to a drum beat, bring to awareness the tree and allow the body to enter its own space. The drum beat is very slow - once every count of eight. This, in practice, means that just as the final resonance from the last beat is heard the next beat is being struck. Because it starts from a restful place, this is not a dance to build up energy, but as a means to meld with tree energy it is a wonderful exercise. It also removes any preconceptions of what dance may or may not be.

Wildfolk Dance

Dance to build up personal power and energy may be more or less spontaneous and unpatterned, but formal dance patterns can be equally effective at focussing and raising a particular form of energy. Outside of any tradition with inherited ritual dance it is easier to allow patterns to emerge in their own time - a gesture here, a sequence of movements there. In this way the tendency to establish a "right" and "wrong" method can be avoided. Certainly where power animals or allies are danced the unique energy interactions all find expression in certain types of movement - this should be observed as it happens rather than anticipated as a sign of success. Nor should the movements be rigidly interpreted as meaning this or that. Dance is for the body - leave the brain out of it as much as possible.

One way to reduce mental diversion is to tie up the thinking processes completely with precisely controlling body position. When we looked for a trance position to help connect with the subtle Nature beings traditionally known as "Wildfolk", we came up with a brain-teasing dance instead.

Starting with a standing position the upper arms are kept tight to the sides at all times but the lower arms should be in continuous motion, though not in any particular pattern. The hands are kept closed into fists but the thumb is fully extended away from the fingers. One foot is lifted off the ground, placed down and lifted again, then the same is done with the other foot. The habit of alternating the lifting of each foot takes some focused attention to break, and to do this whilst remembering to keep the lower arms constantly in motion, occupies the senses in a way that often feels like you've just jumped into a body that doesn't quite fit. Add to this some pounding drums and rattles and an unusual state of awareness soon descends. It has been found that the spirit of the nettle plant or nettle essence can help to get a better attunement in this dance.

Calling the Spirits

A prerequisite for most shifts of consciousness is the establishing of a magical space from which to work. This re-defines the self within the world, the microcosm reflecting the macrocosm. In magical workings it usually takes the form of a protective circle, in wicca and shamanic traditions, an acknowledgement of the directions and elements - the constituents of time and space. These directions and elements are internal, or prototypical, realities and are merely shadowed in the physical directions of the compass and physical matter,: so it isn't necessary to have an accurate compass reading to acknowledge North, South, East and West.

The simplest of sacred spaces can be formed by simply turning to each direction and then bringing to mind the qualities of each archetypal reality. An offering can be the breath, the voice, incense, smoke, drumming or rattling. Attributes of each direction and element are culturally established so variations do occur. This is no problem so long as you stick to the internal coherence of one system. Trying to blend systems, or even draw parallels is usually a confusing, inappropriate activity born mainly of the Western neurosis of "getting things right", for the validation of experience from every possible source in order to justify it. Most people start in the East and move sunwise through South, West and North, but linguistically we tend to say North, South, East and West, and there is no reason why this pattern cannot also be followed. Find which sequence feels the most comfortable for yourself.

The attributes of each direction can become very elaborate, so before adding your own become familiar with some basic correspondences such as:

East: dawn, spring, air.
South: midday, summer, fire.
West: sunset, autumn, water.
North: midnight, winter, earth.

Acknowledging the Upper Worlds above the head, and the Lower Worlds beneath the feet establishes you, not only at the hub of a wheel, but also on the vertical axes of the

Beverley Minster, Yorkshire.

dimensions. I also include the spirits within me and the spirits around me, making a total of eight acknowledgements.

This simple ritual process locks us into the unity of the worlds and acts as a wake-up call to all participating spirits and energies, both within and outside us, that we recognise their existence and may call on their help. It is like knocking on the door of the spirit worlds before crossing the threshold into non-ordinary reality - a sign of good manners and of clear awareness.

Visual Doorways

We think largely in visual terms. Language and verbal thought is simply a symbolic way of codifying the information of the senses. When we understand a word or language we "see" what is behind the sound. In a similar way, when we "see", or understand, what our sense of sight receives, we are creating interior perception of colour, shape, depth and so on.

Establishing a visual setting is one of the fastest ways to shift awareness and move into new spaces. Like any other techniques described here, it is a good idea to experiment with your own variations. Whilst one image may leave you cold, another may instantly transport you to your desired destination. Here are a few that we have found work very well, both with and without an accompanying drum or rattle.

The Doorway

A door or gateway is perhaps the simplest sign to use for indicating the movement from one perception to another, and, very often, nothing else is required. Because it is a quick transition, however, (simply stepping over the threshold into another place), it does usually need quite a vivid portrayal to give enough "boost" to the journeyer to move into the space beyond. In practice it seems the type of doorway is unimportant: a simple curtain will do as well as an ironbound oak door. What is important is to hold the image as sharply as possible. It is a barrier and also a means to pass through into another world. In order to get to your desired destination, intent and a visual cue is needed. Whatever you wish to explore- the nature of a tree or spirit, for example - you must take time to build a strong image superimposed upon the door of something that represents the goal of the journey. To journey to the cherry tree spirit, a bunch of cherries could be imagined there in front of you, upon the door's surface, or a familiar cherry tree you know so well a clear image can be held. What is used is less important than the connection the visualiser makes with the image. If the thought of cherry always brings to mind a bowl of custard, then use that image. We are signalling to the unconscious, the deep mind, that this is our destination. The clarity and strength of the image will help to focus the experience.

Very often, because linear time is left behind, the visualiser finds themselves beyond the door before the conscious mind has constructed the opening and walking- through sequences. If this happens, simply go with it. Where personal conscious control is still in place, the next step after visualising the door and the sign of destination or purpose, is to clearly intend your goal along the lines of "I wish to...(go to place or spirit)...and I ask permission to enter...(repeating the intended goal)". Clearly see the doorway opening in front of you and place yourself so that you are on the threshold. Take a single step with as much awareness as possible, passing over the threshold and then stand still. Allow time to register what it is that you are perceiving. Go through all your senses in turn. What do you see? What do you feel? What do you hear? If you have not been immediately whisked away into scenes and landscapes, you may feel it appropriate to call for a guide to lead you to where you need to go. Some people will enter fully into this Otherworld whilst others may just watch scenes unfolding from their vantage point at the doorway.

What occurs is less important than recognising the significance of what occurs. When you are ready to return, will yourself back to the doorway, pass through it, turn around to visualise it as you did at first - closed firmly shut with no sign or image upon its surface. Bring the attention back to the body and allow the imagery to fade away. Record impressions and experiences immediately. It is a good idea to write clearly the purpose of the journey before you start and then record experiences underneath. Putting the actual words down on paper can help to clarify the events and prevents you from changing the parameters by altering the nuance of wording.

Lower World and Upper World Doorways

The imagery of movement and of transport, or transmutation, is universally employed by shamans to move from reality to reality. Doors, tunnels, bridges, boats, rainbows, birds and animals are all used to draw the mind away from "here" towards "there".

The Lower World is largely associated with the acquisition of power and is where the ancestors can be contacted for assistance. It is usually reached by a descent of some kind. To move into the Lower World visualise a downward-sloping tunnel or cave that enters the earth. It can be of any size, a hole between the roots of a tree, a mouse-hole, a cave, a burial chamber, a well, but it must have reality in this world, it must have an actual physical location. Our starting point must be in the same dimension as we are, though it doesn't need to be in our physical proximity. Call to mind this entrance as vividly as possible, state your intended purpose and then enter the tunnel. Continue the downward sensation until you either emerge into some other kind of landscape, or meet with beings who can assist you.

Long -dead hawthorn tree, Dartmoor, Devon.

The Upper World is usually reached by an upward journey, like climbing a tree, a ladder, a mountain, being lifted up by a bird, or within the smoke of a fire. Often there is a sense of passing through a layer of resistance or a membrane before coming into a landscape. Here the quality of the experience differs in character to the Lower World, even though all sorts of possible and impossible landscapes exist here too. The Upper World is where wisdom can be learned from teachers and guides.

The Middle World is the spiritual correlate to the world we know. Its landscapes and inhabitants can be physically located, though their appearances may be enhanced by the subtle perceptions accessed whilst journeying. Middle World journeys are a movement parallel to the Earth's surface. A Middle World journey might be undertaken to visit the spirit of a known tree or site, or to communicate with or heal some other being.

Despite the intention to travel to one of these three worlds, very often the journeyer will find themselves heading in another direction because their deep awareness will know the most appropriate place to achieve success. A Lower World journey may visit several places in that realm and then move to Upper or Middle Worlds. Simply keep your awareness of the original intention and pay attention to all that is happening.

The Underworld Visualisation

There are several visual meditations that can be used without any form of sonic driving, making them very versatile. R. J. Stewart has created an effective series of techniques for linking very specifically to the energies of the Land and the Underworld of the faery tradition. His basic technique goes as follows. After a period of silence and acknowledging the Four Directions, a circular hatch or doorway is imagined in the floor in front of you. This opens to reveal a rock spiral staircase descending to the right. There is a rope of red, white and black strands fixed into the rock for support. This staircase is descended until a cave, hollow or chamber is reached. Here there is an archway illuminated by a single lamp. Passing through the archway one enters into the experiential or contact phase of the journey. At completion the archway is passed through once more, the stairs climbed, the door closed. Back in your seat the doorway fades once more into the floor.

Although R. J. Stewart's techniques share a lot with other journeying methods they do have a unique flavour and we find that they are one of the best ways to link with a physical location and its core energy. "Earthlight", "Power within the Land", and other related volumes are essential reading.

The Inner Guide Meditation

Yet another neo-shamanic technique devised by Edwin Steinbrecher can be used in a wide variety of circumstances. The Inner Guide Meditation is an amalgamation of shamanic and Jungian processes. Again the book is recommended for full instruction but the basic sequence of the meditation can be summed up as follows.

During the whole process the meditator attempts to experience all sense information within the body, rather than watching it in a dream-like way. Initially a cave-mouth is imagined. Walking straight into the cave all senses are brought into focus. The meditator then moves left along the wall of the cave until a door, passage or entrance of some sort is found. This passage is followed until it emerges into a landscape, which, once more is experienced as fully as possible. An animal of some kind will appear and is then asked to lead the meditator to the Inner Guide. This will involve a movement to the right. The sequence of directions is important here: straight, then left, then right, apparently activates one's awareness in the most appropriate way. The Inner Guide serves a similar function to any other shamanic power animal or ally, acting as an essential protector and interpreter of experience. In this system, because the experience is conceived as happening within the mind, albeit the deep unconscious, or even super-, or collective consciousness, it is considered vital not to act inappropriately as this will inevitably rebound back into the physical realities. Thus, insisting that immediate healing occurs, for example, can open one up to, possibly catastrophic, catharsis. This is because every character encountered, whether real or belonging only to that imaginal world, is simply an expression of an aspect of the self. Changes in one reality will automatically echo into another reality.

We have found that following the guidance of the Inner Guide, once found and established , is a fast and effective way to create desired modifications on the physical level, or simply to investigate, for example, the causes or means to ease a state of disease in a client. The whole process can take as little as ten minutes and is essentially the same as a Middle World shamanic journey.

Each one of these methods has advantages and disadvantages in different circumstances. Each has a unique feeling or flavour, and each will provide a means to acquiring new information about the physical world and its spiritual realities. Each can be used in conjunction with other methods here described to allow a greater understanding of the Tree Kingdoms, and the qualities and characteristics of tree spirits.

Tree Teacher Techniques

The first tree attunement techniques were put together as a way of extending the use of tree essences in the exploration of tree energies during workshops and seminars. For these there gathered a group of "regulars" with whom it was easy to explore the field in some depth. We also continued introductory presentations of these "attunement" techniques. Both of these types of event have been very valuable in expanding our own understanding of tree consciousness, tree spirits and how ordinary people can make significant contact.

The public introductory talks are an acid test for this type of exploration. If a broad cross-section of interested, bored and cynical strangers start sitting up in their chairs with surprised or puzzled faces, volunteering experiences and validating other people's experiences, it is quite clear that something is happening other than wishful thinking on our part.

Taking an audience through extremely simple processes with the minimum of introductory explanation, and seeing the consensus experiences emerge on open questioning is very gratifying. Nearly always there is at least one person in the audience who is so deeply moved by their experiences that they will only mention it in private after the talk has concluded. The tree spirits themselves seem to reach out to these individuals and profoundly touch them. Often the experience is so personal that we never do find out exactly what occurred, which can be a little frustrating, but it is well worth it to see the visible change created for these people.

Introductory talks and lectures are, of necessity, tightly constrained by time. The key is always, at very least, to get the audience aware of the shifts of energy when different trees are worked with, and to outline the possibilities of the various methods used. In group workshops everything can be dealt with in more detail. A larger amount of preparatory research is required and this leads to interesting avenues of investigation. Beginning with a set of appropriate attunements each workshop quickly evolves into a new state where experiences not only validate existing models, but push our understanding into a vibrant state of possibilities. New techniques can evolve and develop from this that, in turn, achieve an even greater perspective on the Tree Kingdoms.

We have called the methods of attunement that we use the Tree Teacher Techniques. This is because they are not teachings in themselves but do give us a means to achieve a direct contact with tree consciousness. Each of the Techniques can be used independently of the others, or they can be combined together as is felt appropriate.

Essence

As has been already discussed, a tree essence is a vibrational preparation that is made in the same way as other flower essences. Tree flowers are collected and floated on a bowl of spring water in sunlight. This simple process binds the energy signature of the tree into the structure of the water. When this is then introduced into the aura or energy field of a person it brings about similar reactions and processes as being in the actual presence of a tree of that species. Because they can be used in a variety of ways in nearly every sort of environment, tree essences are very useful as a key to awareness of the Tree Kingdoms. Because they carry the signature of each tree species, the essences allow a firm initial focus for our experience. Tree essences align our subtle energy systems to each tree signature. Each of the other Tree Teacher Techniques further engages the sensory fields until we become as immersed in the tree presence as possible.

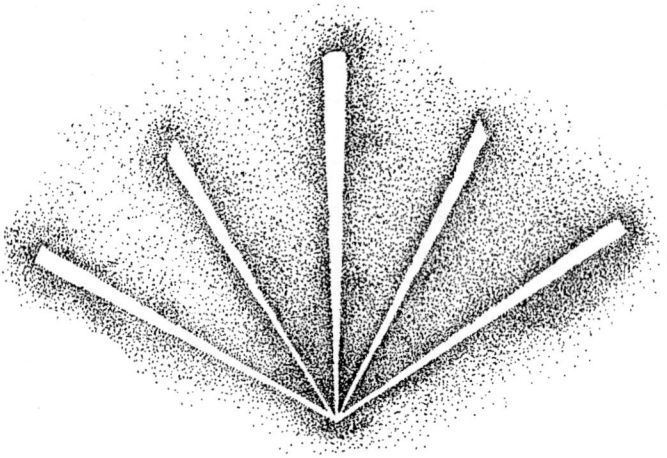

A visual pattern of spindle tree.

192

Mantra

The subtle qualities of sound are recognised in widely different cultural contexts as being the prime formative energy for every sort of form. Sound, subtle compression of space or ether, creates form. Form is seen as light (or energy, or electricity) that is held in place - frozen to become "solid". What holds form in place is a much rarified expression of the energy that our senses perceive as sound - the creation of a "hole" in space (or the "field", or plenum) into which form can flow and settle.

Following this concept through: every form that exists must necessarily have a particular patterning of sound that completely encapsulates, identifies and expresses all the qualities of the object, a sort of energetic hologram of vibration, the seed expression of a thing. Knowing the name, the "hidden name" or magical name, is widely believed to confer knowledge of, and therefore power over, a thing. Human sound used in mantra, chant, magic spell, invocation and so on, is a rough equivalent in vocal terms of this "hidden name". Many mantras, and nearly all "spirit song" or "spirit language" have no intelligible, translatable meaning (or alternatively, they have an unworkable plethora of different translatable meanings), because the sounds themselves carry the significance to a far greater degree than a linear pattern of thought. A mantra, a sequence of significant sound shapes, is a gestalt, a catalyst that, when dropped into the mind coalesces a state or experience of being around it.

To some degree, the effectiveness of a mantra will depend upon the accuracy of the human sound equivalent to the actual subtle vibratory sound. The closer the quality of sound, the greater the resonance with the object. As each person's "instrument" (that is, their energy makeup including the outward physical), differs slightly, so it is that after some time of working with a mantra it may subtly alter its quality, rhythm or emphasis. All repetition of sound tends to take the

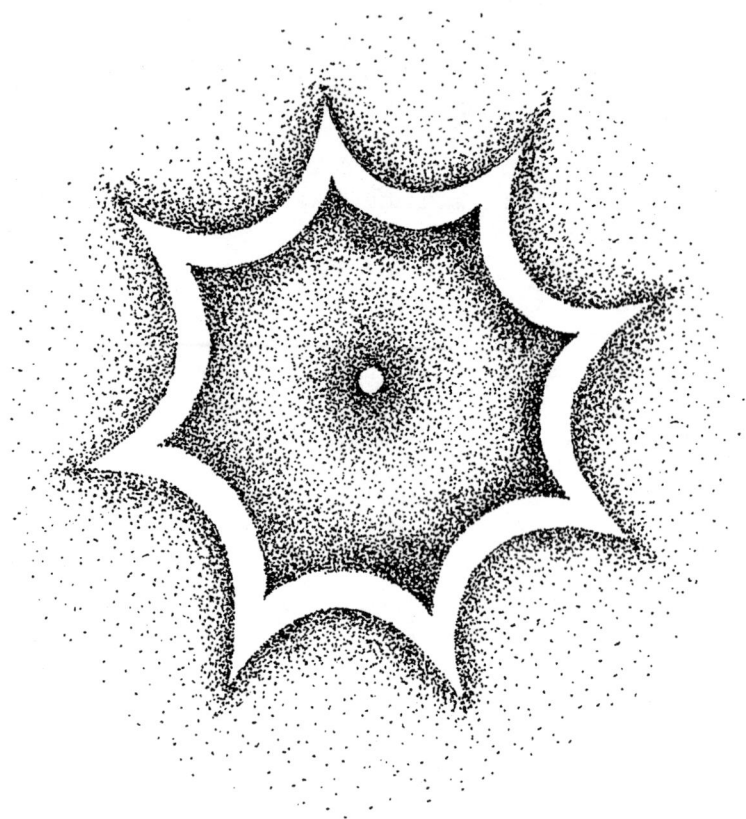

A visual pattern of holly.

194

mind to quieter levels of awareness where subtler qualities of perception naturally change the appearance of all the senses, including sound. The deeper mind, beyond the conscious, usually has a better idea of the nature of things than the structured, compartmentalised belief systems of the work-a-day conscious awareness, so that at these levels modifications of experience can occur. Strain and effort are counter-productive in this activity.

There can be no absolute guarantee of the accuracy of the mantras that have been determined for each tree spirit attunement. Isolating the sound sequences themselves can be a pretty laborious business and many subtle nuances are difficult to describe, pronounce or identify. Many of the mantra elements fall uncomfortably on our own rhythms and sense of language structure, but this itself can create a useful disorientation where it becomes easier to slip out of ordinary awareness into a more receptive state of consciousness.

Whether the mantras identified here are the "best" for their purpose is not for us to say. What we do know is that they do, in themselves, create altered states that are consistent with the tree energies they are defining. Each tree, may, in reality, have a series of mantras, each part of the whole gestalt, each describing or enfolding different aspects of the form and spirit - in the same way that the same tree has many different names: common names, folk names, Latin names and historical names from different cultures. Each of these names too, will contain a certain amount of descriptive energy, or characteristic power, of that tree and it is a useful exercise to use some of these sound-names as mantra. However, because we are usually more familiar with the language and outer meaning of actual tree names, it is very often much harder to convince the conscious mind to let go of its analysing, categorising role, than using a sound sequence that the surface mind considers to be nonsense or "gobbledegook".

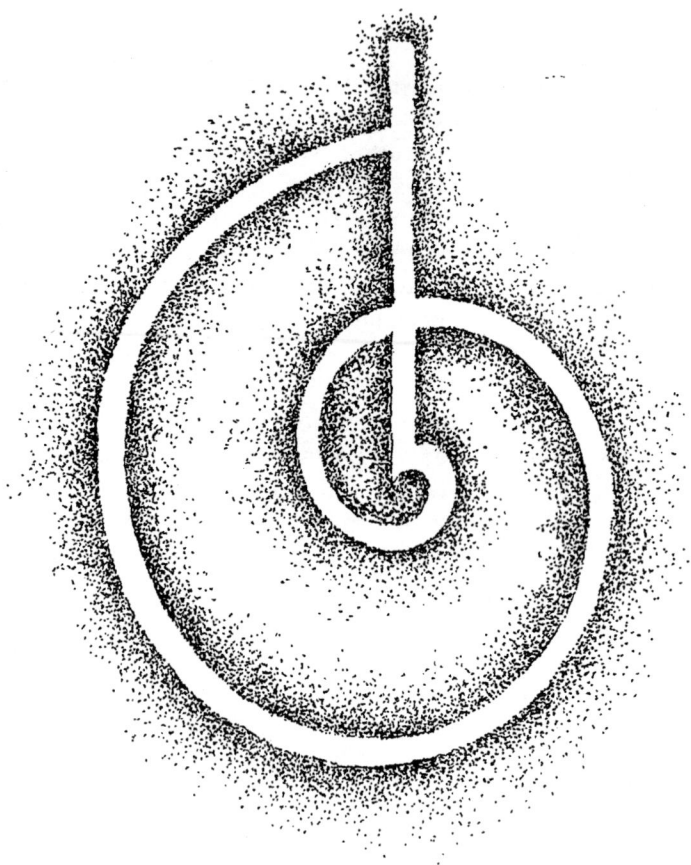

The energy of elder.

Mantras very often have compact and expanded forms. A quite explicit and verbose, perfectly intelligible verse can be conflated into a series of vocables which themselves can be reduced to a couple of vowel sounds - a "seed" or bija mantra of verbal simplicity but enormous potential power. Equally, a bija mantra can be expanded out into volumes of interpretation and commentary. In Hindu tradition, all the many volumes of the Vedas derive from Rig Veda, which itself is an expansion of the first verse, which is a commentary on the first word "Agnim..." which, finally is all contained within the first sound "A".

On a practical level, familiarise yourself with the sound of the tree mantra out loud until you can repeat it without reference to the text, and without getting confused or forgetting bits. Begin by reading it or writing it whilst pronouncing the sounds.

Once the sequence is clear and you have established a comfortable rhythm, begin to speak the mantra more quietly and slowly close your eyes. Continue to get quieter until your lips are moving but there is no audible sound. Then continue speaking the mantra to yourself only with your mind's voice, and allow this voice too, to fade gradually to a level where the quality of the sound can be felt rather than understood or heard. Don't worry about any other activity within the mind, just settle your attention gently on the mantra. If you find there is some strain creeping in sit quietly for a few moments without any thought of the mantra and when you have relaxed, just gently introduce the sounds once more. It should be as easy as turning your attention from looking at one wall of a room to looking at another - just a simple turning of attention from one thing to another.

If you follow this method, try it for five or ten minutes and then just sit quietly and pay attention to what arises for a few moments, and then repeat the mantra again, and so on. You

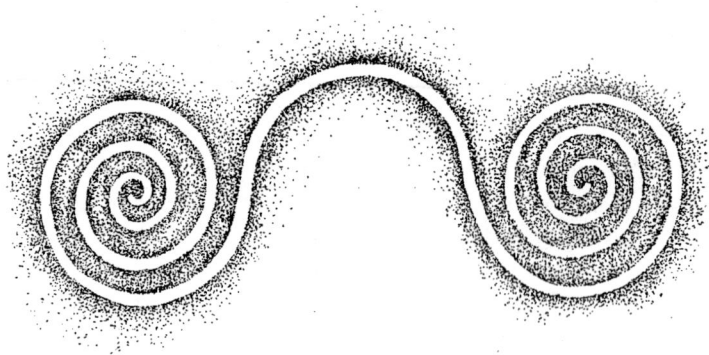

A pattern of hawthorn's spirit energy.

will be likely to have a more focused experience if you use the relevant tree essence before the start. If you become very distracted during the practice use a little more of the essence to bring your awareness back to the tree signature.

Chant

Chant is defined as a separate Tree Teacher Technique though it uses the tree mantra. The experience of chanting the mantra out loud is very different from silent repetition. Rather than dissolving the personal boundaries of the body and taking awareness away from the physical, chanting the mantra out loud tends to build up a tangible energy within the body. Rather than dissolving into the qualities of the tree energy, chant infuses the tree energy into the physical.

How one chants is infinitely variable. Loudness, rhythm, speed will all vary from time to time. Experiment consciously with different qualities to see what difference there is and to clearly establish your favourite approach. A good idea is to chant standing, knees slightly unlocked or to sit in such a position that allows the body to move and sway if it feels like it. If back support is needed make sure it is only the lower back, so that the chest can expand and contract naturally.

Chant can effortlessly move into dance where the whole body can express and investigate the energy flowing into it. Like all spirit dancing it is vital not to be concerned about the form by judging the quality of the movements you are making. This is not ballet, neither is it spectator sport. It is dance spinning out from your centre and is unique to the time and place.

If free movement is allowed the result will be powerful and beautiful whatever the form. But it is easier to move with the eyes shut or where the sight is masked in some way with hair, veil or blindfold. Dancing whilst consciously keeping feet firmly in contact with the ground is practical if you are

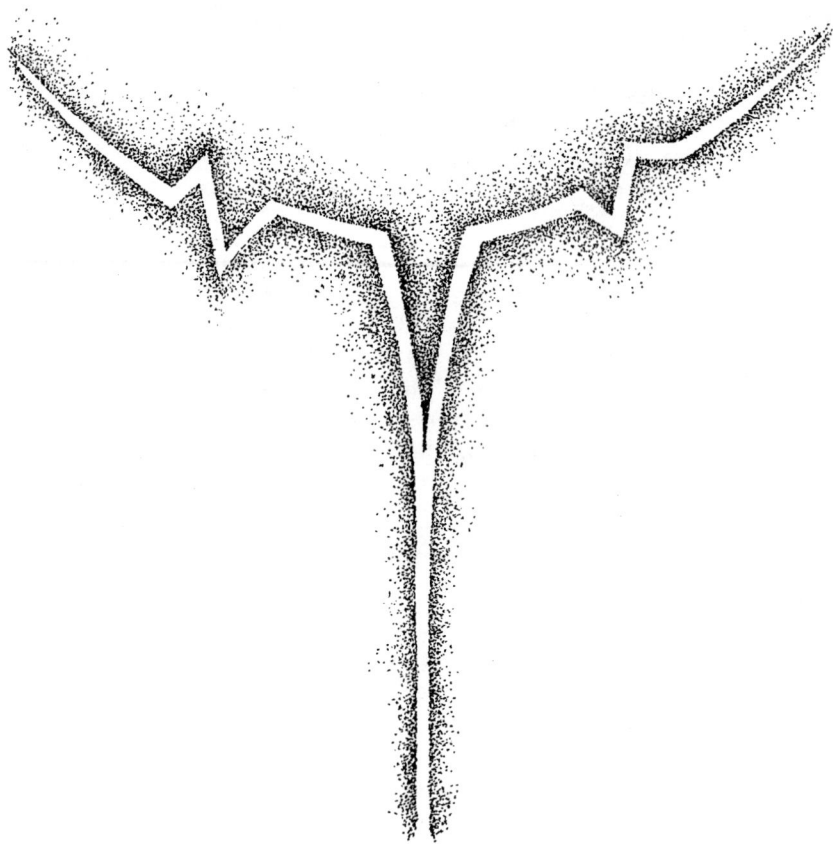

The dynamic balance of oak.

200

moving in restricted space and it can also become a powerful practice in rooting and grounding your awareness.

As human beings we are almost obsessive in our need to move around from place to place. Not moving is most frequently associated with not doing, where "doing nothing" is a moral judgement about value, work and joining in with the society group. Movement is a defining feature of humans, as remaining standing is a defining feature of trees.

Consciously not moving from a spot whilst moving the rest of the body gives a remarkable feeling of freedom with weight, a collecting, rather than a scattering, of energy. If dancing or moving with feet rooted to one spot feels uncomfortable or unnatural, immerse yourself more fully into the nature of trees and allow the movement to be energy, rather than form.

Sound Sequence

Another aspect of the Tree Teacher Techniques can be introduced into chanting by using the notes of particular sound sequences characteristic of each tree species. Note sequences have a very specific emotional effect on our nervous systems - rather peculiar as music is the most mathematical of all the arts. Note sequences for some trees are quite elaborate with repeated or echoed phrases, others are simply one or two notes. Like the tree mantras, these note sequences are suggested from our investigations and recommended by experience. Once the sequences are being used, and once the "flavour" of the sequences have been recognised, it is a natural process to then hear harmonies, developments and new elements. Often the sound sequences themselves can seem inane and boring, with strange intervals and awkward sounds. Working with them over a period of time allows the mathematical, harmonic relationships to become familiar and they take on a life of their own.

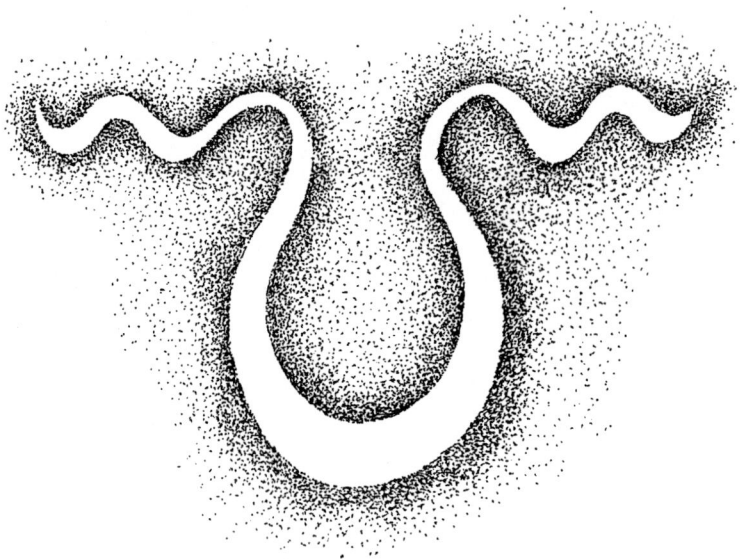

The visual pattern of lime (linden).

If you play a musical instrument the sequences can be a rewarding opening to create improvised musical meditations that can be as trance- inducing as any other technique.

In group situations the combination of mantra chanted with the sound sequences really takes on a new level of power. Start by establishing how the mantra and note sequences are going to work together. Sometimes this is straightforward, note for syllable, but often there will need to be a choice of a lengthened note or a repetition to allow them to work together. Once this has been established, and there may be many possible variations to choose from where one will feel more comfortable than another, start singing the mantra to this sequence all together until there is complete familiarity with it. As the room begins to fill up with the sound allow your heart to find its own pace. Still keep to the note sequence but choose your own speed and rhythms, shorten or lengthen each note or syllable, pause between repetitions or elide sections together. As each member of the group finds their own phrasing rhythms and harmonies, overtones and echoes, will build up. Sing in whatever octave range you feel appropriate and comfortable with.

As the group dynamics develop, weave your own variations of chant. This can be a beautiful and powerful experience for all participants, who can happily continue for an hour or more. The advantage with a large group is that not everyone needs to be singing all the time. Some can rest in silence or subside to a whisper and still be carried along by the sounds washing around them.

Colour Sequence

On subtle levels of creative manifestation, and particularly on those levels that seers call the "devic", the inhabitants are described as working with light and sound to manipulate and direct manifestation to more physical levels of existence.

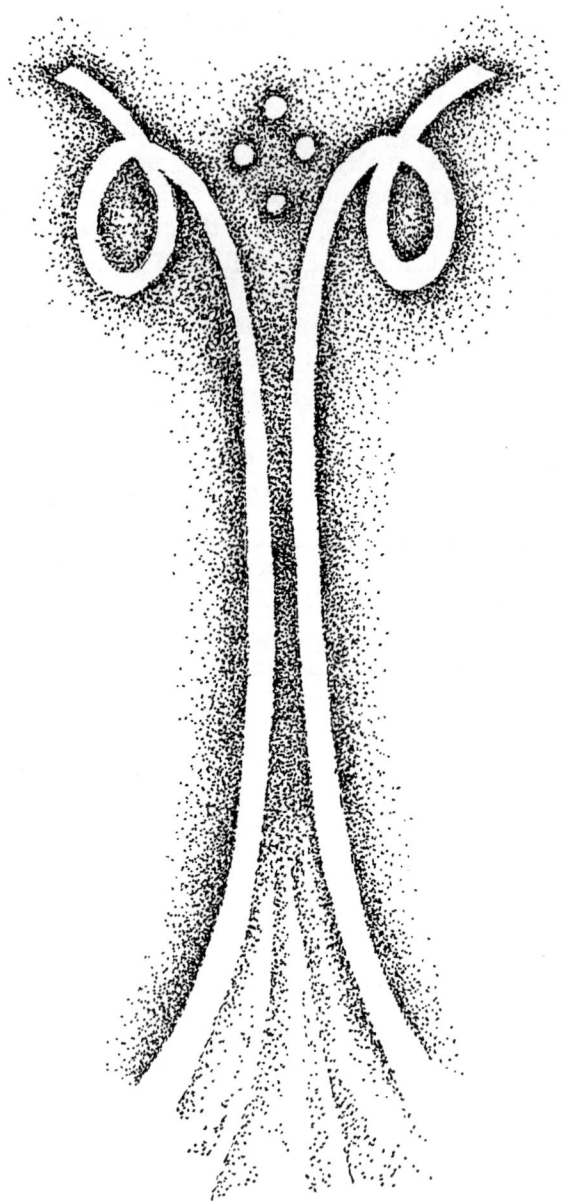

Visual pattern of rowan.

Sound vibration is translated into our world as mantra and music, light vibration is translated as colour and pattern-making.

A colour sequence has been isolated for each tree species investigated, and because each colour carries with it very precise energy characteristics, they can be seen to sum up the tree dynamics in another language - the language of light.

Most people would find it difficult to work effectively with colour sequences unless they have a natural visualisation ability or have trained in visual concentration. Those with some understanding of the characteristics of colour, however, will be able to get a clue to the tree's energy from the unfolding of the colour sequence. Those who are tuned into the vibration of a tree at a visual level may well pick up some aspects of the colour sequence.

We have used slide transparencies made with coloured theatrical gels, projected onto a wall or screen in the appropriate order, whilst other Tree Teacher Techniques were being used. This allows the energy of each colour to subtly alter the energy fields of those present so that they will be better able to, unconsciously, recognise the qualities of the tree spirits present. A bright screen washed with a repeated sequence of saturated colour can have quite a profound entrancing effect, particularly when there are also sound sequences being used simultaneously. At one such event it was afterwards commented by a participant that this was the way for healing to develop in the future: a total sensory immersion in the energy signatures of tree spirits.

Trance Positions

Trance positions are a relatively new discovery made by Felicitas Goodman while studying the characteristics of religious trance. She noticed world-wide similarities of

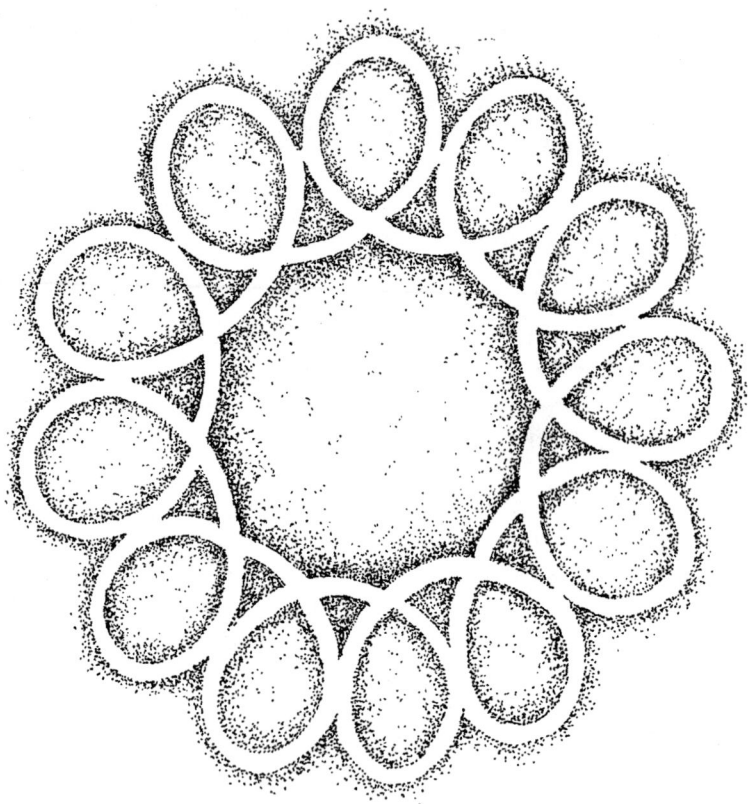

Visual pattern of bay.

206

posture in tribal artworks and experimented holding those postures whilst listening to a simple form of sonic driving, such as a rapid drumbeat or rattle. Each position held modified, quite specifically, the type of experience. There are many cultural models that suggest the physical position of the body can alter states of awareness, the most familiar to us probably being the meditation poses within hatha yoga traditions. (Other notable examples are the seated poses with props and belts within the Long-de Series of Dzogchen, specifically designed to activate the tsa-lung, the subtle channels within the physical body, and the legendary Celtic seer's pose of standing on one leg, one arm behind the back, one eye closed etc.).

Dr. Goodman found that poses were very precise and needed to be held for at least fifteen minutes to get clear results. This involves considerable concentration and effort, even in the simplest of positions. We are simply not used to remaining motionless under tension.

As attuning to tree spirits also involves a shift of perceptions allowing us to glimpse inside a particular Tree Kingdom, trance positions were sought for those trees we were investigating. Some of these positions can be extremely arduous but there are a number that can be tried out by anyone, particularly if the essence has been used beforehand.

Get used to the position first, making sure you have all details correct. If there are no specific instructions for parts of the body, then their positioning is not significant. You will need either a shamanic drumming or rattling tape, preferably with a fast beat, or else someone else who can keep up a steady rhythm without faltering for fifteen to twenty minutes. Subdue the lighting and close your eyes. After a moment or two you will probably begin to be aware of aches and pains, as well as becoming physically disoriented. If you bear in mind that it will all be over in twenty minutes and relax into the sensations, your awareness will soon start shifting into altered states. The first sign of this is often the apparent movement of the sound source or an accompaniment of some sort appearing out of the air. Be open to what you may experience as any of the sense fields might be affected.

Crystal Nets

Placing particular stones on and around the body modifies the energy patterns of the chakras and subtle bodies. Tree nets have been developed that allow us either to change our own energy frequencies and subtle patterning to come closer to approximating the desired tree energy pattern, or they create a field where we become more open and susceptible to the characteristic energy patterns of a tree and its spirit.

Stone placement, together with a specific colour of background cloth on which we lie, "softens" our usual ways of perceiving reality and what we consider to be who and what we are. This added flexibility, or mutability, allows a more fluid state where communication is made easier.

Tree nets, in general, have more idiosyncratic stone placements and more specific types of stone than many other nets we have explored. This is as one would expect when we are dealing with single groups or species, as opposed to more universal qualities such as planets or elements.

Tree nets can be deceptively powerful in their action. It is best not to spend more than twenty minutes at any one time. When finished take at least twice as long as you have spent in the net to slowly acclimatise back to normal reality. Awareness tends to shift levels at intervals of about 4 -6 minutes, so time your exit to make use of these natural energy shifts. (For more details on energy nets see "*Crystal Doorways*", Sue and Simon Lilly, Capall Bann 1997).

Visual Pattern

This is an area only just being touched on in our investigations. Looking at parallels in other traditions, particularly the Indian use of yantras and the European magical tradition of sigils, there is the possibility of finding a visual pattern that expresses the core energy of a tree and its spirit. Working with this in mind has brought up some promising start points, but attempting to encapsulate the "feel" of a tree in a visual form is frustrating. Very often the resulting image seems to only partially reflect the dynamics and it may prove to be that animated graphics will be the most successful method.

Those patterns presented here are mainly the result of shamanic processes of one sort or another, or the combined intuitions of a group exploring the same tree spirit. They are at best somewhere to start from, to allow development into a personally meaningful image. And perhaps this is the best that can be achieved: not a universally applicable series of glyphs, but a very individual way to tune the deeper mind into the signature patterns of a tree's energy.

Certain types and rhythms of shape do, however, seem to be sympathetic to certain tree energies and this is fertile ground for the investigation of repeating motifs in traditional artefacts. Testing some Celtic British spiral designs did come up with alignments to tree types. If this is so there may be a true Celtic Tree Alphabet, or a symbolic or magical language, hidden within the art of our ancestors.

Unlocking the Codes

After several years experimenting with these methods of linking to tree energies and seeing that they were effective, we wondered whether it would be possible to identify the core qualities of the trees from an interpretation of the mantra sounds and colour sequence.

Following the argument that each sound holds an energy pattern enfolded within itself, it was feasible that the mantra could be unravelled to display some of its main qualities. Two templates were used to do this: the concept of root words from Sanskrit and the Pueblo Indians' system of multilayered interpretation of sounds. Both systems come from cultures where language is held to be sacred and where there is profound understanding of the processes whereby vibration becomes form, sound becomes matter.

Root words are a fascinating glimpse into the development of human thought. The Classical languages spoken around the Mediterranean, the Celtic and Germanic tongues, as well as Persian and Northern Indian languages all derive from one common original known to us as Indo-European. From the prevalence of certain groupings of sounds, an original root word can be interpolated. Sanskrit, particularly the archaic Vedic texts, provides a huge amount of information regarding words and their root derivations. In essence, each root word acts like a seed or gravity well around which collects a large constellation of related concepts. In order to define something it is often necessary to define what it is not as well, therefore opposite concepts are often found to have the same root, perhaps with just a simple suffix to denote "not", (such as in Sanskrit: "vidya" - knowledge, and "avidya" - ignorance).

Even in modern English it is still possible to find the threads of these root words. Any glance at a dictionary will reveal clumps of similar sounds that carry a broad, shared concept. For example, the Sanskrit root *Stha*, "strong", can be found in stone, stand, steady, strong, still, where the root concept is clearly to do with stability. On the other hand the sound "Sl.." can be found in slip, slide, sliver, slug, slick, where the core idea, or feel, is: slimy, a thin layer, a motion along, a movement over something.

The Vedic linguists often suggested origins of meaning that a modern scholar would find fanciful in the extreme, but carry with them an attempt to convey some nuance of the underlying reality of the root word. Using language to define itself will always be a rather dangerous occupation. In no way should our suggestions be taken as a definitive statement of factual reality. We were simply curious to see if any coherent patterns emerged that would verify or expand on the information already gathered. Linguistics is a complex subject, there are a bewildering array of language shifts where one sound turns into another so that similar sounding words might derive from completely different roots.

Analysis of Bay

The investigation began with a simple mantra, that of the Bay tree. The mantra found for this spirit was "Pu. Ru." In Sanskrit these sounds are close to the root verbs, "to purify", and "to roar", so possibly interpreted as "Pure roaring".

Using the Pueblo system, described by Joseph Rael (*Beautiful Painted Arrow* of the Tiwa and Picuris Pueblo traditions), the vibrations of each consonant and vowel have a constellation of associated meanings. Using this system, the mantra of Bay becomes "heart carrying, abundance carrying".

If we look at the feeling that the words convey, rather than the words themselves we find:

"heart" - internal, central, belonging;

"carrying" - supporting, helping, enfolding, looking after, possessing;

"abundance" - energy tides, flow outwards, richness, growth;

"carrying" - supporting, helping, enfolding, looking after, possessing.

This might compress down to something along the lines of: "containing (or enfolding) the central energy; the expansion of benefit is helped."

Like the Sanskrit interpretation, the mantra suggests: "beginning with an internal energy, a central something, it acquires energy and rapidly expands".

Turning to look at the colour sequence for Bay this familiar pattern is repeated. The colour sequence is black; red; black; indigo; violet; green. Each colour, or wavelength of light energy, carries with it a wealth of related associations and observations that catalogues the effects each has on our physical body and the total sense experiences. Like the previous examples, only a single aspect of each colour is being examined - many other interpretations could be proposed - but each isolated facet is still expressive of the whole. Retranslating the particular colour sequence for the Bay tree, there is a process of unfoldment:

"Within the hidden potential of the Universe (black), there is a flash of energy (red). A flow of integrating and communicating energy (indigo) evolves and integrates together (violet) to create a space for development of growth, and power (green)."

Here again is the element of an internal focus of energy, (here it is the red within the black), that spreads outwards to stimulate or create a new space (or vessel), to hold and maintain growth.

Analysis of Ivy

With the Ivy mantra (Ki-Ja O'Trrri), there are several possible Sanskrit derived meanings. The first derives from the root words "kuj"- to hum; "ah"- to say, and "trr" - to cross or pass. So there is a sequence of humming, speaking, passing over. This first suggests "an internal vibration (or sound), that becomes clearly expressed (or communicated), and then goes on". A vibrating noise becomes a shaped sound with meaning and, either goes beyond or allows the speaker to move on, pass over or go beyond.

The alternative group of root words uses "ku"- to design or plan, "jaa"- to be born or, to give birth, "a"- as a negative (ie. the opposite of what follows it), and "trr" - to cross or pass. This can become something like: " Thought (or design) that comes forth and remains (ie. does not pass)".

Using the Pueblo system, we find that the sound sequence becomes: "The planting of awareness, guiding the one who knows not (the innocent), into endless (or abundant) time".

Looking at the colour sequence for Ivy, red is followed by a repeated sequence of blue then gold. This can be read as:

"A practical activation of energy (red), creates a cycle of understanding (blue) and wisdom (gold)", alternatively it could be read as "An energy release (red) for an easy flow of information (blue) that leads to knowledge and a creative use of intelligence (gold) that in turn allows greater knowledge, and so on."

In all three examples it seems that we are dealing with the same manifestation of energy in the Ivy. Each describes the creation or shaping of an energy structure that either allows or guides awareness beyond its present levels of experience and understanding. This is a clear parallel to the experiences of the Ivy spirit for many people as a guide and guardian of deep levels of ("forest") consciousness.

Analysis of Elm

When the Elm mantra is examined using the Pueblo model, "Tie Ch'Chaytay. Yow", becomes " A defining, or orienting guide or guardian (shepherd) that is to do with unity or carrying".

The colour sequence of black, blue, indigo, black can appear as "Within the field of potential manifestation (black- black), a flow of knowledge, information and communication (blue), naturally evolves into understanding, acceptance and peaceful slowing of activity (indigo), before returning to its resting state (black)."

With the Elm mantra there is a complex repeat of sounds with the final sound after a pause. Naturally spoken the mantra has a long, slow start (Tie) and a fast, repeating middle section (Ch'Chaytay), a pause and then a long, hollow, encapsulating close (Yow). There is thus an expansion, a stop with a redefinition and a conclusion that acts as a new space.

Looking at the mantra in terms of the possible root words two clear sequences can be picked out. Firstly "There is a movement with light ("di" - to shine or to fly), that movement continues and is directed ("cac"- to leap, "ay"- to go, "day"- to share), and concludes wrapping around itself ("yaa", "yuj", "yaj" - to unite, to offer up, to sacrifice)".

The second sequence begins with: "To solidify into form ("cyaa"-to coagulate), to gleam or, to go, or to share ("ccuc-ay-day"), to unite together or transform ("yaa", "yuj", "yaj")".

Again we must reiterate that this is by no means meant to be a definitive scholastic statement - It is creative play. Along the way, though, there have been some surprising correspondences that have emerged.

From a free interpretation of the mantra elements have emerged the following:

Weeping willow - " To bind together, to give, to free up."

Whitebeam - " Something to cling on to, to be strong."

Great sallow - " To enliven, to sing, to cry/break, to give."

Lime - " To define, to energise and take control, then move outwards."

Alder - " To be sharp, to be unsteady, to swell, to move."

Plum - " To bestow faith."

From the colour sequences:

Alder becomes: "From a place of clarity, energy manifests to create a place for balance and growth."

Great sallow becomes: " Wisdom becomes action."

Hawthorn becomes: " To the self comes the healing of love."

Holly becomes: " Passion and clarity; balance and peace."

Lime becomes: " Integration of healing wisdom and intuition."

One of the most surprising analyses was that of Silver birch, where the mantra turned out as "To formulate or conceive, to gestate and enliven, to bring forth in light, to nourish and protect." Anyone who studies runes would recognise this as a fairly good expression of the energies of the rune "beorc" which most commentators associate with the birch tree and which represents the energies of nurturing, the mother, birth and new beginnings.

The usefulness of such creative play, which could equally have been carried out using alphabets such as Hebrew, and other systems like numerology, is that it suggests possibilities of meaning and significance on a multitude of unforeseen levels. Where these possible meanings coincide and reinforce each other it is then that we can maybe glimpse an underlying facet of each tree spirit and how it relates both to us and the world around it. Only resonance, that indefinable excitement and sudden clarity, that "eureka" of understanding, can show us which correspondences are significant for us and which are redundant. But one moment of resonance, an instant of language-free cognition, that allows us to see the reality behind the tree-form, is worth any amount of intellectual, historical, folkloric, anthropological bits of data (whilst at the same time often allowing us to integrate and understand from a new perspective all such relevant information).

Attunements

Alder

MANTRA: TISH. LEE. PIN. O
Notes: TISH rhymes with "fish" but with more emphasis on the
"s" than the "h"
PIN has a short "i" as in "fit"
O as in "Oh dear!"
The syllables can be run together, they are separated here for clarity

NOTE SEQUENCE: *A *G *G
(* before the notes indicates the octave below Middle C. * after the note indicates the octave above Middle C)

COLOUR SEQUENCE: White - red - green

ENERGY NET:
1) Any sort of pink stone either side of the body, level with the heart.
2) below the feet, 3 stones in a line. Closest to the feet, black tourmaline, then ruby, then a milky quartz.
3) lying on an orange cloth (If a cloth of the right colour is not available, use white spray the area with the appropriate Green Man Light Essence.

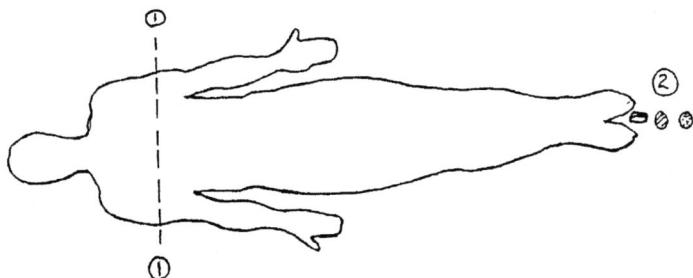

Apple

MANTRA: DOW. PRRRNGAA
or DOW. PRR. N. YA
roll the "r" as in Scots' pronunciation

NOTE SEQUENCE: F. Eb. C#. F. G: F. Eb. C#. C

COLOUR SEQUENCE: Gold - Green - Yellow

ENERGY NET:
1) Orange cloth
2) turquoise by the left ear lobe
3) turquoise by the left hand

TRANCE POSITION:
1) Kneeling on the right knee
2) left foot flat on the floor
3) left hand just below the left knee cap
4) right hand over the right knee
5) head straight forward
6) weight on the right leg

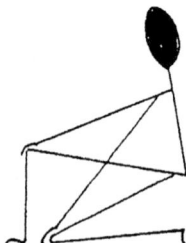

Ash

MANTRA: D' HAA - GAA. D'HRRR - AA. SHRRR
Notes: sounds like - Du Haa Gaa, Drrr Aa
Shrrr-ru (short "u" as in "put"

NOTE SEQUENCE: A. Ab. Ab. Bb.   A. Ab. Ab. Bb.

COLOUR SEQUENCE: Gold - blue - gold - orange - white

ENERGY NET:
1) Green cloth
2) Black tourmalines, in a triangle, point down, shoulder
   width above head
3) turquoise under left foot
4) turquoise by right knee

TRANCE POSITION:
1) Standing, feet shoulder width apart,
   locked knees
2) left arm, bent slightly, forward, palm
   inwards towards "t'an t'ien" (sacral
   chakra area)
3) right arm, same position, but palm
   upwards
4) head and chin held in, eyes lowered or
   closed

Bay

MANTRA: POO. RU (x6)
Notes: rhymes with "two", "rook" - similar to "poorer"

NOTE SEQUENCE: B. G.

COLOUR SEQUENCE: Black - red - black - indigo - violet - green (repeated)

ENERGY NET:
1). Black cloth
2). left side, elbow level - azurite
3) right side, level with hand - sodalite
4) right side, ankle level - citrine
5) above head - black obsidian

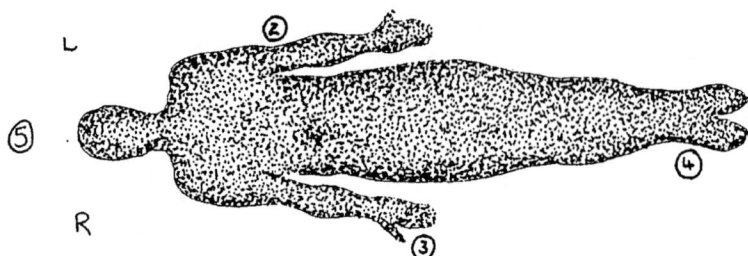

Beech

MANTRA: DESH. LAA. CHI
Notes: CHI rhymes with "see"

NOTE SEQUENCE: *G. *G. *F. *F. D. C.

COLOUR SEQUENCE: Orange - white - blue - black

ENERGY NET:
1) at heart gold/yellow petrified wood
2) at arch of left foot - aquamarine
3) pink cloth

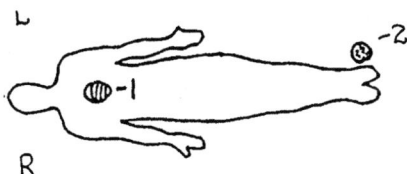

TRANCE POSITION:

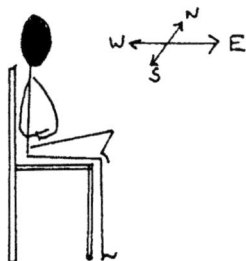

1) seated on chair, right foot on the ground
2) left foot on right knee
3) hands folded in lap, right on left
4) head looking straight forward, facing east

Crack Willow

MANTRA: PL. OO. G'DHOO.   JI - NOW

NOTE SEQUENCE: Ab. C. Ab. C#. A. Eb.

COLOUR SEQUENCE: Violet - indigo - yellow - turquoise

ENERGY NET:
1) Blue cloth
2) blue quartz on the heart
3) mid calf, away from body - turquoise
4) by right hand - rhodochrosite

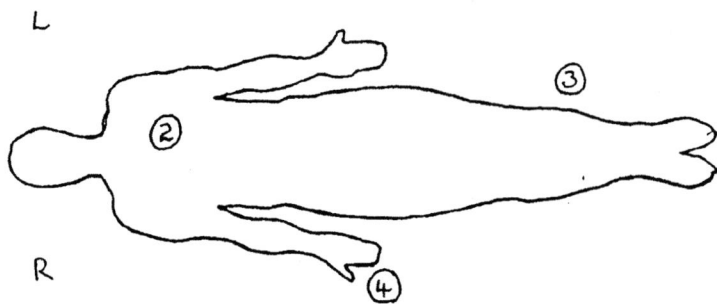

Elder

MANTRA: MOO. GUS. GAAAD

NOTE SEQUENCE: *E. *G. *B. *F. *F.   (prefix * shows
notes in octave below Middle C)

COLOUR SEQUENCE: Blue - gold - pale pink

ENERGY NET:
1) pink cloth
2) red amber on right side of chest, level with armpit
3) smoky quartz in each hand

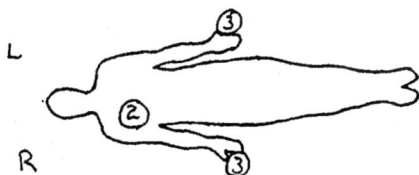

TRANCE POSITION:
1) lying on back
2) hands on torso, left hand over right shoulder
3) right hand over navel
4) legs apart

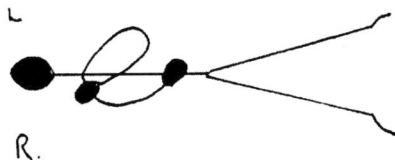

English Elm

MANTRA: TIE. CH...CHAYTAY....YOW
Notes: TIE.CH as one sound. CH with a very
short "u", as in "chuck"
CHAYT rhyming with "plate". AY the same
YOW is a distinct sound with a pause before it.
Rhyming with "cow"

NOTE SEQUENCE: C. *G. C. D

COLOUR SEQUENCE: Black - blue - indigo - black

ENERGY NET:
1) White fluorite on the heart centre/ centre of chest
2) azurite in both hands
3) a white cloth

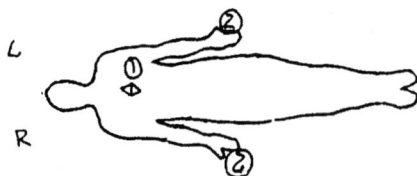

TRANCE POSITION:
1) half kneeling (either foot) - left shown here
2) left hand on ground to left side of left foot
3) right hand on top of left hand
(vice versa if kneeling on right knee)

Gean (Wild Cherry)

MANTRA: CHO. PAA. T. R. PAA
                Notes: CHO to rhyme with "blow"
                       T as in "touch", R as in "rut"
                       PAA rhymes with "car"

NOTE SEQUENCE: D. D. G. A. B. G. E. C. *A

COLOUR SEQUENCE: Turquoise - gold - turquoise - pink

ENERGY NET:
1) Pink/cherry opal at second chakra
2) gold citrine, point downwards, between feet
3) red cloth

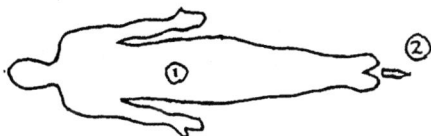

TRANCE POSITION:
1) lying on left side, knees drawn up to the chest
2) left hand, palm down on second chakra
3) right hand, palm down over heart chakra

Giant Redwood

MANTRA: NAA. FAA. KOO. SHI
Notes: SHI sounds like "she"
NAA sounds like "now" without the "w"

NOTE SEQUENCE: *B. F#. Eb. F#. G. C#.

COLOUR SEQUENCE: green - gold - violet - red

ENERGY NET:
1) amethyst on right side at heart level
2) amethyst beside right foot
3) smoky quartz between feet
4) white cloth

TRANCE POSITION:
1) on all fours (on hands and balls of feet, heels up)
2) hands facing forwards
3) arms straight
4) eyes closed

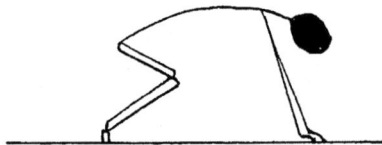

Great Sallow

MANTRA: SHOO. GRUHUH. ROO. DAA
Notes: GRU has a short "u" as in the "a" of
gorilla
HUH is an aspirate as in the expression
Huh!

NOTE SEQUENCE: *G. Bb. C#. Bb. C (x3)

COLOUR SEQUENCE: Gold - red

ENERGY NET:
1) a pink cloth
2) green calcite held in the left hand
3) red jasper held in the right hand

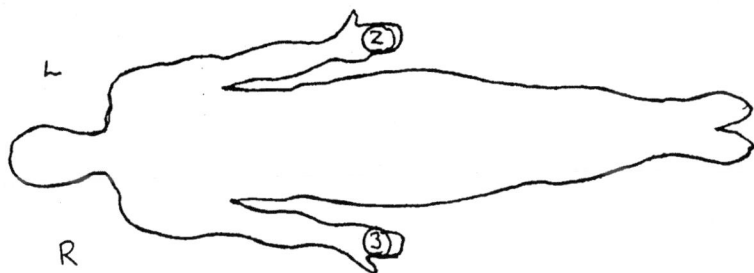

Hawthorn

MANTRA: MAA. ILCH. DUH. HUH. RRR. FIY
Notes: DUH and HUH are a short "a" or "u"
sound
RRR is a long rolled "r"
FIY rhymes with "fly"

NOTE SEQUENCE: D. B. D. D.

COLOUR SEQUENCE: Gold - orange - pink

ENERGY NET:
1) an emerald above the head
2) yellow/ gold topaz below the feet
3) on the left side - blue quartz
4) on the right side - yellow apatite
5) gold/deep yellow cloth

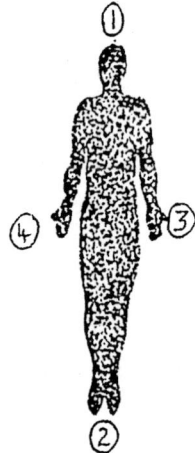

TRANCE POSITION:
1) sitting, standing or kneeling
2) hands, palms down, fingers stretched,
placed comfortably
3) arms out towards front or back, elbows
not locked
4) move hands around the body in a slow
swing

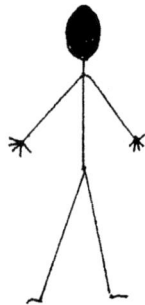

228

Hazel

MANTRA: TOO-O'CHU. N'YAY-SHOO. JAY-SHAY (x3)

NOTE SEQUENCE: F#. C.

COLOUR SEQUENCE: Gold - magenta - turquoise - indigo

ENERGY NET:
1) white cloth
2) amber either side by shoulders
3) lapis lazuli either side by fingers
4) dark blue fluorite beside ankles

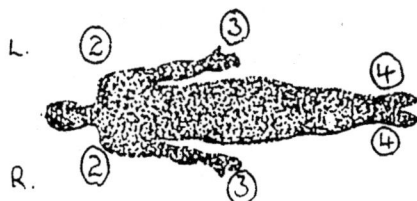

TRANCE POSITION:

A   1) kneeling, knees apart, buttocks on the ground
       2) hands on hips, elbows close to body

B   1) feet shoulder width apart
       2) hands on hips, elbows close to body

229

Holly

MANTRA: T'SHAY. TOE. CHOOL
                Notes: T'SHAY rhyming as O'Shea, say, play
                etc. but with a shorter "y" sound

NOTE SEQUENCE: A. C. C. D.

COLOUR SEQUENCE: Red - white - green - blue

ENERGY NET:
1) dark blue cloth
2) below left hand - a red garnet
3) below right hand, an amethyst

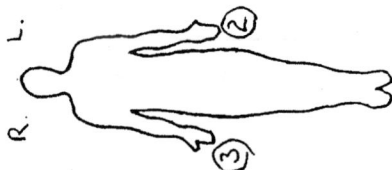

TRANCE POSITION:
1) seated, base of spine on floor
2) right leg straight
3) left leg - sole of foot on the ground, knee bent
4) right hand on left hand, resting on left, bent knee

230

Horse Chestnut

MANTRA: GAASH...T'HAASH. DAA. R. NAA. Y

NOTE SEQUENCE: * Ab

COLOUR SEQUENCE: Pink - red/orange - yellow

ENERGY NET:
1) blue cloth
2) by left and right shoulders - blue lace agate
3) on heart - rhodonite

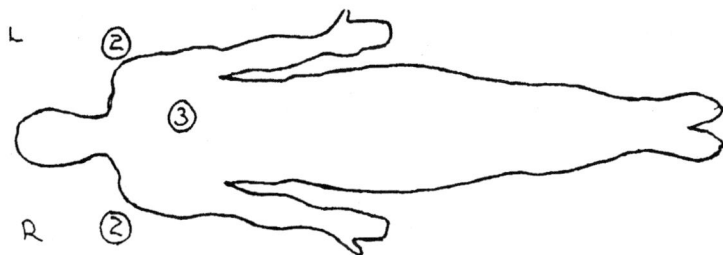

lʊy

MANTRA: KIJA. OH. TRRR

Notes: KI as in "kill", JA as in "just", OH as in French - "autre" or as in Oh! Tree

NOTE SEQUENCE: E. F. Eb/ E. F. Eb./ E. F. Eb.

COLOUR SEQUENCE: Red, followed by blue - gold, blue-gold repeated...

ENERGY NET:
1) gold cloth
2) turquoise either side, level with hands
3) kyanite on right side of head, at crown level

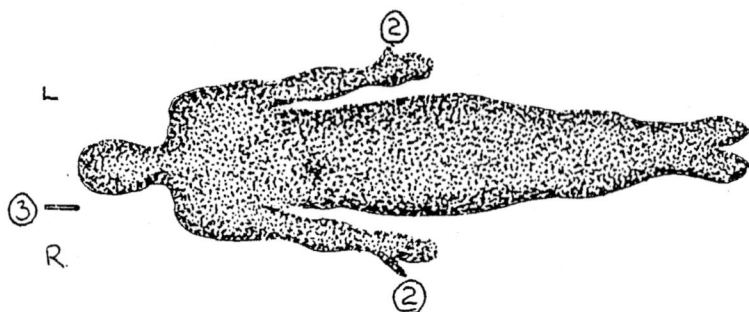

Lawson Cypress

MANTRA: PAI. VAU. KHI

NOTE SEQUENCE: C*. Bb. G. G.
(suffix *, denotes notes an octave above
Middle C)

COLOUR SEQUENCE: Violet - turquoise - yellow - black

ENERGY NET:
1) indigo or violet cloth
2) lapis lazuli near to and below hands
3) turquoise beside, near to hands
4) clear quartz above head

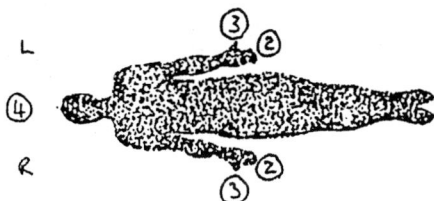

TRANCE POSITION:
A.   1) sitting on heels
      2) forehead forward onto ground
      3) arms and hands extended backwards, close to body,
         relaxed, palms upwards
B   1) sitting on a chair with back relaxed forwards
      2) hands dangling loose

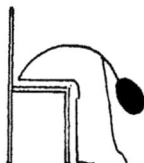

Lime

MANTRA: DAA. GI. HAY. DAA. GI. HAY. DAA. GI.
HAY
Notes: A threefold repetition and then a pause
before the next repetition, and so on.
GI has a hard "g" and a short "i" as in
"give". HAY is a short "Y" somewhere
between "hay" and "hair". Emphasis is
on the first syllable, DAA.

NOTE SEQUENCE: C. G. E. F. Eb. C.   C. G. E. F. Eb. C.

COLOUR SEQUENCE: Orange - turquoise - indigo

ENERGY NET:
1) yellow cloth
2) a sugilite at the centre of the forehead
3) a handspan across upper chest below collar bones:
   left, iron pyrites - right, green calcite
4) at front of ankles, yellow fluorite

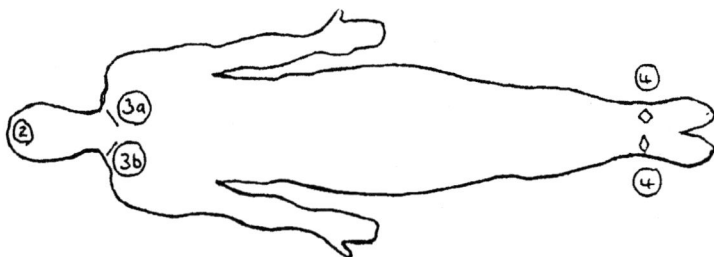

Magnolia

MANTRA: RU..KOO..AA..RU
Notes: RU as in "run", KOO as in "cook",
AA as in "are" with the "r" pronounced

NOTE SEQUENCE: F. G. Eb. Bb. F.

COLOUR SEQUENCE: gold - turquoise - white - dark blue

ENERGY NET:
1) red garnet below the feet on the midline
2) sodalite below the garnet
3) white cloth

TRANCE POSITION:
1) lying face down, with support for the forehead
2) legs together, straight
3) arms out from the body about 45 degrees
4) palms down, fingers splayed

* Please note: Magnolia helps to attune to "sambhogakaya", the sphere of energy where light and sound are form (i.e. similar to "devic" realms)

Monkey Puzzle Tree

MANTRA: SHOW. KLE. KAA
Notes: SHOW as in "shower"
KLE as in "CLEanse"

NOTE SEQUENCE: G. Eb. G. G. F#. D. B.

COLOUR SEQUENCE: Orange - yellow - pink - magenta - orange

ENERGY NET:
1) at both sides of neck, under jaw, yellow quartz/citrine
2) smoky quartz at base chakra between legs
3) citrine between feet
4) at base of each foot a rubellite
5) orange cloth

TRANCE POSITION:
1) standing upright
2) head forward
3) torso twisting from side to side

Monterey Pine

MANTRA: YEAR(uh) . EH. TURR (uh). HO. SHAY

NOTE SEQUENCE: Bb. F...Bb. F....repeated

COLOUR SEQUENCE: Blue - yellow - blue

ENERGY NET: (As for Scots Pine)
1) red cloth
2) blue sapphire at brow
3) amethyst at left ear
 (if pointed, point inwards)

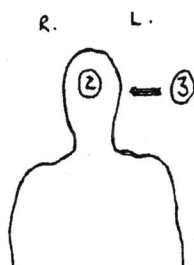

TRANCE POSITION:
1) standing, feet together
2) spine turned to left so that right shoulder is forward
3) head turned to the left as far as possible
4) arms held to the body as far to the left as possible
5) hands open, with fingers splayed, held against the body

Mulberry

MANTRA: TEE...SHOOED...NYAI...NYAA
                    Notes: SHOOED as in "rude"

NOTE SEQUENCE: B. A. B. G.

COLOUR SEQUENCE: Indigo - violet

ENERGY NET:
1) red cloth
2) turquoise on the right thigh, where the middle finger
   of the right hand can reach (Gallbladder Meridian)

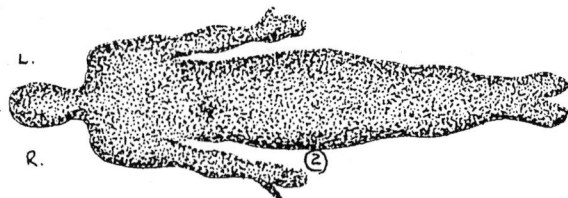

Oak

MANTRA: DOW. TAR. BEY. PEY. DHEY
Notes: TAR as in "ta, very much"
BEY and all following syllables are
short "y" as in the "ai" of "dairy"

NOTE SEQUENCE: Bb. Bb. C. Bb. E

COLOUR SEQUENCE: Red - yellow - blue - white - indigo -
black

ENERGY NET:
1) red cloth
2) beneath the feet, a white opal
3) below this, to the left, a turquoise
4) below this to the right, a clear selenite
5) below these, centrally, a haematite

TRANCE POSITION:
1) sitting on floor, one leg bent and tucked, like a half-lotus close to the body
2) other leg with foot placed flat on the floor, knee bent
3) head looking straight forward
4) hands resting on raised knee
5) use oak essence to activate trance

Persian Ironwood

MANTRA: DAA. SH. T' HRRIY
Notes: SH has a short "i" sound after it.
T'HRRIY like "hurry" with rolled r's

NOTE SEQUENCE: G

COLOUR SEQUENCE: Violet

ENERGY NET:
1) on the arch of each foot, an amethyst
2) amethyst held in both hands
3) below the feet, further out than the other stones, an amethyst on both sides
4) black cloth

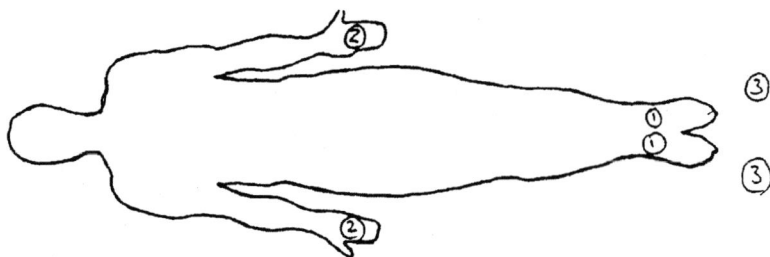

Plane Tree

MANTRA: NI. YO. TIE. YO
               Notes: NI as in "nip", YO as in "yo-yo"

NOTE SEQUENCE: G#. C#. *Bb. *F#.

COLOUR SEQUENCE: green - orange - blue - yellow

ENERGY NET:
1) blue cloth
2) by each ear a red (iron) quartz
3) at right side of chest, level with elbow, a white selenite

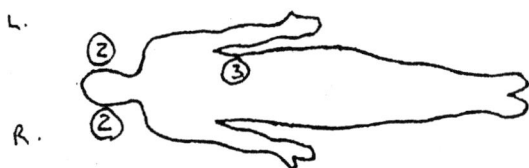

TRANCE POSITION:
1) lying down on back
2) knees bent and raised, feet on ground
3) hands by sides, left palm up, right palm down

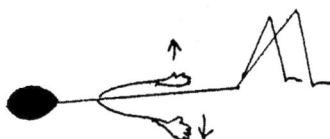

Plum

MANTRA: DAA. SHUT

Notes: the vowel sound in the second syllable
is a short "a", sounding close to "u"
The final T should be an emphatic
explosive without a vowel echo, i.e. said
without opening the jaw

NOTE SEQUENCE: G. Db. G. A.

COLOUR SEQUENCE: Pink - rainbow - pink

ENERGY NET:
1) pink cloth
2) three stones in a row above the head
   left - jade, right - thulite, central - jet

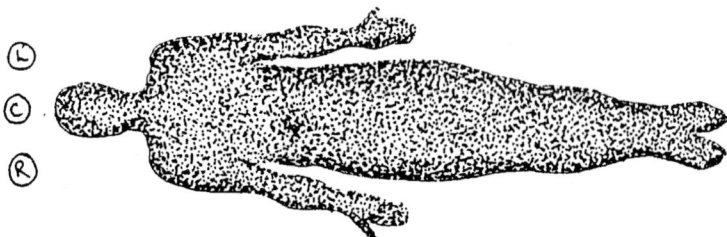

Red Chestnut

MANTRA: BEE. TIE
               Notes: BEE has a slight aspirate: B(h) EE

NOTE SEQUENCE: C#. E. G. D.

COLOUR SEQUENCE: Blue - yellow - blue - green

ENERGY NET:
1) sternal notch at the base of throat, violet fluorite
2) on left hip - black tourmaline
3) on right hip - pale rose quartz
4) red cloth

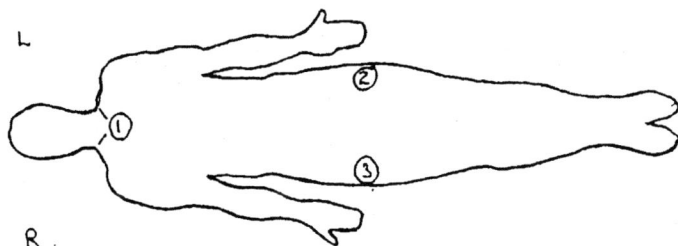

Rowan

MANTRA: AY..NOO..AY
Notes: AY rhymes with "say"
NOO as in "put"

NOTE SEQUENCE: G. F. F. G. *F. *C#.

COLOUR SEQUENCE: red - yellow - blue sparkled with
white

ENERGY NET:
1) on top of right shoulder an amethyst
2) at centre of top of right wrist a ruby
3) at right knee a red jasper
4) lapis lazuli at right ankle on outer
edge
5) blue cloth

TRANCE POSITION:
1) kneeling, right knee on floor
2) left leg/knee at right angles to foot on
floor
3) left elbow, arm straight is resting on left
knee, hand straight, palm up
4) right arm rests along right leg, palm down
over knee
5) head turned and gaze fixed on left palm

Sequoia (Coastal Redwood)

MANTRA: TAA.TER....SHUSHAA.....KOOK...A
Notes: TAA.TER sounds like "father"
KOOK.A sounds like "cooker"

NOTE SEQUENCE: C#. C. F#. G. Eb. C#. C.

COLOUR SEQUENCE: yellow - red - turquoise - blue - turquoise - gold - red - green

ENERGY NET:
1) top of right instep - a turquoise
2) obsidian on right hip
3) red cloth

TRANCE POSITION:
1) standing, feet shoulder width apart
2) face forward, both hands making fists
3) knuckles together at level of hara (second chakra)
4) hands held slightly away from body

Scots Pine

MANTRA: MA-FRRUK. T.DAA.VA

NOTE SEQUENCE: G. A. C*.

COLOUR SEQUENCE: red - magenta

ENERGY NET:
1) red cloth
2) blue sapphire at brow
3) amethyst at left ear (if pointed, inwards)

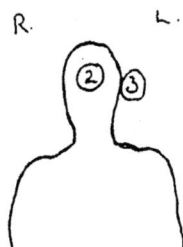

TRANCE POSITION:
1) kneeling on a cushion, knees apart
2) body forward, head on the ground
3) arms stretched out in front, palms down

Silver Birch

MANTRA: KOO. SHOW. TIE. PAA
          Notes: emphasis on the third syllable i.e. close
          to k...sh..TIE..paa
          SHOW rhyming with "toe"

NOTE SEQUENCE: G. G. F. Eb. G. Eb. F

COLOUR SEQUENCE: magenta - gold - indigo - white with
          blue shimmers

ENERGY NET:
1) red or pink cloth
2) rose quartz in both hands
3) citrine, point down, on sternal notch
4) red granite on centre of chest

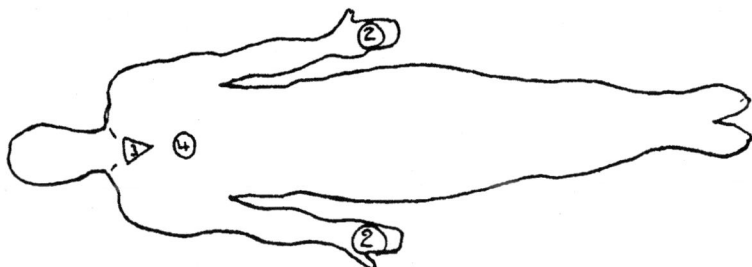

Silver Maple

MANTRA: TESH. YOONOOSH..NOW

NOTE SEQUENCE: A. Bb. G. C*. G.

COLOUR SEQUENCE: Green - yellow - magenta

ENERGY NET:
1) just above left knee a rutilated quartz
2) white cloth

TRANCE POSITION:
no physical position
1) visualise being buoyed up by the air, surrounded by cloud, high in the sky. All parts of the body supported gently

Stags Horn Sumach

MANTRA: J'CHO. K'LA. B'RA
Notes: CH as in "loch", K'LA as in "colour",
B'RA as in "borough"

NOTE SEQUENCE: A. C*. C*. Bb. F. *A~ A
Note: there is an octave slide between
the last notes

COLOUR SEQUENCE: green - violet - turquoise

ENERGY NET:
1) blue sapphire by outside of left knee
2) indigo cloth

TRANCE POSITION:
1) sitting, left hand on left buttock, right hand on right
   buttock
2) head tilted upwards and back as far as it goes, relaxed
3) feet or leg position not important

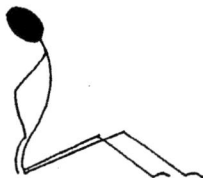

249

Sycamore

MANTRA: SH. AW (as in "shower", "found")

NOTE SEQUENCE: G. C. *Bb.

COLOUR SEQUENCE: Green - orange

ENERGY NET:
1) green or yellow/green cloth
2) left hand - carnelian
3) right - iron pyrites

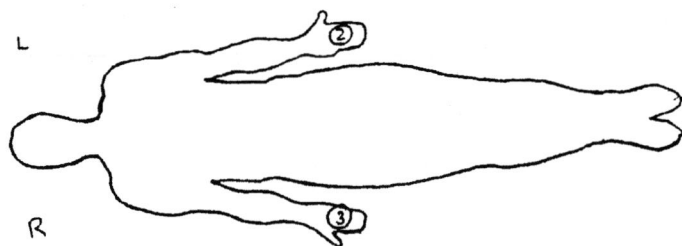

Tree Lichen

MANTRA: KUCK. IN. YAA. TAY (x3)
Notes: KUCK as in "cuckoo", TAY as in "say"

NOTE SEQUENCE: D. *G#. *B. C#.

COLOUR SEQUENCE: Green - yellow

ENERGY NET:
1) opal on left hip bone
2) opal on right hip bone
3) indigo cloth

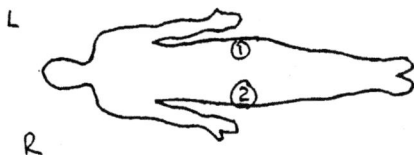

TRANCE POSITION:
1) lying down on back
2) knees apart, thighs spread with ankles crossed
3) hands palms up
4) left arm out straight, level with shoulder
5) right arm up above head

Tulip Tree

MANTRA: SHA...S.HO

Notes: SHA rhymes with "car", S.HO rhymes with "show"

NOTE SEQUENCE: *G. C. *E.

COLOUR SEQUENCE: turquoise - yellow - green

ENERGY NET:
1) white cloth
2) red jasper in each hand
3) citrine at solar plexus
4) red jasper between the knees

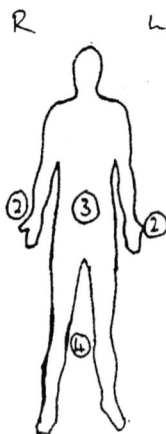

TRANCE POSITION:
1) lying down on right side
2) knees drawn up together
3) palm of right hand over right ear
4) palm of left hand over heart
5) the head can rest on a pillow

Weeping Willow

MANTRA: Y. RAA. TIE
Notes: Y has a definite stop afterwards with no
vowel sound, as in the 1st sound in
"yes"

NOTE SEQUENCE: F#. Bb. C. C.

COLOUR SEQUENCE: Turquoise with green flashes and
sparkles of gold

ENERGY NET:
1) green cloth
2) above the head, iron pyrites
3) below the feet, blue tourmaline

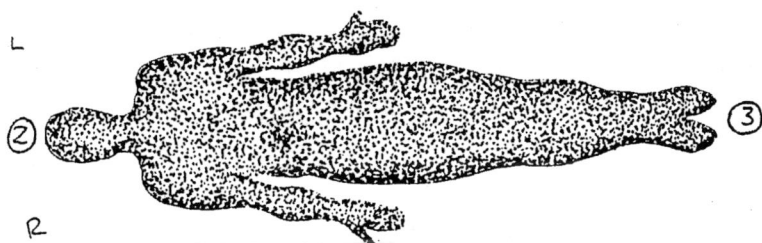

Whitebeam

MANTRA: LAID. TOO
                  Notes: there is a slight "h" after LAID

NOTE SEQUENCE: C*. C. G. F.   C*. C. G. F.

COLOUR SEQUENCE: red - violet - rich yellow

ENERGY NET:
1) below navel (hara) a dark blue tourmaline (indicolite) or a
   kyanite, placed at right angles to the central axis of the
   body
2) left side, knee level - violet fluorite
3) right side, knee level - pink calcite or pinky garnet
4) gold cloth

TRANCE POSITION:
1) lying on back with knees raised and bent to flatten the back
2) feet on the floor, placed apart
3) arms fully extended straight out from body, palms upwards

White Poplar

MANTRA: N'GAI. B'HOO

NOTE SEQUENCE: C*. B. D. D. F. C.

COLOUR SEQUENCE: White - blue

ENERGY NET:
1) white cloth
2) amber at level of diaphragm, left side
3) amber at level of navel, left side

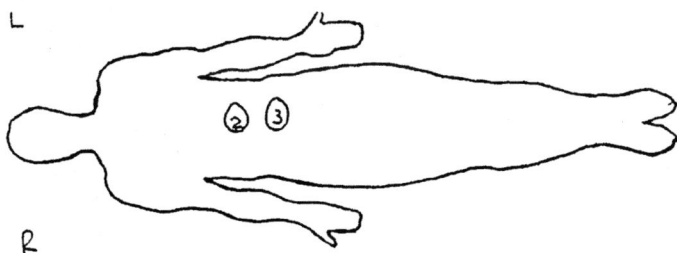

Yew

MANTRA: DOW. DAY. VOW. DAA

NOTE SEQUENCE: B. Eb. B. C.

COLOUR SEQUENCE: indigo - red - orange - yellow

ENERGY NET:
1) magenta cloth
2) below and between feet, red garnet
3) beside mid-leg, left side, purple fluorite
4) at hara/second chakra, moonstone
5) beside mid-arm, right side, green jade
6) in or taped to right ear, clear selenite

TRANCE POSITION:
1) stand straight
2) left hand to right clavicle
3) right hand to second chakra/ hara
4) eyes closed

Yew - The Root of Power

"I am flying low over rolling green hills marked out with hedge and field with small copses of woodland between. Dipping down into a small river valley a church tower comes into sight between churchyard trees. To the southeast of the grey stone walls is a tall mass of dark green. Gliding down into the dense shade I stand on grass looking at the dark red bulk of an ancient yew's trunk. From about three feet above the ground the trunk splits into four huge boughs leaving a flat bed of rotted needles large enough to seat three people comfortably. But it is not this that draws my attention. With the eyes of the spirit the trunk dissolves to become the entrance to a small cave. Sitting cross-legged inside is a male figure, young looking but of indeterminate age. My vision slips into a double exposure: the human head is also a snake's head, the body at once human and serpentine. The yew spirit suggests that I dance, and so I dance, at first around the tree under the dark boughs but then in amongst the branches, even through and between the internal structures, the cellular spiralling of the yew's growth, and then down again onto the ground around and around.

With a shift of perspective the tree becomes the hub of a silver wheel that spins out for miles across the landscape. Silver roads and gossamer thin infiltrations; a wheel that stretches through time as much as it moves through space. A wheel that anchors a certain reality, that feeds, transmits and supports the structure of the lives in the land around it. A sure, timeless hub, measuring the ebb and flow of seasons - green tides and brown tides, weather, wind and centuries.

To the cave of the spirit once more: the one who sits, who is still and dancing simultaneously. The one who smiles and measures the offering of dance with flickering tongue. But

deeper yet, beyond and beneath, there is a chamber, round with inset niches an unknowable distance beneath the soil. There is no movement here, no playful, sharp smile or deep seeing pupils. It is the silence of maintenance, the silence of feeling, the wielding of profound awareness. Around the chamber, within the alcoves, facing inwards towards the centre are those that watch. It is like a chamber of remembrance and a chamber of generation. It is of the yew and yet beyond even the yew. It is numinous, ancient, profound and vital."

This is a record of a spirit journey to an ancient local yew tree. It presents motifs and seed-concepts that keep re-appearing with those who choose to work with the energies of the yew (or perhaps more accurately, those whom the yew chooses - for such a smoulderingly powerful tree, the yew spirits will make themselves clearly felt at every opportunity with the enthusiasm of boisterous, very large puppies!).

Right from the beginning of our work with trees and tree spirits, yew had a prominent place. In introductory talks it was simply one of the best essences to demonstrate as it created a strong, palpable and weighty presence in the room or hall. The change of energy can be clearly appreciated by all, and when contrasted with a second essence that has a light energy, such as lime, few are left in any doubt that something is going on.

Having a very old yew just over the hill from us was another reason to explore the tree's characteristics early on, and the yew essence was gathered from the flowers of this tree. Testing the efficacy of the yew essence immediately gave us a healthy respect for its energies. Power of this stature cannot be ignored, but not everyone is able to cope with the intensely grounding, energising, uncompromising presence. Very often yew essence will have an energising effect. This can act on the physical level of the circulatory system, possibly including a general increase in oxygenation and aiding the liver in the purification of the blood. This increased circulation may, in some cases, be aphrodisiac. The essence also may help with the assimilation of nutrients within the digestive tract.

At its most basic the energising effects of the essence are related to those issues to do with survival and protection. Therefore it has a tendency to activate the functions of the base chakra. The solar plexus chakra is also stimulated and this works on the memory and the faculty of self-discrimination, particularly when this concerns survival and protection. Yew brings these basic instincts and drives to the very finest levels of the individual - the subtle body called the spiritual - a level of activity well beyond the "Higher Self" where individuality and perception open out into multi-dimensional realities. Such an energy might represent the upholding of the integrity of creation. The energy of the tree itself, as perceived through the essence, is strongly linked with the protection of the planet, the Earth's immune system, purification and alignment with nature's energy flows - particularly the cycles of the sun, moon and tides.

Yew essence is thus deeply energising, having a potentially beneficial effect on the immune system. It has a relationship with existence within self-existence that suggests far memory, the cycles of time and the planet Earth's connection to solar energies. With such a signature no wonder the tree itself gives many people the willies!

There is no tree that excites such fear and folklore as the yew. It is true that all parts of the tree, except the red aril around the seed, are toxic, but there are many other plants of equal or greater danger in our surroundings which are generally unknown or unconsidered. With the yew it is as if the toxicity merely verifies other, less tangible, fears and associations. In some lectures this irrational fear manifests directly. We have had people get up and leave the room rather than be subjected to a few droplets of much diluted essence from a diffuser sprayer. Had there been access to strings of garlic and crucifixes, these would no doubt have been waved in our direction too. The greatest poison is ignorance that breeds fear. Fear prefers to destroy the object of fear rather than understand the reality. Poisonous plants and animals have always attracted great respect in traditional cultures because it has been found that the strongest poisons are also, very often, the strongest medicines when treated with care, knowledge and respect. From a shamanic viewpoint we always feel threatened by spirits with more power than we ourselves possess, and the power of life and death is one that few of us have any knowledge of at all. The yew is powerful because it does have the power over life and death - and this must always have been understood.

The death aspect of yew is nowadays immediately associated with churchyards where the tree is ubiquitous. It is so obviously a tree of the dead. This aspect of the connection, though, is a comparatively recent one - less than half the life of one of our oldest yew trees: a mere thousand years or so, since the establishment of the Christian religion. As has always been the tradition with religious takeovers, the most sacred sites were appropriated by the new beliefs. So, churches were built within, upon, or close to the sacred groves, enclosures and temples that would often have contained ancient trees, and especially the yew.

Nothing Living So Old
"If this tree is gone, then we will no longer exist." (Allan Meredith)

Two hundred million years ago, *Paleotaxus rediviva* lived during the Triassic period. Its fossils show the tree to be one of the oldest conifers and a direct progenitor of the modern yew. In its current form the yew tree can be distinguished

Sampford Courtney, Devon 15" c. This area of mid-Devon was the site of a large sacred forest and its churches contain many Green Men.

from fossils one million years old. Yew is one of the world's great ancestors and bears the characteristics of its longevity. Scattered about the temperate zones of the planet, never appearing in great numbers, it hangs on as a variable and resistant, hardy species. It grows very slowly yet lives for a very long time. Yew once constituted a major part of the forests of Europe between the Ice Ages and its decline is due primarily to its continuous harvesting by mankind. There is little, except continually sodden soil, that will prevent a yew tree from establishing itself and thriving.

There are few beings so numinous, so still and dark, so turbulent and frozen in writhing force as an old yew tree. Each characteristic of habit and quality of use simply reinforces the atmosphere of watchful power. If it is so easy to feel uneasy in the presence of the tree today, how much more awesome in previous ages?

The *Book of Lismore* sums up this knowledge of the tree's longevity in the following verse:

"A year for a stake,
Three years for the field,
Three lifetimes of the field for the hound,
Three lifetimes of the hound for the horse,
Three lifetimes of the horse for the human being,
Three lifetimes of the human being, the stag,
Three lifetimes of the stag for the ousel,
Three lifetimes of the ousel for the eagle,
Three lifetimes of the eagle for the salmon,
Three lifetimes of the salmon for the yew,
Three lifetimes of the yew for the world from its beginning to end."

The yew represents the ultimate measure of time. No living thing can be measured against it, only the changing backdrop of the heavenly bodies.

Know Thyself - Yew and You

The folklore and history of the yew tree coalesce and clarify with a conscious, subjective experience of the tree itself. Noting how our perceptions and internal reactions change in the presence of yew is an essential introductory experience to the spirit's power.

It is not so important to find an ancient yew to explore - even a youngster tree can be several centuries old. A single tree or a grove of yews will bring the necessary energy. Begin by standing for a while under some other kind of tree. This will help to clarify your experience by giving a flavour of your emotional "weather". Take note of how your thought is moving, its quality and content. Pay attention to the senses and to how your body is feeling. Once this is clear move with awareness towards the yew tree. Notice at what point changes begin to be felt in the atmosphere both outside and inside. Watch any emotional shifts from a neutral standpoint and don't be too concerned if the normal processes of thought seem to alter or disappear entirely!

Most surviving yew trees are in churchyards and you might wish to locate a tree in another sort of environment to check whether the feelings you pick up are in any way influenced by the quality of these surroundings. Though different trees will present some individual personality most people will easily distinguish the "yew effect". Broadly speaking there is a bubble of denser atmosphere, a stillness and weight that descends from above yet also creeps up the legs from the ground. The mind easily loses its bearings - thoughts have a habit of spluttering out. An interminably slow wave of energy and power builds and crashes over consciousness. The immediate response to such a wall of Time is fear, a desire to back off into the sunny world, or to resist the sinking feeling where individual boundaries lose their importance. Learning to swim in the void-ocean of yew may take a good few lessons, but once familiar with the dissolution of small things, it is often possible to cognise (to understand wordlessly), huge vistas of existence; though it is not always possible, once back in the world, to verbalise the experience.

Timeless Time

The yew is a difficult tree to date accurately where it has been left to take its natural form, not trimmed or disturbed by man. Most other trees have an average increase in girth of one inch per year, and this can be seen in the annual growth rings of a cross-section of trunk. Yew grows so little that annual rings are almost impossible to distinguish. Even when they are visible the growth habit of the tree often prevents a clear measurement. The bole of a mature yew tends to hollow with age leaving a ring of living wood around a slowly decaying core. The lower branches of the tree sweep down low to the ground and whenever allowed it will root and send up daughter trunks. So as the centre becomes hollow the tree itself expands outwards. If the tree is a female producing seed one or more may take root within the protective space of the hollow and grow to once more fill the space. Other old trees become a ring of daughter trunks simply marking the void where the original single trunk once stood. In such instances the age can only be guessed by the overall girth of the tree. Some yews send roots down from higher branches into the deadwood and from there back into the ground. Even a tree that appears completely dead may begin sprouting once more as the yew is able to regrow over areas of dead wood. The habit of sending out shoots from the base of the trunk can mean that even a large space surrounded by younger daughter trunks can eventually fill in again with fused and amalgamated new growths.

The timely re-examination of the remaining yews in Britain, which seems to hold the greatest number of old trees in Europe, may prove that the yew can outlive even the bristlecone pine and be the oldest living creature on Earth.

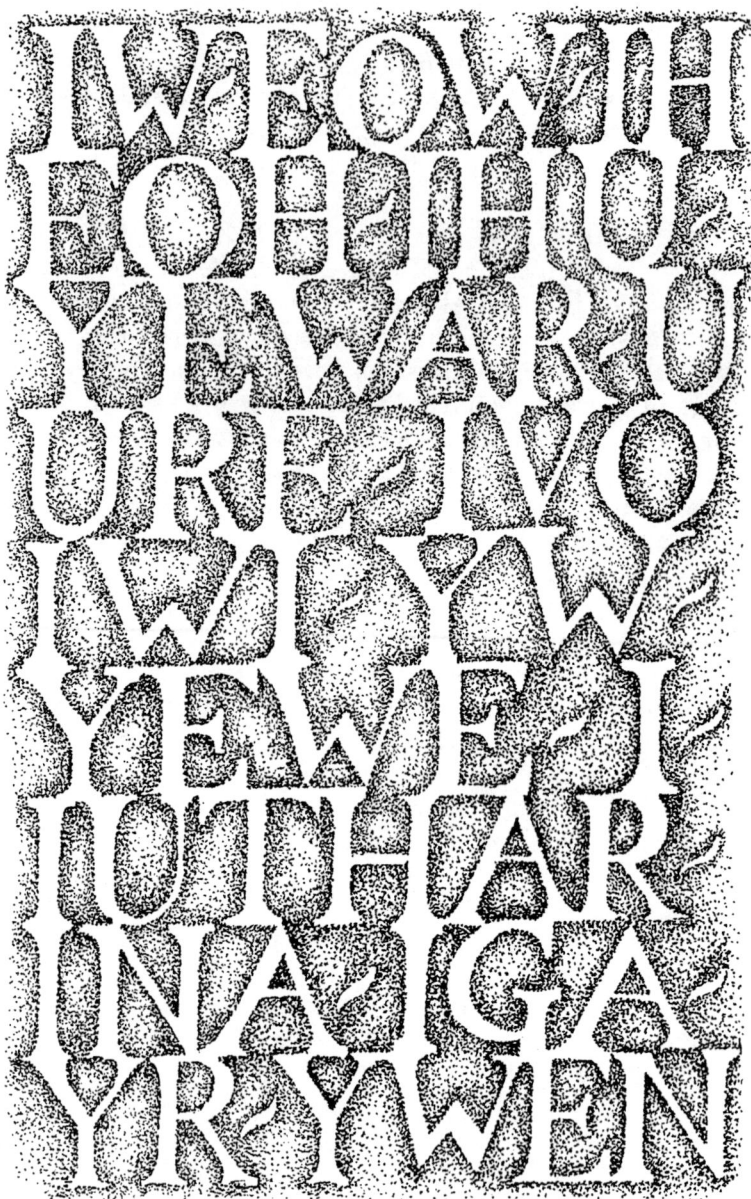

Ancient European names of yew. The similarity of sounds suggests a very ancient common origin. The sequence makes a powerful basis for chant.

Red Tree of Death and Life

All parts of the yew but one are equally poisonous. The exception is the cup-like aril that surrounds the seed on female trees, which is edible. Birds eat this fruit with impunity as the poisonous seed itself passes through the bird's digestive system intact. The toxicity of yew is due to a combination of alkaloids called taxines. (The word "toxin" itself derives from the Greek and Latin name for the yew tree). These alkaloids remain intact in fallen or cut branches and needles. Some animals seem to escape serious harm from casual browsing on yew, whilst others succumb so rapidly that undigested yew leaves can still be found in their mouths.

The active compounds are absorbed very quickly from the digestive tract and once in the bloodstream begin to interfere with the functioning of the heart. The mildest of effects would be slight nausea and abdominal pain. A lethal dose produces lethargy, trembling, staggering, coldness, a dilation of the pupils, a rapid pulse that weakens, convulsions and finally coma and death.

Yew was the preferred wood with which to make bows. The natural qualities of the yew make it unsurpassed. The wood is light and the white sapwood is very flexible whilst the red heartwood gives the strength and compression needed for range and speed. Cut and shaped by a master bowmaker all these qualities combine in one piece of yew wood. The Greeks record using not only the yew but also the habit of dipping their arrows in a poison brewed from yew-wood. Thus in the Classical world the yew became associated with the Death aspects of the Goddess, the dark Goddess or Crone.

The Eburones, a Celtic tribe named from the tree, had a king Cativolcus, who committed ritual suicide after defeat by drinking yew juice. Very often yew-wood was carved as votive offerings to be thrown into sacred pools, wells and pits in the Celtic lands.

Archaeological evidence shows that yew was often the choice for weapons like bows and spears from the Stone Age period onwards. The short hunting bow gradually evolved, towards the end of the 12th century, into the six-foot longbow extending the range of an archer from 50 to 250 yards. For the next four hundred years until the 16th century, the yew-wood longbow was the pre-eminent weapon in battle. So important was the archer that it had become obligatory for a free man to own a bow and arrows and be able to shoot them effectively. Archery practice even became a legitimate activity on Sundays and holidays. The English yeoman, is the "yew-man", the owner of a yew longbow.

So vital were yew bows to the aggressive territorial conquests of European monarchs that the demand for wood soon threatened to exceed supplies. Yew was planted throughout England during the 15th century but during the 16th century yew for bows was having to be imported from Continental Europe. By the time of the Civil War, during the first half of the 17th century it has been suggested that the stands of yew trees were so depleted that the far less accurate and slower pistols and muskets were the only choice of weapon. Modern warfare and the development of the gun arose directly from the need to find some replacement for the over-cropped yew tree!

Among the Native tribes of the North West Coast of America, yew wood was favoured for many of the day-to-day and ritual implements. Spears, bows, paddles, wedges, harpoons, fish-hooks, bowls, drum-frames, tool handles and boxes were all made from the wood. One of the names for the yew meant "plant used for warring".

Yew also had medicinal value. The Canadian yew was used for pain, rheumatism, digestive ailments and paralysis. The needles were used to make an astringent bath. Crushed needles were used as a poultice for wounds and yew bark made into a tea for lung complaints. An infusion of crushed yew will produce quick and healthy root growth in cuttings if other plants are soaked in this mix.

In the 1960's it was found that a compound within yew, named taxol, seemed to inhibit the growth of cancer cells. This led to a great reduction in the number of yews in the natural forests of Western America, as the bark was stripped off to provide the compounds for medical testing. Once again, the very existence of the yew tree is put in serious jeopardy because of its properties. Once it was because it was an efficient bringer of death, now it seems to be a viable prolonger of life.

Yew is inextricably linked to these qualities of existence - life and death. The Germanic and Anglo-Saxon tribes summed up the yew within the magical runic alphabet. Here the glyph for the rune "eoh" or "ewaz" is an upright shaft bent down to the right at its top but acutely upwards at its base to the left. In this form the rune resembles part of a spinning sun-disc or swastika, the ubiquitous Indo-European symbol for solar energy and good fortune, apparent as the wheels and solar crosses of the Neolithic peoples and developed by the Celts into the Celtic cross. (Our later phobia about "good" clockwise/sunwise and "bad" anti-clockwise swastikas is irrelevant both in its present-day Hindu manifestations and in its early medieval usage, where less attention seems to have been paid to which way round a symbol or sign was drawn.)

The yew tree and its rune-energy are solar in nature because the tree has the quality of inner fire, the fire within. One spark of life can regenerate a seemingly dead, stripped tree. It is a tree and rune energy of hope, regeneration, revitalisation and restoring energy.

Like the rotating symmetry of the rune's shape, yew exists to remind us that death emerges out of life and life grows from

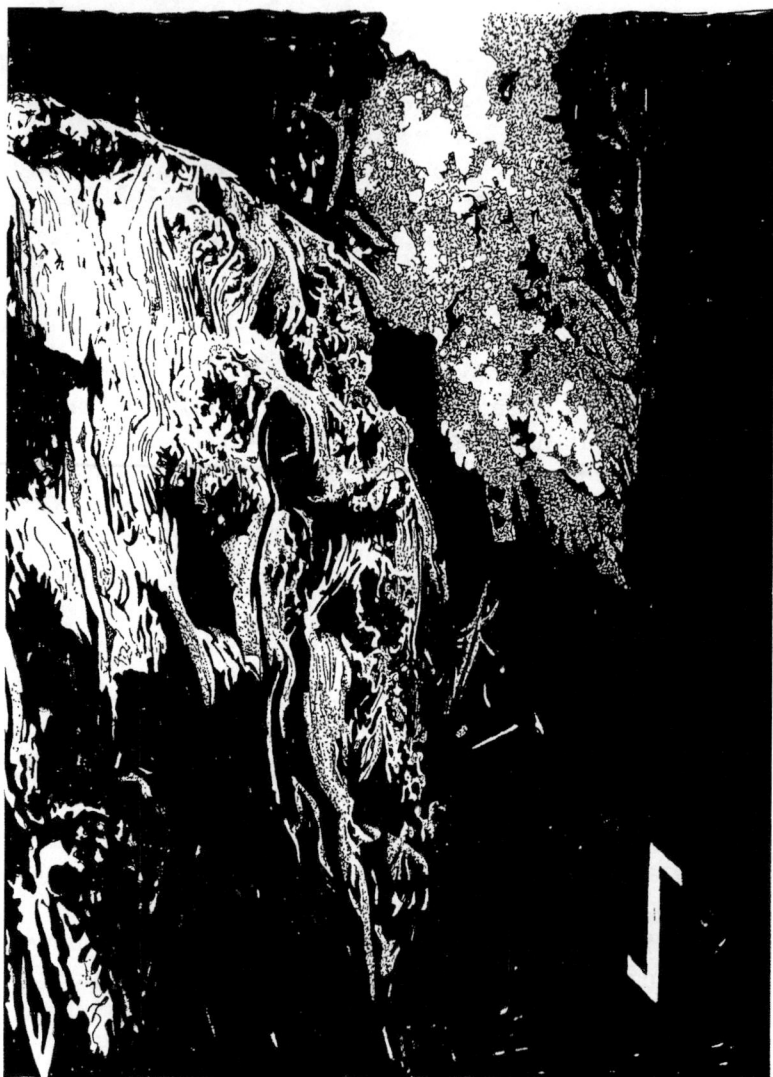

IN YOUR DEEP SHADE
TIME'S WHISPERS
DULL AND FALL.
THOUGHT GLIDERS:
FEATHERS OF FLAME.
CENTURIES REVOLVE,
A ROUND VOWEL
IN THE POET-BARD'S
RECITATION,
THE HISTORIES
IN YOUR DEEP HEART'S
REMEMBRANCE.
RED, DARK HUB
OF THIS LAND'S
WHEEL.

SIMON LILLY

death. There is only an apparent difference between these states of being. The yew tree is the vertical axis, the constant of existence, the immutable substance of being which nonetheless can be manipulated or integrated by humankind as a life-taker or life-giver, a tree of life or a tree of death, a poison or a medicine, darkness or light.

The spark of life within yew may be the spark that regenerates and maintains life itself. To eradicate a being so old from the planet, simply because in some cases it may prolong human life for a few more short years, may be one of humanity's last great gestures of arrogance on this Earth.

The Yew Initiation

As befits a tree of such mystery and obvious power as yew, the actual initiation is the simplest of any we have so far found. An initiation is what it says it is - a beginning. Initiation is the beginning of a possible relationship between one energy and another. Initiation is planting a seed. The seed in some cases might fall on fertile, already prepared, ground and so will shoot up strong and healthy immediately. It may, on the other hand, remain a dormant possibility for some time, or not germinate at all. The act of initiation or of planting a seed is simply the beginning. It is what is done afterwards that will determine the outcome for each person. Initiation is opening a door and letting two distinct energy patterns meet each other, face to face. It will usually require both parties to step forward, greet each other and learn to communicate in the same language or to find a mutual link of some kind to continue the relationship beyond such a formal acknowledgement.

Each Tree Initiation that we have worked with, is suggested by the spirit itself. The spirit can direct the pattern whereby we should come into its presence, but it cannot dictate who will or will not be suitable for that meeting. This has been left up to individual choice and circumstance. So far in our work at this level of commitment with tree spirits, we have been happy to offer such initiation to all who wish to attend, understanding that not all those present will necessarily experience profound or even recognisable energies.

Wherever possible, however, we always start with the Yew Initiation. Although it may not be an energy that feels comfortable to many, it has the root of power, the pre-eminence of ancient being, which we feel is right and proper to acknowledge first of all. Although other Initiations may provide more material for group discussion, the Yew Initiation stirs the depths of the cauldron and can enliven the deepest sparks of potential so that even a slight breeze blowing from the right direction will kindle a fire.

Preparation for all initiations should include working with the appropriate attunements and Tree Teacher Techniques so that the subtle bodies and perceptions are already familiar with the tree spirit energy. Knowledge of any traditional lore or associations can also be helpful to put symbolic experience in a meaningful context, although equally, this information may colour and seem to influence the direct personal involvement. On the one hand traditional imagery may help to frame or give form to rather subtle, numinous energies. On the other hand, such detail may also limit or circumscribe the direct experience. In most cases, however, the available lore is scanty and very generalised, offering little substance for the fact-hungry conscious awareness to crib from.

The Yew Initiation is accomplished by lying down with the head towards north. A piece of yew-wood is placed at the brow chakra in the centre of the forehead. Make the simple intention "to receive yew initiation". There is no specified duration for the process to be completed - usually we use periods of journey-drumming interspersed by silence, depending on whether participants are familiar with journeying to drum or not. Twenty minutes or so should be sufficient. The simplicity of this initiation means that it can be carried out by an individual or within a group and that it can be repeated whenever there is a wish to re-enter the yew spirit's presence for teaching or healing.

Song of the Yew Teacher

Dow. Day. Vow. Daa

This is a song of the Yew Teacher:
The spiral snake, the dragon healer;
Strong song and silent teacher.

Before the dawn, before the first day,
I knew the sun's name
As it called me forth.

Pollen, heavy ,yellow on the wind.
Red apple, sweet heart of death.
Green tongues and lifeblood fire.
Patient roaring, passion turning:
"Come not with your mind, nor your chatter,
drown in me, die in me, join the centre:
The hub, the wheel, the word, the laughter.
The fire inside, concealed, concealing.
Wood and weather, warm and winter.
In my shadow, dance, dissolve."

Past the sitting one who sees all,
Past the root into the chamber
Where the watchers weave and gather,
Where the dragon's breath is potent,
Where the silver wheel is woven,
Where the time is marked and measured,
Where the space is held and hallowed,

Where the land is named and numbered.
"I am fire
And I am water
I am earth
And I am ether."
This is the heart of Time, the heart of matter,
The drum of centuries, the door, the silence.....

Dow. Day. Vow. Daa
Dow. Day. Vow. Daa

Green Man, St. Mary Redcliffe, Bristol.

276

The Elm - Silence Reaching to the Sky

The Ghost In the Hedgerow

It is frightening how quickly we can forget what was once so familiar and commonplace. Only thirty years ago the lanes of all the Midland counties were bordered by mature elm trees. They framed every landscape view, rose from every horizon and led the eye continually upwards to the topmost branches and beyond into the sky. It is now difficult to find records of how things were for so long - the devastation of Dutch Elm Disease was so rapid that only a few out-of-print tree books and even older black-and-white rural photographs can bring back that forgotten landscape.

Simon remembers working on a country bus service in Warwickshire during the summer of 1976. Already the largest trees had been felled and the skyline was half summer, half winter, with dead and dying elms visible everywhere. Now few people can see elms older than forty to sixty years. Elm is still there in the hedges, its vigorous suckering habit ensures that, but apart from the plantings on motorway embankments, most new growth is removed each year by hedge flailing machines. Those that are already too large a diameter to be flailed either succumb to the chainsaw or fall prey again to the disease and within a year or two die off. From being a tree that grew to over a hundred feet tall and living up to 300 years, most elms now barely reach thirty feet or live for more than sixty years.

What is the energy effect of such a rapid withdrawal of a species from its habitat? The psychic effect was felt immediately by those who knew and lived amongst the elms -

the countryside was no longer theirs, it had become unrecognisable overnight, another place that no longer fitted with memory. By the Seventies chemicalisation of the planet had become the norm; industrialisation of the traditional occupiers of the land was spreading inexorably - larger machines, larger fields, factory farming processes. Personal computers began to become available, videos, colour TV and all aspects of electronically dependant information technology had increased significantly. Politically and economically the early Seventies were increasingly unstable with the three-day week, power cuts and monetary chaos. The Conservative Party grew in ascension, was put in Government and remained in power until 1997. You might ask what all this has to do with the disappearance of a single tree species. How can one be linked to another? It is not possible to look at such coincidences ("co-incidence" - parallel event), in terms of cause and effect but it is always fascinating to juxtapose different event and timelines. Hidden trends, underlying patterns, currents that are deep and strong can sometimes be discerned in this way.

Changes of State

By 1977 the elms were gone. In 1977 the planetoid Chiron was identified and soon linked to the energies of teacher-healer. Like the English Elm, accidentally infected by a shipment of wood from abroad, the centaur Chiron was accidentally wounded by a poisoned arrow and chose death rather than an immortality of pain. Chiron was translated by the gods into a constellation of stars. Where did the estimated twenty million elm trees go to?

We tend to see the death of anything, be it individual or species as an end, a full stop. From a spiritual viewpoint (and a much more traditional one), death is a part of life where there is a change of state. The dead are still with us, they're just working in a different office! The energy signature and its concomitant energy function (in terms of the whole), doesn't necessarily vanish along with its physical vehicle or focus - it may merely shift to another level of focus. To draw a rather irreverent parallel - wipe out a race of, say, North American Indians or Tibetans and before long they are turning up as your spirit-guides and inner plane teachers. The intent of the race or species leads it to continue with its purpose in different ways, and of course genocide creates a pretty strong karmic bond between perpetrators and victims that will last for centuries of mutual argy-bargy (ie. the Balkans, Middle East, Northern Ireland etc. etc.)

The elms' susceptibility to this recent devastation was due in part to its popularity with landowners in the 17th and 18th centuries. To fulfil demand elms were grown from the suckers of a few trees in nurseries, which meant that genetic diversity was restricted. Thus a disease that hit one would hit all equally hard, with little chance for immune strains to emerge. Six thousand years ago though, at the beginning of the Neolithic period, there was another elm decline. It has been suggested that such a disappearance of a quite significant part of the native tree cover enabled man to clear and farm land until then covered with impenetrable forest.

The New Awareness

Whatever the ramifications of the current elm decline in subtle energy terms, we can at least deduce a few likely outcomes. Firstly, a large proportion of British trees have a life-cycle three or four times as long as the human average. With such a perception of time, responses to change and understanding of other life-cycles would be seen from a very non-human standpoint.

Now imagine the Elm awareness having a physical existence reduced from an average of 250 years to the almost certainty of losing physical form after 60 years. The understanding of

the short lifetimes of humans and their preoccupations would become immediately more vivid and relevant.

The presence of elm in the energy environment, particularly in those areas adjacent to large human conurbations (West Midlands and Greater London), would have fulfilled a necessary balancing role. This can be said with some certainty or else some other entity would have filled that particular ecological and metaphysical niche. Having had a close interrelationship with man at least since the 17th century, Elm spirit is unlikely to have dropped that concern or relationship as soon as it entered non-physical states.

The obvious and catastrophic nature of the elms' decline created a shift in consciousness for a large number of people whose feelings of devastation, sympathy, sorrow, shock would have forged a stronger bridge between the two species. Like the hurricanes of the late Eighties the massive loss of trees served as an effective reminder of the presence of these silent standing energies in our world and spurred some people to consider a more beneficial relationship.

Contact with the Elm spirit energies is certainly a particularly poignant and uplifting experience for many people. There is a quality of humanity and understanding there that is less obvious in other tree spirit contacts. There is always an ambience of protected space and personal recognition.

Uxlemitanos

We were first introduced to that energy one evening when we were working on other subtle energy matters. Sue noticed a sudden shift of vibration in the room that she couldn't identify. All she knew was that whatever it was, was very big! After a lot of testing we found that the energy could be identified with the Celtic High Elm God Uxlemitanos. As the ambience increased in power we slipped into half-trance and received our first teaching from the Elm spirits. Each tree spirit interacts in its own peculiar manner: Elm is characterised by terse, gnomic but poetic phraseology and many evocative images that explain and elucidate the meaning of each teaching. Sometimes there is just a phrase that is open to several interpretations and at other times there is a deep silence with a sequence of visual images. Working in a group there tends to be an interchange and mutual clarification of each lesson from different viewpoints, but whatever communication method is being used one characteristic of Elm is an underlying blissful silence or shiny peacefulness. Like on a still pool each phrase or image creates ripples that spread outwards into our human awareness.

In order to give a flavour of Elm Spirit Teaching here are some extracts from some of our own early sessions. When the process first began we were asked to start with a repetition of the phrase "Activate, Green Man Uxlemitanos, Now Please." Doing this Sue saw an image she took to be a representation of Uxlemitanos. First of all there was a circular white or silver disc like a mandala and by it a teacher in a loose robe with grey hair and a grey beard. When the hands were held out there was a rune stave in each. On the left was Haegl, the forces of Nature and an esoteric symbol for the essence of creation: the snowflake or ice-egg. In the right hand was Mann, the rune of inter-relationship, humanity and the power of the mind (from the Indo-European root meaning thinker, human, mind, mental etc.).

The first words received were: "I hear your thoughts speak. Slowly. Clear." In response we asked a couple of questions firstly about protection on subtle levels (the reason for that evening's work in the first place), and then about our work.

The Elm spirit replied:

" Breaking twigs underfoot,
  they believe they are silent.
  Owls see them."

This is a wonderful image relating to those dabblers trying to
manipulate on subtle planes, events in the physical world. In
reality they clomp carelessly through territory they cannot be
in harmony with and are watched by the all-seeing eyes of the
inhabitants, portrayed here as the birds of wisdom, death and
dreams, the owl.

" Our spirits are at your service.
  In this form we cannot be slain.
  One tree is a forest."

Here we get a glimpse of the wry humour of the Elm and also
the quality of energy: two million spirit trees, no longer able
to be felled by axe or disease acting with one accord for those
who ask. Indeed, following this guidance we have asked the
Elm spirits to help with protection on several occasions, both
for ourselves and for others. If you can imagine a couple of
thousand full grown trees appearing in close ranks around a
needy person, energetically blanking out or making invisible
the activities that need secrecy, and at the same time
neutralising any harmful intrusions, that is exactly what it
feels like - the depths of a safe, protected forest.

At a different time, in a different context, we also heard that
elm trees are one of the few trees that seem to survive on, and
help to neutralise, harmful geopathic stresses. It was
suggested that the planting of elms in strategic places would
greatly enhance the natural balance of a geopathically
disturbed area. If this is true it would also suggest that the
loss of harmony in the English countryside was much more
significant than just on the physical level.

Energy and inspiration flow from the quiet expression of this Green Man from a woodcarving at Poitiers, 13th c.

Later we asked: How shall we progress? This was a personal question, but also can be applied more generally. The answer anyway is good guidance for all:

"By defining, by revealing, by sending more roots downwards, deeper than any other, and letting the light draw them up."

We asked about the nature of these roots, whether they were best made using shamanic types of techniques or by some other means.

The answer was direct and simple:
"Earthing!
We offer to teach you - the invisible tribe of Elm."

Asking how we should avail ourselves of this, the reply came:
"Ask.
We are preparing for you teachers and warriors."
Then we asked if there was a particular process or ritual that was required:
"Binding and weaving of water with light. Accomplished through gold."
This is the essence of the Elm Initiation and it was suggested that we began each future session with this process.

The Elm Initiation

Two ways of how to interpret these instructions presented themselves. The first was to use a magnifying glass to focus the sun's rays on water contained in an elmwood bowl, the second is the technique which we adopted and use whenever we wish to link closely to the Elm spirit. After a few minutes of chanting or drumming to build up energy we put some spring water in an elmwood bowl. A small nugget of native gold, that is, gold found in its natural state before being worked in any way, is dropped into the water which is then stirred around with an elm stick. The stirring is done in a gentle, conscious manner with the idea of the mingling or weaving of the water with light, (as symbolised by the gold nugget). When it is felt that this process has been done sufficiently the elm stick is carefully laid aside and the hands are dipped in the water. With a few drops from the bowl the hands are symbolically washed together, and then taking a few more drops from the bowl with the fingertips, the forehead is touched and a line is drawn from there to the crown of the head and then back to the nape of the neck. The ears, eyes and tongue are then also touched with the water.

This simple act has a remarkably profound effect on the consciousness and it is then very easy to sit back and sink into a deep, energetic quietness. It is in this state that teaching may take place: either in the form of voice, vision or insight, interspersed with a silence few will have experienced except those familiar with long periods of meditative retreat. If a lack of clarity occurs, or if awareness slips, focus can be reintroduced by repeating the anointing ritual.

Key Qualities

Clarity and communication are the keywords for the effect of elm both as an essence and as a herbal remedy. Traditionally the inner bark of various species of elms have been used to clear up skin complaints and infection such as herpes, ringworm and itch. Slippery Elm (an American species), can be found in any healthstore as a soothing ointment for inflammations and to promote the healing of wounds. As a tree essence the vibratory energy of elm seems to re-energise and motivate a desire to progress and move on with enthusiasm. Feelings of being overwhelmed either emotionally (heart), or by the weight of perceived responsibilities (mind), are brought into balance so that there is a new chance for clarity in decision-making and study situations.

In folk culture the ability of elm to act as a vehicle for true communication appears in various guises: tiny pieces of elm hung in a bundle from a child's neck would ensure eloquent speech; elm twigs bound with a yellow cord and then burned would prevent gossip; elm was thought to be popular with elves and so the wood was helpful in communicating with the subtle realms of nature; a favourite tree of crows and rooks to nest in, the elm is connected to the Northern European Odin/Woden, god of eloquence, farsight and seerhood - crows and ravens were important oracular birds well into the Middle Ages and great attention was paid to the direction of flight and the nature of their calls.

Taking the Path of Water

Further contacts with the Elm Spirit gave a whole series of techniques that can be used as meditations and healing processes. Some are simple and can be brought to mind at any time whilst others are more involved and require time and a quiet place. The process we have called "Taking the Path of Water" is a meditation ideal for creating a state conducive to contact and teaching by the Tree Spirits. The title gives the instruction succinctly. The nature of water is to settle, to come to rest, at the lowest point that gravity allows. It will sink downwards until its way is blocked and there it will rest. In the tree, water is transported to the highest leaf - a flow of water against gravity up to the sky.

First of all clearly imagine a tree. It can be one you are very familiar with or it can be an imagined tree. It is important to be very aware of the height of the tree. It may be useful at this stage to merge with the tree or identify with it enough to get a clear awareness of the size.

Find yourself a comfortable place to sit in the crown of the tree, a place that feels secure and stable. Take your time to become fully settled in that place.

Then allow yourself to gradually sink down through the tree, much as if you were relaxing fully into the presence of the tree.

Sink down until you are at its lowest level, probably perceived as being among the deepest roots or at the base of the trunk.

You will see a narrow, round tunnel extending away from where you are. Follow the tunnel until it opens out into a light-filled space. This space may be defined but generally it is experienced as a vague, bright area. As you rest here you will gradually become aware of a pulsing. It may be a sound, a vibration or a feeling. This is the pulse of the tree. Stay listening to the pulse until it naturally fades from your attention.

As the pulse fades you will naturally find yourself rising upwards. The sensation here is often of climbing to a great but undefined height. You will come to a place or a space where you are able to experience some kind of teaching or communication.

Again, the space may be a definite landscape or room that may contain spirits in human or some other form. A sequence of images or scenarios may pass before you, or you may simply rest in stillness, aware of subtle tides of change passing around and through you.

Remain in this state for as long as you wish and whenever you feel like returning, to bring yourself out of the meditation, visualise water drops falling into a pool and see the ripples spreading outwards. This simple image will almost immediately break the spell. It is an important visualisation to remember because sometimes with Tree Spirit energies one can feel so overwhelmed that it is difficult to remember how to get back to where you started. Dropping water rippling the surface of a pool will always safely and instantly return you.

Spinning Bowl

Another time the Elm spirits were saying:

"We travel out on the rays of light: the roads we have built through our lives in form."

and at the same time came a vision of the following meditation.

Called "Spinning Bowl", this technique will quickly disrupt any negative forces or negative energy around you, and so is of use in any situation where there is a feeling of oppression or threat, or simply a dullness of energy.

Imagine a golden spinning bowl inside you; a spinning bowl of light; as if it were a seed in spinning form. Allow the speed of the bowl to increase and increase until, when it is spinning as fast as you can imagine, it shoots out golden roots and branches. There is no need to carefully construct the image of the roots - if you have spun the bowl fast enough, the rest will naturally explode outwards into the surroundings.

Seed Heart

A more gentle variation of this is called "Seed Heart",

It is a meditation that will especially nourish the heart. See the image of your heart like a seed. From this seed allow roots and branches to grow, simple and slow at first, then more rapidly spreading and becoming complex until they extend out into your surroundings. Feel them bringing in energy and nourishment. Feel yourself relaxing and allowing the flow and interchange of energy and information. Feel yourself becoming blended into and part of your surroundings.

This is an excellent technique for getting to familiarise and harmonise your energies with new surroundings. By altering the colour of the roots and branches it is possible to tune into different aspects of the environment. Pink will tend to dispel fear and tension both within you and in those around you; yellow will help to identify what is present - useful when trying to locate specific objects; blue will open fine communication channels; both violet and pink will help to heal disturbances. It is worth experimenting with this technique in a familiar environment using different colours to see what you are able to pick up.

Breathing in Light

Finally, the Elm suggested a technique that bears close resemblance to many classic meditation procedures. It focuses on following the breath - a simple way for quietening the mind and allowing an awareness of the present moment to naturally arise. One purpose of such an exercise is to establish a real relationship with the world-as-it-is, free of projection, conceptualisation and judgement. We are conditioned to react to the world constantly from the viewpoint of manipulation, management and control. Each experience is weighed up for its value to us as individuals: whether it is "good" or "bad", how it might turn out, how we could do things to alter the outcome, whether it is important or can be ignored. This obviously is of biological survival value, but due to our way of living and belief systems, it has become a major neurosis stemming from a deep lack of personal security, fear of loss and continual need to establish an apparent control of external power. The very opposite to internal power, which arises from a sense of place in the world.

The inability to accept change as the one constant - a rather fundamental shortcoming - together with a fear of death, and a sense of identity assumed to be one mind located in this one and only particular body, creates a constant turmoil where everything is seen in terms of our perceived needs. Choices, new values and wider perspectives are excluded almost completely from this loop of action and reaction. The unfolding of events is seen as unavoidable and inevitable. We understand that we are reacting to the world but fail to understand the other half of the deal - that the world reacts to our reaction. Mind becomes the shaper of reality, yet rarely sees the world as anything other than "object", "out there", an adversary that must somehow be overcome or subjugated - psychological projection par excellence!

Meditation procedures that aim to quieten the mind enable the stark subject/object, me-versus-the-world, that antagonistic relationship between me in here and everything else out there, to dissolve a little - to melt the boundaries so that we can find ourselves sitting within our experience of the world in a more comfortable and natural way. To simply enjoy things as they are , as equal fragments of Being.

This tree-taught technique does much the same and maybe a little more. There are two stages involved. The first is breathing in and imagining light filling the body. The second is breathing out and allowing awareness to flow out as if our senses were carried on the breath beyond the body's boundaries. Here is the exercise as taught to us, we will examine it some more shortly:

"Now
Open wide your senses.
Breathe in Light,
Breathe out form.
Breathe in Light - extend the senses outwards.
Let your senses flow like water where they will.
As you breathe in light your form becomes fluid with light.
Your senses belong on the outside.
As your senses flow outwards they merge with the world until they are no longer yours -
they belong to the world.

All that needs to be done is to breathe in the light and let the senses flow like water.
This is how we know, this is how we talk."

So the language is quite straightforward and the instructions simple and clear. It will, however, probably take a little experimentation to tune the focus of your practice. There are two simple stages: to imagine drawing light into your physical form with the inbreath, and on the outbreath to allow your awareness to take note of the source of sense perceptions. The first stage establishes the boundary of our physical presence - we become aware of being "in" our bodies because it is that space we fill up with the light drawn in with the breath.

The second stage turns attention outwards to whatever signals we identify as belonging to the world -sound, sensations, feelings and so on, and this leads us to the experience of being "in" the world. The world we then inhabit is as large as the furthest sense vibration that we can pick up. If you imagine the flow of the senses like waves making their way up a beach, coming to their fullest extent and then returning to the sea, to return again a little further, exploring a little more, stretching inland a little more: that is the same effortless motion of awareness that we should cultivate during the exercise. Once you are familiar with the process sitting with the eyes closed, have a go with the following variations: eyes open throughout; eyes open on the outbreath only; eyes open on the inbreath only; standing; walking; and during everyday activity.

Breathing in light gives a subtle nutrition to the body that is also purifying, cleansing and quietening. It is not necessary to perceive the light as a colour, but if that happens by itself just allow it to be the way it is at that moment. This can be thought of as paralleling to a tree drawing in the sun's energy as a source of life and its interaction with the world around it by means of leaves, branches, flowers, roots and bark.

Initially, your outward attention will be held by whatever sounds are going on around you, and you will be automatically identifying the sources of each sound as they occur. As you become accustomed to the process more subtle tides of information will become part of your experience. Habitually allowing our awareness to flow into the world stabilises our own sense of presence and creates a deeper belonging. The me-versus-the-world, subject/object scenario, loses its rigidity and, feeling more at home, we relax enough to pick up much finer expressions of communication from other beings. The last few words of the teaching make this clear: knowledge and communication among the Elm spirits is simply accomplished in this way.

The Ivy Doorway

Walking through a Dartmoor oak woodland assimilating energies for the forthcoming Oak Initiation workshops, we became aware of the presence of Ivy and the necessity to work with Ivy before introducing the Oak Spirit energies.

This seems a familiar pattern when working with the Oak - one thing leads to another and before you know it you're delving into areas tangential to your original purpose. In fact it may not be possible at all to come truly before the Oak spirits until we have fully assimilated all the libraries of mystery they throw at us. Hercules himself was linked to the Oak as guardian via his trusty club and look what a series of quests he kept getting himself into! The Oak Spirit is for most people, perhaps, a teacher who teaches by setting tasks, labours and quests and getting us to learn through personal exploration, rather than sitting us down and saying: "Here it is!".

One particular oak, hidden away back from the path on a boggy bilberry slope, had an enormous girth and an equally impressive straight, very tall trunk. Wrapped around this huge trunk was a venerable ivy - almost large enough to be called a tree in its own right. So enveloping was it at human height that the oak could only be reached "through" the ivy. Brief linking to this dual partnership gave the core of information for developing the Ivy Doorway techniques.

Most people are pretty ambivalent when it comes to ivy. It seems no one can decide whether ivy actually damages the tree it climbs, though this is certainly the pervading common view. Certainly ivy is not parasitic. It doesn't rely on its tree host as a source of food, only as a means to gain access to greater amounts of sunlight. However, the winding stems of

295

ivy will eventually restrict the expansion of the tree's branches and, though there is some accommodation in the tree's growth, there may be a reduction in nutrients reaching some parts of the tree leaving it more susceptible to damage. The weight of a mature ivy plant and its leaf cover would affect a tree's ability to withstand heavy winds, yet in other ways this extra covering may act as an insulator from harm.

It is easy to assume that a dead tree covered in ivy has succumbed to the ivy, rather than the ivy is flourishing on an already dying tree because it has more light available and will continue to remain well and growing long after the tree has completely died -until such time as the tree rots and both fall to the ground.

Ivy becomes associated with a duality - the taker of life, strangler and bringer of death - and, being evergreen, with the power of life, the everliving. If you were of a morbid Victorian frame-of-mind, the ivy might be named "The Eternal Bringer of Death", or "Deathless Death" or some such. But this would be only part of the story. Firstly there is no creature that will not take life in order to itself survive. However, this is more a trait of animals than of plants - most plants do not NEED to absorb the life of others to sustain themselves, though they may compete for the same nutrients, light, water and soil. Ivy doesn't require the death of its host but this may be the consequence of the partnership. This, and other traits, gives ivy animal-like characteristics.

Remaining evergreen throughout winter, ivy is one of the few native plants to carry the green hope of life through the dark part of the year into springtime, and in most parts of the country will certainly have been the commonest evergreen, though perhaps more humble than the others. Ivy flowers late in the year, well after other trees in autumn and the starlike globes of strangely smelling flowers give the last nectar to many flying insects before the frosts descend. Likewise the black-blue berries that ripen afterwards give food for birds throughout the cold.

Ivy is a plant of darkness and of death. It is one of the few plants that can flourish in deep shade, in nooks, crannies and forgotten places, and yet it is always striving towards the light of the sun. Once ivy has climbed its way along and upwards into the light, the characteristic three and five-lobed leaves become smooth and undulating oval and it will produce flowers and fruit. Climbing by means of its rootlets and twisting in a spiral growth, ivy supremely demonstrates the power of life and the lifegiving sun - the spiral path is the sun's path through the year and the spiral of life from birth to death, ignorance to knowledge, darkness to light.

The leaves of the ivy contain much symbolism: three lobes that then divide into five points, the triangle becomes the pentagon and then a clear pentagram, the five-pointed star. Three is a well-known Goddess number, five is the number of intellectual man, upholder of universal law and balance. The pentagram is the human body: head, arms, legs or five fingers and toes, five senses, five openings in the head, the four directions and the centre, the five elements. The Egyptian hieroglyph for "star", (which is the same as the Chinese character for "person"), neatly schematises the shape of the ivy-leaf. The triangle is the cave of birth, the vulva from which emerges the new being, the five-pointed human.

On early Celtic coins the ivy leaf is quite a common motif. This may be of tribal, totemic or religious significance, or simply that ivy is closest to the grape-bearing vine in its characteristics - the Celts were inordinately fond of Mediterranean wine!

Now that we are onto the subject of intoxication, ivy is said to have the peculiar properties of making a sober person deranged and making a drunk sober. It has been suggested

297

KI JA OH TRRI

that this is the reason why the Greek god Dionysus is wreathed in ivy. This seems a pretty lame rationalisation.

Ivy is certainly a plant to be used with caution, though it has extremely useful properties. Five leaves (only) infused in half a pint of water will reduce swollen glands and calm fevers. The dose is one tablespoon of infusion three times a day (from *"The Magic of Herbs"*, David Conway 1973). Externally the pulped leaf in an ointment helps to soothe stiff joints and aching muscles.

Ivy contains the useful anti-bacterial and anti-parasitic agents emetine and triterpine saponins, which when properly administered, are effective against liver flukes, intestinal parasites and fungal infections. However, the wrong dose will cause irritability, diarrhoea, severe vomiting and destruction of red blood cells, so do-it-yourself treatment is not advisable! Young leaves and berries are particularly powerful and can be a severe skin irritant and allergen.

Holding a small mature ivy leaf in your mouth will allow you to move quite safely into the plant's domain, but if you decide to chew be prepared for a sharp, astringent bitterness that sticks at the back of the throat for a lot longer than one would wish.

Let us look at the metaphysical characteristics of ivy some more. Ivy is a plant that behaves like an animal -specifically a snake, which it so obviously resembles. It creeps and wriggles throughout the undergrowth, it wraps itself around tree trunks. An image of the deep forest: mature old trees within a darkened, clean forest floor. As though in a time-lapse film nothing much changes except the flicker of day and night, the occasional leaf fluttering down into the humus. And then a movement on the corner of sight: a thin snake-like tendril wriggles its way into view. It writhes and twists and scrabbles as though sniffing out something. As time flickers on, the tendril thickens to become python-thick; aerial roots, like legs, support and stabilise; new tendrils spread outwards across the floor searching more of that essential food: light. Soon a wave of ivy, a tide of shiny green, is washing up the tree trunks and as time flickers forward the main Ivy Snake wriggles on out of sight deeper into the forest silence.

Ivy is a tree that moves; a vegetal snake; a green sea of leaves; it can become a gatekeeper and a useful guide.

Our first encounter with Ivy energy was in the use of a protective phrase "Gort for Dryssawr". Gort is the Irish ogham name for a tilled field or garden (gart, gard - as in, protected enclosure, demarcated space, land, farm). It has become associated with the ivy in recent tree calendars via the concept of the vineyard as fertile tilled land. "Dryssawr" is a name that appears in Celtic references to god-names and means "god-of-the-oaken-door". So the phrase means something like "protected space for the god of the oaken door", or "Ivy for the god of the oaken door".

This conjures an image of a sturdy arched oak doorway surrounded by a mature ivy plant as it would be portrayed with significant symbolism in a Pre-Raphaelite painting. The sense is that "gort" as ivy, protected, disguised, guarded and locked or bound shut the already formidable oak door. There is no tree that is not protective in one aspect or another, but we have found on several occasions that Ivy will surreptitiously disguise and hide from view something we want to remain energetically hidden - much as an ivy will quickly cover old walls, doors, windows, tree roots and so on.

When Ivy is viewed with spirit-eyes there is no clear image that emerges. Somewhere there is the presence of a slender, white female form but behind and through this is a definite male energy - more like a warrior. Most to the fore is the image of an enthusiastic dog - a gun-dog, sniffer or retriever of some sort. This is the guide aspect of Ivy, the one that will lead you into, through and out of unknown regions safely and with care. There is a link with this rather homely image to the more potent, powerful presence of Lord Anpu, (known via the Greeks as Anubis), Lord of the Underworld, Guide of the Dead, Protector of Souls, and more particularly to the much more cthonic jackal deity Wepwawet (Apuat or Upuat), the Opener of the Ways.

Dogs as guides and guardians are also familiar in Northern European tradition, though often with more sinister intent as fierce guards at the entrance to the lands of the dead or as hunters of souls like the Wisht Hounds of Dartmoor, or like the baleful black dogs that still stalk the old lanes of England, silent and intimidating.

The snake aspect of Ivy is more initiatory: it is quite likely to dump you just out of your depth to see whether you can come up with the correct response to extricate yourself, or without questioning, lead you helter-skelter to EXACTLY where you said you wanted to be - which is more than likely well out of your depth! Just then, in the nick of time, the snake-dog Ivy will throw you a tendril and whisk you back onto energetically safer ground.

One thing seems certain: unless you travel via the intermediary of Ivy or some other similar tree spirit, it is not easy to gain access to the deeper levels of Tree Wisdom that we call "the Deep Forest". Like a wild wood in this physical world, the Deep Forest can be a dangerous and forbidding place without directions and a sure guide to show you how to get in, and more importantly, how to get out in one piece.

In his inimitable style Kaledon Naddair also hints at the significance of Ivy in "Celtic Fairy Tales": "for the bindwood snake that spirals round trees sunwise also leads to the Lord of the Forest". Is it perhaps the ivy that winds above the

antlers of the Horned God on the Gundestrup Cauldron, or the heart-leaved black bryony?

Using the Ivy Doorway with intent to open the Tree Doorways will help to access significantly deeper levels of tree energy and information when that is appropriate. It is a useful exercise to do on its own as it quickly shifts awareness to non-ordinary states. The process is a combination of chant and vision. Within a semicircular doorway is silhouetted a large five-pointed ivy leaf. The archway is black and the leaf white.

With the intention "to open the Tree Doorways", gaze steadily at the image whilst chanting or mentally repeating the Ivy mantra "Ki Ja Oh Trri". All the vowel sounds here are short and clipped but it is useful, if you can, to roll the rr's. Particularly if you chant out loud you will find your own rhythm and emphasis. Don't strain as you look at the image: allow it to flicker and change. Don't be concerned if you can't hold focus, and if you like, continue with eyes closed for a while. Make sure the image is flat on a wall and placed so that you can comfortably look at it from a relaxed position. Fix it so that the leaf you are focussing on is slightly above eye level, but not so much as to cause strain.

The commonest experience with this exercise is the sensation of rapid movement of some kind. Whatever your experience may be, doing the Ivy Doorway exercise demonstrates your desire to travel deeper into the Tree Kingdoms and so sets up a sympathetic resonance and an added receptivity to any subsequent meeting. With the Ivy Doorway we are acknowledging the presence of boundaries over which we must move only when permission has been given and with the correct frames of reference. It is like the traditional ritual processes recorded in folk and fairy tales. One must travel in the correct manner, with the required gifts and must know what questions are required of you to ask and to answer. Without knowing the right knock or the right password, and

certainly if we don't say "please" and "thank you", and unless we accept the need for guidance, we can walk through endless worlds without realising or enter castles and palaces seemingly devoid of life except for the fragments of whispers from their hidden inhabitants.

We have ourselves used the Ivy Doorway mainly in the context of the Oak Initiation. The colour of the Doorway may therefore be particularly suited to this work. Certainly the colour black has Celtic associations with that tree, and from our own work the polarity of white and black is energetically linked to the creative and manifesting roles of Oak. It may therefore be interesting to try the Ivy Doorway image in other complementary colours, such as green - red, blue - orange, purple - yellow, turquoise - magenta. Make sure that the colours are truly complementary, that they "flash" together, so the full visual impact is not lost. It is likely that each colour Doorway will "open" onto different energy landscapes and it may be that every individual will find a combination that works much clearer than any other. However, before you try these other possibilities get used to working with the black - white image. Trace or copy the Doorway outline given here, enlarge it to a useable size and colour it in so that each area is a single saturated colour with as little variation as possible in tone and shading.

Once the Doorway image is memorised it may be that you can use it in many different ways: as a means to enter a receptive meditative state; before sleep to alter the quality of dream; to quickly alter awareness in order to access the subtle energy of a tree or other site; to acquire the aid of the Ivy spirit. As the attunement colours for Ivy are red followed by blue and gold alternating, a blue and orange/yellow Doorway should access the Ivy energy itself in a very clear way.

When it is made into a flower essence ivy continues to demonstrate the same constellation of concepts and effects -

Misericord, Southwell Priory, Nottinghamshire. Bard or teacher?

namely, that of guidance, clarification and identification. Ivy essence seems to particularly act on the heart centre and its related energy pathways. This centre is primarily concerned with relationship: the relationship between who we believe we are and what we consider to be "outside" us. Thus the heart is not just concerned with human relationships but relationship in all its aspects and manifestations, and with the expression or demonstration of this relationship. It is the heart energy that reaches out into the world to "feel" and understand, to balance and weigh the external with the internal.

When the heart centre is unable to "feel" or understand a particular aspect of the outside world, we experience anxiety and fear. We are unable to bring that aspect into a harmonious relationship with ourselves and so begin to perceive it as potentially harmful or dangerous. If we cannot accept it into our energy field, if we cannot feel comfortable when that aspect of power is close to the power we consider as under or within our control ("within our grasp"), it threatens our own power relationship with the world. Fear begins. And with fear comes endless projections of uncontrollable futures that may or may not have a basis in likely realities. It is at this point that ivy essence can come into its own. By clarifying our own feelings towards the external, we are able to clearly identify our true needs, and once we know our own basis of energy the fears and anxiety disappear. Lost in a forest, fear increases with the inability to control our surroundings and the lack of knowledge of the way out. Ivy is the guide out of the fearful places.

The ambivalence of Ivy - the life-death tension - and the relationship it has with fear and acceptance, admittance and doorways, links it with the Anglo-Saxon rune Ior. The exact translation of this rune in terms of traditional symbolism is unclear and it is usually associated with either some aquatic mammal such as the beaver or otter, or with the sea-monster Jormungand. Jormungand is the World Serpent who surrounds the circle of the ocean forming a boundary of the world, and yet it continually gnaws at the roots of the World Tree threatening to undermine the foundation of the Universe. In both symbolic forms Ior is to do with duality. The former is the duality of existing equally harmoniously on land and in water ie. in contradictory environments. The latter has to do with the acceptance and necessity of perceived "evil" or "destructive" energies. The lesson of the rune Ior is not to attempt to right the world's wrongs, not to become over-whelmed with the perception of right against wrong, but to see opposites as equally valid environments in which to exist. Equanimity and poise, non-attachment and clarity are what will allow us to exist in harmony with the universe. The Forest is life and death, good and evil, knowledge and ignorance, fear and control, the known and the unknown. Ivy helps us to weave our way among the trees so that we can always come back to "our place". The serpent, the wise snake, is the Ivy that lives in the duality of dark and light, summer and winter, intoxication and sobriety, life and death. Only a teacher who has travelled every possible path can know every step of the way and be for us, a safe guide.

Oak - Door of the Year

"As the oaken cup holds the acorn, the seed of life, so the oak tree holds safe the world of form."

There is no tree more pre-eminent in European and Indo-European tradition than the oak. The labyrinth of its associations turns and winds upon itself back into the distant centre of origin. Links of linguistics and lore interweave and reinforce each other. Traditions live in the oak as abundantly as the multitudes of other life-forms the tree sustains. Over five hundred insects, moths, spiders and beetles rely on the oak tree for food and shelter. Fungi, ferns and lichen populate these city oaks that are also inhabited and visited by numerous birds and small mammals. Of all European trees the oak is the finest symbol of symbiotic microcosm - the universe or World Tree apparent within one being.

The Stability of Oaks

Even the oldest oaks in Britain, the giant pollarded trees in parklands and estates, are young when compared to the ancient yews - they may, at most, be 800 years old. Oaks seem to naturally live for about 300 years, so it is curious that oak lore attributes to them a much greater life-span than this. When oak woodlands were managed, regularly harvested by pollarding and coppicing, there may have been many more of the ancient hollowed-out giants around, but it is quite likely that the aura of oak itself brought about this assumption. Very few trees feel as rooted, as solid, as at home in their energy fields as oaks. Teeming with life in every nook and cranny, yet still and established in their own awareness.

There is evidence from tree ring dating that oak has been the main timber tree in Europe for at least nine thousand years and yet despite, or perhaps even because of this close

Oak on skyline, Kenn Valley, Devon.

310

technological relationship with mankind, the oak has maintained a firm link to deity, especially the primary sky and thunder gods of Indo-European pantheons.

The tree's name: darroch, dair, derwen, daur, derry, durr, duir, in the Celtic languages are directly linked to the god-names Zeus (Deus), Jupiter (Dis Pitar), Taranis, the Dagda, Perkunas, Thunor and Thor. The most ancient place of worship in Greece at Dordona was where the father of the gods was believed to be immanent within an ancient oak. All throughout the Classical world, trees and gods were held in close association, but the oak was chosen to represent or hold the energy of the father of the gods. The evidence of Classical writers suggests that to the Celtic druids, the oak was the pre-eminent tree and some suggest that the name druid derives from "oak-man" (though others with a more sound linguistic footing, rather see its descent from the Indo-European root words for "wise man" or "man of knowledge" i.e. seer). There are Greek texts that suggest much of Greek philosophy, including astronomy and mathematics, was learned from the Celtic peoples dwelling to the north of the Hellenic tribes - and it is unlikely that such a notion would have been mooted had the Greeks of more Classical times not considered the Celtic tradition to be one worthy of emulation. Historians rarely promulgate unpleasant truths about the source of their culture, just as a matter of expediency and self-interest.

Despite the possibly different linguistic origins, an association would have been readily apparent between these names for the oak, and the words "dur" meaning hard, durable, unyielding; "duranta" meaning mysterious; "duir" meaning door; "dag" meaning door and day; "druid", the wise men and law keepers; "droen" the wren, one of the most sacred birds of the druids; "dubh" meaning black or dark; "dryad", the sacred spirit of the oak. (Sanskrit roots: "turv" - to overcome, "du" - to burn)

Thunderbolt of the Sky God

The relationship between oak and lightning furthers the link to power. Oak is very often struck by lightning, perhaps because it can be the tallest tree in an area. More likely because its large taproot travels deeply into the earth where it maintains a steady contact with sources of water, acting as a powerful grounding for the massive electrical potential of a thunderstorm. Thunderstruck oak has been a sought-after talisman in many countries. In Indo-European cultures the lightning and the storm are seen as fertilising sources bringing much needed rain and the magical presence of wild - fire to the dry, parched lands of summer. It is no accident that the sky gods such as Thor, Jupiter and Zeus are wielders of the thunderbolt and also renowned for their virility (and in many cases, promiscuity). Indra, the Vedic storm god of India carries the vajra thunderbolt, that, in Tibetan Buddhism becomes the dorje, the indestructible diamond thunderbolt of realisation, also a powerful symbol of the manifestation of form out of emptiness - the play of wisdom (female quality) and compassionate activity (male quality).

The vajra is a symbol of the emergence of the universe and it echoes the form of a tree. The central point of the vajra is the sphere, symbolic of the primordial creative void, the true nature of both emptiness and form. This is the seed or the heart, (the core or trunk) of the Tree of the Universe. From this sphere arises differentiated aspects of energy - the primal elements and their characteristic play and interaction. This is where the trunk begins to divide into separate boughs and roots. The vajra next expands further into clearly separate parts, each diverging from its neighbours as manifesting creation seems to proliferate distinct entities and awareness throughout space and time. These qualities, space and time, are created by the apparent separation of form and emptiness - represented by the alternating bands of metal and empty space. The enclosed space within the tines echoes the original creative void - the true nature of all apparent manifestation and the realisation that nothing else exists. This void is recapitulated as each divergent tine returns to unite in a final point, where all apparent individuality and difference merge together once more.

The branches and roots of the tree spread out from the point of origin, yet in terms of both electromagnetic energy patterns, movements of the water cycle and other natural processes within the tree, this divergent manifestation forms a closed circuit of energy, a continual return to the source and further outward expansion.

So the attribute of the sky-god, the thunderbolt of protection and fertility (or the hammer, in Thor's case), can be seen as also representing the tree. The indestructible, durable, sustaining tree is the oak within which the deity can reside and which is often visited by his heavenly fire - the lightning vajra meets the tree vajra. Fire unites with water, heaven with earth. The many instances where runaway kings and other god-chosen individuals hide in oak trees rather than any other species may well be a continuation of this concept of the indwelling god-spirit that shelters and protects from harm the rightful rulers of the land. (This theme appears again in the aspects of sovereignty and the Goddess of the Land.)

Rune of Day

Yet another constellation of meaning can be found in the associations of the oak with doorways, both in time and perception. We can follow this through an exploration of the rune-sign "dag", the Germanic and Anglo-Saxon glyph which has a similar meaning to "duir".

Our present name for oak comes from the Anglo-Saxon word "ac", which has its own rune in the Anglo-Saxon expansion of the Germanic rune rows. Under the influence of existent British traditions and a changing vocabulary and pronun-

OAK CHARM (1)

OAK FAST.
HOLDING
LIGHT AND DARK.
SPINNING FORM FROM
THE CRACKS OF
NOTHING.
FIRM FRIEND,
ROOT AND ARCHING
BOUGH.
THE FIRST,
KNOWING THE LAST.

OAK CHARM (2)

FIRM FIXED.
FLOW FAST.
FORM FINDING.   SIMON LILLY

314

ciation of vowel sounds, the Anglo-Saxons augmented the original rune system adding another five and finally, eight more runes.

"Dag" is "day", day-time, specifically the height of noon or the stroke of midnight. That is, "dag" is the moment when one state reaches its apogee and becomes another: when morning becomes afternoon, where one day ends and another begins. "Dag" is thus a doorway from one state of fullness to another, a rune energy of fulfilment and transformation. As "dag" is a turning point in the runic cosmologies, so is "duir" a central pivot in the ogham cosmology. It marks the point of the longest day of the year, Summer Solstice, when the nights once again begin to lengthen towards the dark cold of winter.

The oak is traditionally linked to this time of the Summer Solstice, for the Oak King is thought to have ruled the year from Winter Solstice until this point, when his rule is overthrown by the Holly King who will take his place until the light once more begins to advance at midwinter.

Such a clear cut division of the year into dark and light halves seems to be blatantly intellectual and dualistic (and therefore perhaps a true Indo-European relic!) - which could have only a limited relevance to the more pragmatic and earth-based existence of the average hunter or farmer. But since when had mankind ever favoured a balanced perception of life when offered a memorable simplistic model of opposite forces?

Doorway

Certainly oak and its associations link it quite firmly to the abundance of life and fertility of summer storms, and both its magical attributes and its qualities as a tree essence indicate that the tree is both a doorway and an anchor of realities.

Both the rune "dag" and the ogham "duir" display the same magical properties that therefore transfer to the wood of the oak tree itself. Of its many attributes the most widespread is strength. As the primary source for building material, ships and furniture, oak is the epitome of durability and reliability. Its close-grained solidity meant that until the widespread use of iron tools, brought westward by the Celtic cultures, oak would have been difficult to fell. Where other trees would be cleared, the old oaks would be left standing. Most of the oak's other magical attributes are associated with the doorway. It acts as a gateway to other states of awareness and inner experience; it bars the way for negative energy but allows positive forces access. It reveals the hidden means whereby strength can be gained and it also protects by conferring invisibility or being able to see the invisible realms.

The Essence

All these magical qualities also agree with the qualities of the tree essence made from oak flowers. The initial assessment of the oak essence was quite surprising. For such a central, culturally important species, oak seemed to have a limited range of functions, especially compared to other native tree essences. However some of these functions are central to well-being. Primarily the essence seems to focus at the heart chakra and the Heart meridian where it has a calming effect. With other subtle energy systems oak tends to give a general energy boost without any re-balancing or reintegration.

The essence, on the other hand, focusses very specifically on two energy centres outside of the physical body. Quite a way above the top of the head are five chakras that continue the axis of the seven main chakras in the spinal column into very rarified energy levels. As most people have enough difficulty balancing the first seven centres, these rarified vortices, numbered from eight to twelve, rarely play any prominent part in healing or everyday states of consciousness. The eleventh chakra, said to integrate the individual energy pattern with the planetary consciousness (that is the collective consciousness of all awareness-beings within the sphere of the physical planet earth), is specifically energised by the oak essence. The second extra-physical chakra stimulated by oak is below the feet. In fact it can be located by mirroring the triangle between the base chakra and the soles of the feet downwards into the ground so as to form an elongated diamond. The lower apex of this diamond is the position of this small energy centre. Sometimes called the Earth Star or Earth Heart chakra, this point is our main anchor into this physical reality, the taproot into Earth's nutritious support. Without this focus point it becomes very difficult to feel as though we belong and there can be a profound lack of confidence, energy and motivation.

Combining these two energies, and remembering also that oak essence acts at the heart, the main balancing centre for all other energy systems of the body, it can be seen that oak helps with the absorption and integration of very profound, hidden energy levels that exist at the primal sources of being. Linking to the supra-physical levels of existence at either extreme of the individual auric field, oak funnels energy into the desire for growth in solid reality and the delight of expressing this in as many ways as possible.

Sutra

Attuning to the tree itself, its friendly familiar nature disguises the force within the oak's being. Working closely with the tree for the first time it became clear that its primary energy function was to maintain the balance within physical reality. The drawing in of polarities, the harmonisation of opposite forces, the tying together of dark and light, sky and earth, void and form, existence and non-existence gauged from the consolidated tension within the large boughs of a mature oak. It seems, then, that each oak tree is a stitch,

(Sanskrit: sutra - that which brings together or explains) holding our very reality together in its present form.

Each oak tree becomes a vortex of energy, simultaneously a white or black hole, drawing down to itself the tendency of things to separate and fly apart, to dissolve back into the initial matrix of potential being. Oak seems to be the means by which the individual, the distinct, can manifest from out of the many possibilities of how reality might be constructed. Oak absorbs within itself all these possibilities and then reveals new patterns. Chaos, after all, is not an absence of things but a eternal indecision about what things are to be - an inability to define and clarify the nature of anything which therefore ends up being everything and nothing simultaneously - the ultimate frustration. Oak enables the communication, the flow of energy, from the hidden sources of existence. This can appear to enable manifestation from "nothing", the weaving together of impossibly thin threads to create an unbreakable web that will hold all perceptions fast.

Timeless Return
Yet oak, whilst maintaining this pull of opposites seems to be held free of time, outside the flow of events and can bring with it a sense of timelessness, a place of uttermost calm in which to consider possibilities.

Perhaps it is these qualities of the Oak Spirit, felt surrounding the physical presence of the tree, that encourages us to perceive oak as the steadfast ancestor, the spiritual heart of the land. Certainly working with oak is an odyssey of adventure through the parallel possibilities of myth, meaning, symbol, history and nature. Like a fractal pattern or an infinitely detailed tapestry, focussing on one image or lesson offered by the Oak Spirit opens a door onto vast unexplored territories, a Glass-Bead-Game of intersecting significance, a redefinition of the play of Creation. Just as one fragment is thought to be fully explored and understood, another angle reveals a greater unthought of perspective. Depending on your nature this can be either exhilarating or exhausting, but following the path oak offers is a labyrinth. There is only one way to go and each turn, though appearing to be leading backwards on itself, takes one closer to the centre (where the only thing to do is to begin the journey back to the starting point).

Oak Initiation

The oak and Oak Spirits are a doorway, and a door is either a means of entrance or a means of obstruction; it is either open or shut. The Oak Initiation can be like this also. The initiation process may hand the participants a key but the door and its keyhole still need to be found before what is beyond the door can be revealed.

Firstly a circle of oak leaves is placed upon the floor, large enough so a person can stand or sit comfortably within the space. The oak leaves are placed in a clockwise direction (that is, the stalks are pointing anticlockwise). The initiate then enters the circle and stands or sits facing the direction where they feel most comfortable. If desired a personal power object can also be taken into the circle. A horizontal door or hatchway is then visualised within the circle. If there are witnesses or other participants present they also hold the image of a doorway in the floor. The intent is clearly held: "to allow the door to open". Then the following variation of the oak mantra is repeated for about five minutes - out aloud or subvocally: "Or. Tar. Bey. Pey. D'hey". Here the change to the first syllable of the mantra acts as a door key to the initiation process. There follows two minutes of silence, where all participants remain aware and listening. After this silence those present walk clockwise once around the oak leaf circle and then once anti-clockwise. If the process is carried out by oneself, then "all present" are those spirits that are witnessing. In this case the person in the circle visualises these beings circling around. The circle is then left and the next participant enters or the initiate sits alone quietly for a while, with awareness.

In our experience many people feel as though they are sinking downwards through a doorway of some kind, though often the process isn't complete and they feel "half-in and half-out". Further attunement and work with the energy of the oak, and using the oak leaf circle as a preliminary exercise to meditating with the tree spirit may allow the doorway to open more fully. Also becoming familiar with the Ivy Gateway will encourage a deeper experience. Remember that not every initiation process will be the most appropriate at the time of participation. An attitude of sharing the experience of the presence of the tree spirit is more helpful than the expectation of receiving hidden teachings and self-gratifying revelation. Two types of awareness-being are meeting each other, perhaps for the first time. Both are equal in significance. Both may find a doorway that is open or shut.

Talking With Dragons

After working with the Ivy and Oak for a little while it became apparent that one line of enquiry was to explore the links between tree energies and the energies of the land itself. There are many systems that define the Earth's energy fields and many definitions of its channels, emanations and patterns. One organic model that ties in with the legends and lore of Britain, and that remains redolent with power and rippling energy, is the land's consciousness as seen as the dragon.

Dragons belong to the same symbolic family as snakes, serpents and wyrms. They have a historical, objective reality as our ancestors - those great lizards who lived here on Earth successfully for millions of years. In this aspect alone, the

dragons have undeniable power of presence within the planet's noosphere, the sphere of mind or vibration that can be likened to the memory, genetic and subtle, of the Earth. Dragons still dwell within the deep caves of our own genetic makeup and cannot be expunged.

The seed ideas to which dragons and serpents are linked clearly establish their nature. Both have a power that is dangerous - in the same way that high power electric cables are more dangerous than domestic wiring. Both have a sinuous movement and they are also conceived as being intellectually or emotionally insinuating and wily. This brings to mind the (sinuous) sine wave, the pattern of vibration, and also the movement of wind, the movement of water and the movement of earth (for example, "rolling" hills). To the Celtic peoples the sacred rivers were fertilising and sustaining snakes, dragons of water and light. Many river names derive from the words for "bright" (such as Clyde and Clyst), or "snake" (for example Ask, Nidd, Esk and Exe). Indeed, dragons in lore do have much in common with the sources of water within the earth: they live in caves, on mountains, in lakes, pools and wells. They are long-lived and are nearly invulnerable. They rest undisturbed and out of sight and they guard or collect, or hoard, great treasures. Dragons are depicted as underground guardians with great knowledge and power that can be of harm to humans - perhaps symbolised by the withering fire that they are often said to exhale. A connection made between serpents and druids, in many primary and secondary source material, may lead one to the conclusion that the dragon's fiery breath is a kenning for the curse of satire that druids were able to bestow upon those that had displeased them.

The evolution of the dragon image has developed from many different sources and cultures. Like their origins, dragons display many disparate features. They are scaly like fish or reptiles, they often have a tail like a scorpion. The head is like that of a horse, teeth like a crocodile, talons like an eagle and wings of a bat. As well as combining the realms of animals, dragons also seem to amalgamate the elements: they breathe fire, dwell in the earth, they are winged and so are at home in air, they are sinuous like water. Whether a distant memory of dinosaurs, interpolations from fossil remains, combinations of the frightening aspects of nature's forces, or a real spiritual entity at non-physical levels of existence, the image of the dragon is a useful one in which to encapsulate the cthonic, mysterious power of the land. It can rise up when working with the spirit energy of trees. Like all powerful things dragons need to be treated with discipline and caution. Face to face the energy can be seductive or utterly terrifying - compared to an individual human the Earth is, after all, a very large being! To meet a completely non-human consciousness requires courage and confidence in one's own existence.

Dragon Dance, Dragon Trance

A particular rhythm can be useful for invoking the dragon/ earth snake, heart beat of the land. The rhythm can be used in silence or as a beat of a drum. In a count of eight slow beats, the first beat is struck. Just as the resonance dies away from this beat a double beat (equivalent to the count of one) is sounded: ONE (two, three, four, five six seven eight) ONE ONE (two, three, four five, six seven, eight) ONE (two etc...) and so on. While listening to this rhythm stand firm with your feet on the earth. Let the rest of your body move with the earth dragon energy. To begin the whole process you could visualise walking into a tree's form and then end by becoming aware of the tree's roots and exit out of the tree, giving thanks.

A trance position to help contact dragon energies can also be used with this beat or with regular journey drumming. Stand with the body very straight. Hold the upper arms tight to the sides and hold the lower arms horizontal with palms facing towards each other at waist level. Very quickly an energy will build up between the hands, and with the beat of the drum will transform into interesting energy patterns! An alternate position is to hold the arms straight, unbent at the elbows with the hands held at waist height.

Meeting Dragons - A Guided Journey

The following exercise can be a powerful method to journey into the presence of the dragon energy. Remember to ground and centre yourself before and after the process.

Begin by entering into the presence of a tree that you find powerful in its relationship to the Earth. Any tree will work where you feel this connection, or use the energy of oak, yew, ivy or Persian ironwood. If you know the attunements, the mantra or the colour, repeat the sequence a few times to yourself.

Asking permission to enter the tree itself, see a door or opening of some kind appear to open. You are aware that you have with you a small bundle wrapped up in some way.

Enter the doorway and find yourself within the energy body of the tree. Take a minute or two to acclimatise yourself here. Then frame the clear intention of travelling to meet with the dragon energies of the land.

Become aware that you are moving down through the large roots of the tree. Keep your attention as clearly as possible on following the roots. Be aware of the decreasing size of the roots the deeper they travel. Follow them as if in tunnels or with your vision. See them become as thin as arms, as thin as rope, as thin as string, as thin as thread. See them as the thinnest you can, and beyond this to where you can only sense the finest feeling of the root's presence.

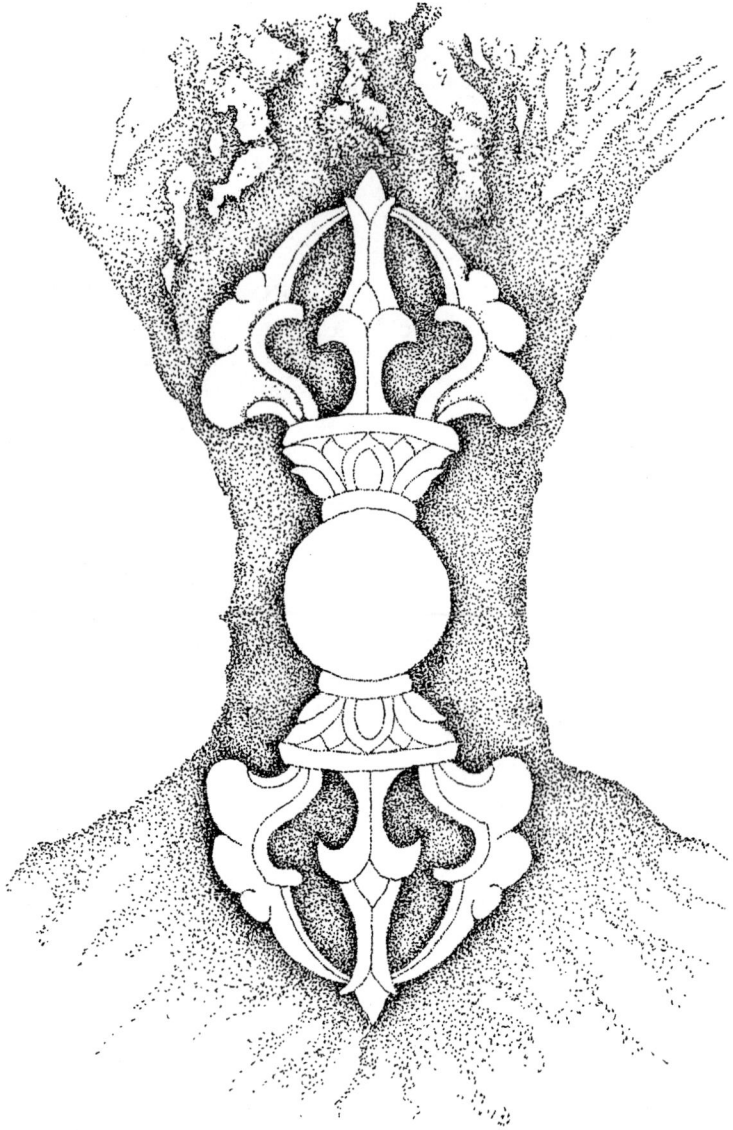

Oak and vajra. The vajra, or "dorje" in Tibetan, is the indestructible thunderbolt. It symbolises the lightning of full Realisation and the process of Form manifesting from Void. Its shape echoes the balanced duality of the tree. So tree and universe have the same shape: World Tree, Tree Universe.

Now there is just a tickle of thought, the slightest variation of vibration as you follow the minutest root downwards into the earth. As the root thought vanishes, you become aware that you are, as it were, floating on a mist or sea, of gentle silver vibration. There are pulses of energy like waves or breezes that play across your awareness.

With a conscious intention, allow yourself to sink within, or under, the surface of this silver sea. Become aware of the sensations of silence and the fleeting patterns of vibration as they pass over you. Although you have now no sense of direction, you will still feel that you are passing deeper into the earth.

Quite suddenly, but gently, you are aware that your feet are on a solid surface, although all is still swirling silver stillness around you. Now, again frame that conscious intention: "to meet with the dragon energies of the land." (If you have a personal addition to this intent ie. ".... in order to...", make it now also).

Feel the place you are in come into focus: what is beneath your feet, what sort of space you are in. Can you recognise things, such as rocks, walls, windows, trees, people and so on. Don't, as yet, look around - just focus on what is in front of you. It may be very clear or it may be fleeting and not clear enough to make much sense. Will yourself to understand with clarity as much of the place as possible. Wait for a minute or two for your mind to settle down.

As yet, you have not moved from the spot. You have not turned around or explored where you are. Now with a very clear intent, have the thought: "When I turn around to face the opposite direction I will come face-to-face with the dragon energy of the land." Quickly turn around and hold in your mind the image of what you are aware. It may be very clear or difficult to discern. Take a while to understand what you see.

It may be a recognisable dragon form. It may be some other form, or it may be a feeling of energy or a pattern of vibration. Whatever the form, be courteous and curious.

If when you turn, nothing is present, quickly turn around again. If after several turns you have no sense of a presence, take one step forward and look downwards. You will find a small pool or a mirrored surface of some sort. Gaze behind your reflected image in the surface and you will see the dragon energy take form.

You may now be communicated with, you may have questions come to you mind. Ask and answer courteously and truthfully. When you feel that it is time to leave, ask permission to depart from the presence. Say thank you. Turn around and close your eyes. You will now have the sensation of rapidly rising, or of a quick transition from one level to another. When the sensations ease and stop you will be once again within the body of the tree. Take a minute or two to merge once more with the harmonious balance and stability of the tree-being. Feel well-rooted into the earth, yet able to reach up into the air and sunlight.

Find the doorway or opening and enter into the world again. Turn and thank the tree for its help. Become aware of your body and the room you are in. Take a while to run through your experiences, then, when you are ready, open your eyes and record the journey.

Holly - Fire of Compassion

In the two-fold year of light and darkness the holly is said to rule the dark months between midsummer and midwinter, opposite the oak. Both trees have many fiery associations and share some key concepts. Some of the regional names of the tree are hollin, hulver, poisonberry, Aunt Mary's Tree, Christmas tree and Christ's thorn. The holly was *"holegn"* in Old English, *"holin"* in Middle English, *"cuillen"* in Old Irish and *"bein-viar"* in Old Norse. In the Ogham Tract the tree is known as *"smir guali"*, fires of coal, because holly was an excellent source of charcoal for making fine weapons. In Cornwall holly was known as *"gas-tann"*, the green sacred tree, and it has been suggested that the English verb "to tan" comes from the use of holly bark in tanning leather. If this is so then both oak and holly share this attribute. More oaks were grown and cropped for the tanning industry than for the whole of the needs of the Royal Navy and domestic building.

Like oak, the holly is connected to the same deities Tannus, Taranis, Thunnor and Thor the fertilising sky and storm gods of Northern traditions. In the ogham alphabet it has become associated to "tinne", which means fire, and which is the same root as the word for tinder. In bright sunlight holly is certainly a tree of fire. It's glossy evergreen leaves catch and reflect the sun's rays so that from a distance the tree turns from a sombre green to a flashing brilliance. Few British trees "spark" so much as the holly does. Perhaps this too strengthens its associations with lightning (for which it is planted near the house as a prophylactic). The sharp leaves together with the combination of darkness (storm clouds) and light (lightning flashes) of holly further conjure the elements.

Detail of the veins of a holly leaf. These delicate skeletons can be found in the leaf litter beneath the tree and can provide a powerful focus for meditation.

The New Sun, the Holly, the Crown

Holly's folk associations with Christ and the Christian myth are at once more symbolically apparent and yet offer the real possibility of new jargon replacing an older, parallel system of religious identification. The most well-known association with the Christian Passion can be found in the Christmas carol *"The Holly and the Ivy"*:

> "The holly and the ivy
> When they are both full grown
> Of all the trees that are in the wood
> The holly bears the crown......"

The carol continues to draw parallels between the tree and Christ's Passion, yet still carries as strong a pagan flavour as can be found within the Church. Carols always were the music of the people and so present a view less liturgical and more seasonally celebrational. A very similar carol from Cornwall is the *St. Day Carol* and one is left wondering whether those who sang the words were interpreting the symbols in a completely non-Christian way:

1.   "Now the holly bears a berry as white as the milk,
      And Mary bore Jesus, who was wrapped up in silk.

Chorus: And Mary bore Jesus Christ our saviour for to be,
         And the first tree in the greenwood, it was the holly!
         Holly! Holly!
         And the first tree in the greenwood, it was the holly.

2.   Now the holly bears a berry as green as the grass,
      And Mary bore Jesus, who died on the cross.

3.   Now the holly bears a berry as black as the coal,
      And Mary bore Jesus, who did for us all.

4.   Now the holly bears a berry, as blood it is red,
      Then trust we our Saviour, who rose from the dead."

It must be remembered that the season of mid-winter was sacred in many European pagan religions. In fact, so stubborn was the upholding of solstice celebrations by the people that Christ's birth was purposely moved to coincide with the birth of the new sun. If the holly was already a central symbol at this festival it would have been adopted with little change into the new, official, Christian symbolism.

In the *St. Day Carol* the tree becomes an image of the Mother of God, Mary and its fruit, the berry, with her son, Jesus. The association of holly with this thinly veiled Mother Goddess might explain why in these songs the holly is given very obvious pre-eminence. It "bears the crown" and "is the first tree in the greenwood" even though it is generally a small, understorey tree in established oak woodland. Of course, it may bear the crown because it has sharp spines and red berries therefore reminiscent of the crown of thorns. It may be "first" because it is an evergreen and so the first green tree in the winter wood, but even so, other trees fit these categories well, if not better. Other folklore also strengthens this pre-Christian Goddess/God association. A 15th century poem stresses the sacred nature of the tree:

> "Whosoever ageynst Holly do crye
> In a lepe shall he hang full hye...
> Whosoever ageynst Holly do syng,
> He may wepe and handys wryng."

Holly is seen as a protective tree, as many sacred to the Goddess would be: drinking from a holly-wood cup could cure illness. Holly would protect from evil spirits and witches as well as misfortune on the road. Cutting the tree was often done furtively so as not to stir up retribution.

Whilst the early carols stress the mother-son attribute of holly, other sources seem to emphasise the male aspects. Holly and ivy are seen as a pair where holly represents the male and ivy, the female qualities. The festival of Saturnalia at mid-winter between the 17th and 23rd of December was a period outside of normal time and order where masters served slaves, cross-dressing and other role reversals were acceptable and presents were given and received. The holly tree was the representative of this time ruled by the dour father of the gods, Saturn, whose club was fashioned from the wood.

Green Holly Knight and Winter Initiation

Saturnalia and Samhain both celebrate a period of initiation where doorways usually closed are flung open. A famous Middle English poem *"Gawain and the Green Knight"* seems to take the theme of the year's ending and intermixes a series of Celtic beliefs that are very relevant to our examination of the Holly spirit.

It is New Year's Day at Camelot and King Arthur and his knights are all gathered in the hall for feasting. Arthur remains unseated and will not eat until a marvellous adventure is recounted or until a challenge is made. The first course has just been served when a fanfare sounds....

"There pressed in from the porch an appalling figure,
 Who in height outstripped all earthly men .....
Amazed at the hue of him,
A foe with furious mien,
Men gaped, for the giant grim was coloured a gorgeous green
And garments of green girt the fellow about....."

Both the giant and his horse are decked out in the finest accoutrements of green and gold.

'GREENMAN AT MIDWINTER'

Greenman at midwinter

"Lightning like he seemed
And swift to strike and stun.
His dreadful blows, men deemed
Once dealt, meant death was done."

It is also interesting that the simile of lightning is used where it is not the obvious choice, reflecting perhaps the traditional links with holly trees and lightning, and fire generally.

His huge size and appearance clearly denotes his Otherwordly nature and this is confirmed by what he is carrying - a holly cluster in one hand and an axe in his other. Holly became Christianised as a symbol of good luck but was used prominently in the Saturnalia festival. The Green knight offers "a Christmas game, for it is Yuletide and New Year, and young men abound here."

He offers to strike one blow in return for another, using his great axe "And I shall bide the blow first." After a year and a day's reprieve the return blow will be given. Not surprisingly there is a lack of willing volunteers, so Arthur himself steps forward, but Gawain offers to accept the challenge - which everyone readily agrees is a good idea.

Gawain strikes a blow that severs the giant's head from his great shoulders. Red blood gushes from the body as the head rolls away but the giant remains standing, then retrieves his head and swings onto his saddle. He reminds Gawain of his promise to find the Green Chapel and receive the return stroke of the axe "in the gleaning New Year - such a stroke as you have struck."

What is the Green Chapel, but a sacred grove? And what is a knight but a warrior guardian of his land?

Gawain remains at court until All Saint's Day (All Hallow's E'en - the festival of Samhain where the doors to all worlds are opened) and then leaves on his search for the Knight of the Green Chapel. So Gawain leaves on the Celtic New Year's Day, his shield marked with a golden pentacle - the magical knot of protection, the ivy leaf, the "druid's foot".

On Christmas Day Gawain arrives at a great castle where he is welcomed and feasted by a knight and his beautiful lady. He discovers the Green Chapel is only two miles distant from the castle and the host bids him stay and rest until the appointed hour. Whilst all the others go hunting Gawain stays at the castle where he is continually propositioned by the lady in no ambiguous terms. For a man who knows he is going to have his head chopped off in a day or two, Gawain is surprisingly steadfast in his honour. When the host returns each evening he gives Gawain his catch of the hunt, whilst Gawain gives him the chaste kisses he has been given. Gawain is even offered, by the lady, a silk girdle that has the properties of protecting the wearer from harm, which he accepts and hides away. On New Year's Day Gawain sets out with a guide to find the Green Chapel. As he nears, the guide attempts to dissuade him from going further

"No man passes that place, however proud in arms,
Without being dealt a death-blow by his dreadful hand."

(It has been suggested that the Green Chapel is located in the Peak District, where Cheshire, Staffordshire and Derbyshire meet around Swythamley Park, where Lud's Church, a natural ravine can be found, echoing the poet's description. Interestingly enough, this exact area is described as being one of the last areas of England where Celtic-derived pagan traditions could still be found up until the present day.)

Gawain enters the ravine and looks around for a chapel but all he sees is:

"a fairy mound apparently,
A smooth-surfaced barrow by the side of a stream."

The Green Knight appears and Gawain prepares himself to receive the blow. As the axe descends upon his neck Gawain flinches slightly. The axeman stops the descent and berates Gawain for his cowardice. The second time the knight threatens to strike but doesn't. The third time he leaves "A mere snick on the side so that the skin was broken."

The Green Knight then explains that the first two were feints because Gawain had shared honestly his gifts of the first and second days. For taking and keeping the braided belt he received the "tap". The Green Knight tells Gawain that his wife was testing him all the time and invites him back to the castle for the feast. Gawain refuses and returns to Camelot.

The whole sequence is reminiscent of an Initiation - though the Christianised version peters out in a rather unsatisfactory pious fashion with Gawain grumbling that he has been "caught by cowardice and covetousness".

Caitlin Matthews associates the Green Knight with the Wild Herdsman - "The Lord of Wild Things; instructor and guide; Lord of Death and Rebirth" whom she titles: "Guardian of the Totems, Lord of the Wheels." The guardian is the one who gives tests and challenges to the hero. In Celtic tradition the beheading game is a common motif of Initiation. But if the Green Knight is the Lord of Wild Things, the lady would be an aspect of the Goddess, embodiment of fertility and the land. The sacrifice, or beheading, can thus be seen as an offering to maintain the relationship with the land itself. That this process is related to the midwinter rites and to the Holly spirit may give some insight into the nature of holly's energy.

Holly and the Goddess

There are a sequence of narrations that deal with Gawain and some retell the story of the Green Knight. By far the most important is "Sir Gawain and the Green Knight" but it must be remembered that the tale has come down to us through the exacting lens of Christian patriarchy. The age of Chivalry, begun in south-western France, can be seen as an attempt to redress the male-female imbalance created by the Church, where women were becoming increasingly proscribed and vilified as the cause of all sin. Even seen at its best, however, the Chivalric ideal was a sublimation of negative attitudes rather than a true freedom from prejudice. Attempting to look at the story from a more balanced perspective, several important points become clear. In the hall after he has retrieved his head, the Green Knight specifically addresses Guinevere, though his words are directed towards Gawain. Many consider Guinevere to be a "light", summer aspect of the Goddess, so this throwaway line may suggest a deeper level of meaning to the entire poem. The Green Knight appears at the initial challenge and during the final test with the axe. However, a much larger proportion of the poem is concerned in detail with the tests of discipline and honour as Gawain faces the erotic temptations of the Lady of the Castle. And this testing turns out to be the most significant because had he failed, the Green Knight would have struck off Gawain's head instead of giving him a mild reproof.

In another version of the story, the entrance to the Green Knight's castle is guarded by a hawthorn on one side, with a hazel growing opposite it. Of all the trees to chose, these two have perhaps the clearest of traditional associations. Hawthorn or May, is the energy of the Goddess in her role as bringer of fecundity and fertility, the Lover. Hawthorn represents the heart. Hazel has, from the earliest Celtic period, been seen as the tree of wisdom, revealer of knowledge and food of druids. It represents clarity of mind. So here the entrance to the Green Knight/ Goddess/ Holly Spirit can only succeed by passing between, that is balancing, the energies of desire and wisdom, head and heart.

Essence of Holly

This balancing quality is very apparent in the essence of holly. Edward Bach was drawn to make an essence of holly flower as a remedy against anger, envy, jealousy and suspicion. He saw it as an antidote to hatred: "holly protects us from everything that is not Universal Love." Bach used holly when all other remedies seemed to fail because lack of love he saw as the ultimate foundation of any negative emotional state. In other words, holly essence heals the fractures of separation that lead to a withdrawal from universal support.

Our own assessment of holly essence agrees with this and also parallels the hawthorn-holly-hazel doorway image. Holly reinstates a fundamental level of balance and justice that is supportive of healing and evolution. It provides a sense of security and contentment whilst energising the ability of intelligence and discrimination.

At the heart chakra, holly greatly helps to strengthen self-worth and acceptance of one's true energy potential. At the brow chakra holly reduces irritability and nervous mental chatter, so that a deep peace can be realised within which creativity, passion and expression can be found.

The Holly Initiation

Of all the Tree Initiations so far covered, holly is the most complex in its engagement of all the senses and the mind. The Holly Initiation is also the one that has the strongest sense of polarity within it, and in the personal experiences of the participants. Light and dark, life and death, fear and bliss can all be encountered here, in the balance of the Holly Spirit.

339

Begin the process by spraying the essences of hawthorn and hazel within the room. Now visualise yourself standing in front of an oak doorway. At one side of the door is a hawthorn tree, and on the other a hazel tree. Take time for the picture to clear. Are there details on or around the door that can be seen or sensed? Allow all the images to clarify.

Wait in front of the doorway until it opens. As it does you will see a passageway where the left side is in darkness and the right side is in bright light. Move down this passageway until it becomes a dark tunnel where the only light is now coming from the far end. As you emerge from the tunnel you will find yourself in a light space of some kind. Allow time to perceive what sort of space you are now in.

At this point, keeping the eyes closed, a drink is brought up to the lips and a little is sipped. This drink represents blood, the blood of the earth, and can be made from an infusion of edible fruits and berries. As a base, sloe gin is ideal, comprising as it does the fruits of blackthorn and juniper. What is added to this will depend on local availability, but rose hips provide a good body and richness. Crab apples, cherries, strawberry tree fruit and other autumn hedge foods can be added as felt appropriate.

Once this drink has been tasted, frame the intention: "to meet the Lord of the Forest". Now an incense is lit and inhaled. This too can be a personal mix - but best to use plants from your locality or that you yourself have gathered and blended. A rich mix can include cypress, cedar, lavender, sage, dried mushroom (non-toxic!) and thyme.

Opposite: An unusual Green Man portrayed as a knight with shield and sword. 14th c. Winchester Cathedral. The knight is the protector and guardian of his lord and lady's land. The Green Knight is thus the protector of the Land of the Goddess.

Now you will find yourself entering a light, warm direction-less cloud. The Holly Tree Spirit Teacher will come to you here. Take as much time as you like to communicate with each other. When it is time to leave this space you will notice an ivy tendril somewhere close to you. Follow it until you come to a white archway through which all you see is darkness. This is the Ivy Gateway. Take time now to remember and clarify your experiences and note any new thoughts or ideas that come to you now. When you are ready, step through the Ivy Gateway. Complete the process by sounding or listening to a high-pitched gong, bell or bowl that will help to centre you within your body.

In our experience the Ivy Spirit is of great importance in this initiation process because it allows a clear and rapid means to return to the present. If the inner experiences are challenging the appearance of the ivy tendril can be as welcoming as a rope to one drowning. If the inner experiences are of a blissful nature it can be a less welcome, but equally necessary, reminder of the world of form.

Like other Tree Initiations, the Holly Teacher can be met by repeating this ritual until such time as it seems no longer necessary or specific teachings have given you personal instructions. The engagement of each of the senses in turn, make this Initiation particularly pleasing as a sequence for meditation and ritual contemplation. When it has been memorised, each section flows effortlessly together: spray the essences, begin the doorway visualisation and the passage, taste the drink, meet the Lord of the Forest, light the incense, talk with the Holly spirit, follow the Ivy, exit the Ivy Gateway, sound the bell.

Lord of the Forest

Information about the nature and appearance of the Lord of the Forest has here been kept vague so as not to necessarily colour the personal experiences one may have. Such a primal, ancestral energy can appear in a great many guises and manifestations. The experience may be of a single being of any sex, or of a numinous intelligent atmosphere, or of a series of vignettes, animal, vegetable, mineral or mind. Remember that the Forest has been the home of the greatest variety of life on the surface of this planet. Hundreds of millions of years have passed since trees first grew in the Carboniferous Forests we now burn as coal.

For those who wish to experience this energy more directly there is a trance position that can be used either at the appropriate time in the Holly Initiation or as a separate practice. There are three possible variations to the posture and it will be necessary to find the one best suited to each individual. The basic position is to be kneeling down with a straight back and head looking forward. The arms are held out from the sides at a slight angle and the hands are open with palms facing the front. Variations of this position are to sit back on the heels, so that the buttocks are resting on the feet, kneeling upright so that the upper legs and body make one vertical axis, or kneeling, sitting on a cushion with the feet splayed out to either side.

Like the story of Gawain and the Green Knight the Holly Spirit tends to work by presenting a situation and getting you to notice how you are reacting. Holly can appear to be a trickster-like spirit but the intention is to expand self-awareness and the ability to balance extremes of reaction, not to judge or condemn. That we do very well for ourselves.

Hazel coppice, Dunsford, Devon.

Hazel - Tree of Knowing

(Using your nut)

Hazel is a common hedgerow plant though it is rarely seen as a mature tree. It can grow to thirty feet, but the young hazel rods are so useful that most plants are coppiced or laid back into the hedge. It can be quite surprising to come across a mature hazel tree with broad spreading boughs. Usually they are only found thus in gardens or in remote, unfarmed areas. Hazel is not a particularly long-lived tree but when coppiced regularly it can live for as long as a thousand years.

Hazel rods and sticks are very pliable and tough which makes them ideal for weaving hurdles, making baskets, as a framework for temporary buildings and for stakes. Well over twenty products have been listed as being made from hazel. Such a fast-growing and useful resource is this tree that it is little wonder that the Irish Celts counted hazel among the seven chieftain trees, which meant that felling one was punishable by death. Ah! The good old days!

Hazel catkins, "lambs' tails", are the tree's yellow male flowers that appear in the hedgerows before almost any others from January onwards. They shed pollen from around mid-February when the very small female flowers, looking like green buds with bright red hairs, become fertilised. Around September what fruit has not been collected by squirrels and mice is ripening in clusters of twos, threes and fours. For those who appreciate a more subtle taste, or who are impatient to wait so long, the green cobs provide a sweeter nutlet. Hazelnuts are one of Britain's few native

345

fruits and would have provided a useful source of storable protein through the winter months. As a food it is high in proteins and fatty acids, containing significant amounts of potassium, phosphorus, magnesium and copper.

Hazel nuts are certainly "brain food". These minerals are of major importance to the proper functioning of the nervous system and the activities of the brain, especially memory. They also help with energy production and the repair of damaged tissues. If we look at some of the symptoms associated with deficiencies of potassium, magnesium, phosphorus and copper, we find an increase in mental confusion, irritability, tiredness, weakness, general malaise and a feeling of being run down.

The Doctrine of Signatures works perfectly with hazel: the shell is the skull; the green bracts, the hair; and the soft nut is the brain itself. Or again, the fruit is heart-shaped and is known to improve the functioning of the heart and helps prevent hardening of the arteries. In traditional societies either the head or the heart are often understood as being the seat of the soul or the container of wisdom. The Celts saw the head as the source of power and there would have been a clear correspondence between these qualities and the status given to the hazel tree.

The colloquialism for head, "nut", clearly derives from the physical form of hard shell and soft interior. "Using your nut" would therefore have the meaning of using your head or thinking processes. It would be interesting to see if this terminology simply arose from the physical parallels or whether the associated Celtic lore played a part in its development as well.

The Doctrine also determines that hazel would be an aphrodisiac - with its long, dangling male flowers and paired nuts (the other colloquial meaning of the word), how could it be otherwise? As further verification, the Celtic god of love, Aengus, is said to have carried a rod of hazel. The appropriateness of this connection can be clearly seen in the nutritional content, particularly phosphorus which plays a fundamental role in the structure and maintenance of RNA and DNA.

Herbal uses for hazel do not seem to be that numerous but the nut powdered and sweetened has been used to help chronic coughing, and when added to pepper will draw mucus from the sinuses (whether this explosive mixture is snuffed or swallowed isn't mentioned).

Connla's Well

For all its modest stature and practical, homely usage, the lore for hazel is more complete and specific in the remaining Celtic literature than for any other tree. In "Dindsenchas", the sacred geography of Ireland, Connla's Well near Tipperary is described as being overhung by nine hazels of poetry. These trees contained knowledge of all the sciences and arts, and as the nuts fell into the well they were eaten by the salmon who swam there. Each bright spot on his skin represented a nut that he had eaten. This fish was thus the repository of all wisdom. The trees were said to produce flowers and fruit simultaneously and this has been interpreted as standing for beauty and wisdom. But it is also a common characteristic of Celtic Otherworldly trees- spirit trees - and can also represent the immediate fulfilment of an inspiration, that is, no sooner is one inspired than the fruit of that inspiration appears, complete and whole.

Finn

There is a well known tale of Fionn (Finn) who was instructed by a chief druid to cook a salmon but was strictly forbidden to taste it. While busy in his task he accidentally touched the

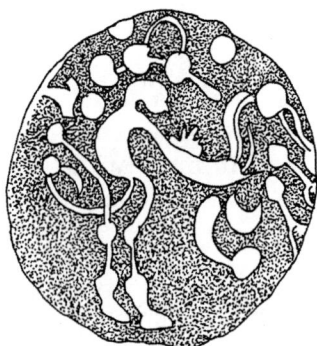

fish, burning his thumb. Without thinking he put his thumb in his mouth to cool it and immediately became inspired with all knowledge and all arts. The salmon had fed on the sacred hazelnuts, Fionn got lucky, and the chief druid cooked his own fish from then on!

Fionn is again associated with another hazel, this time the "dripping hazel", a leafless tree upon which perched vultures (probably buzzards or some other raptors) and ravens which continually dripped poisonous sap. He made a shield from the wood of this tree that gave off fumes killing thousands of enemy soldiers. This story has been seen as a poetic kenning for magical protection, probably a satire or cursing poem and hence the destructive or defensive use of knowledge - the dark side of inspiration.

A leafless tree is seen in winter, the time of introversion and death. The only fruit are vultures (buzzards?) and ravens, that is, birds with intimate knowledge of carrion and death and so able to act as messengers between the living and the dead. The poisonous sap and the wood that produces toxic fumes are the antithesis of the fertilising, health-giving nuts and the versatile flexible timber, (closer in nature to the cthonic darkness of the yew than to hazel). So the sacred tree

---

Opposite: Two Celtic coins showing the hunt for plant spirit wisdom. Top: the shaman turns hog / bear / hunting dog in the forest and succeeds in sniffing out the precious fungal (?) prey which is held between his open jaws. Below. shaman turns mushroom. Surrounded by the characteristic shape of psilosybin mushrooms the wise one extends a hand and receives energy from the mushroom spirit. The mushroom cap cut in half makes a characteristic incurving spiral form that appears frequently in Celtic art, as it does in art throughout the world. In many cultures fungi are described as trees. The close relationship between the two kingdoms would not have gone unnoticed nor would the healing, death-dealing and entheogenic properties of fungi.

of wisdom, guardian of the well of knowledge, is shadowed by this dripping hazel. It is easy to produce a moralistic view with a neat commentary along the lines of "knowledge can be used for good or ill", but it seems a rather tame conclusion, too sanitising and not very Celtic in spirit. Satire and satirical curse was effective because at its basis was truth - albeit a dark truth. The dripping hazel perhaps represents those elements of knowledge and truth that most people will fear to look at - the "poisonous fumes to the thousands". Fionn being of heroic stature, and a truthful warrior, can approach and use the wood without damage to himself because he knows that the carrion birds are as much a part of life as the salmon. When we are looking for answers, for inspiration, the vision we receive may tell us things that we would prefer to ignore. Turning away from "dripping poison", we may fail to learn how it can be used to heal - the strongest poisons are also the strongest medicines.

The motif of putting the thumb into the mouth appears several times in Celtic literature and it is always associated with gaining knowledge or inspiration. This will be looked at again in a little while.

Hazel has a strong connection to sacred wells and springs. Hazel nuts have been found as offerings to the spirit guardians of such places, and the tree was clearly understood as a gateway to the numinous Otherworld.

The hazel wand was used as a mark of authority for Irish heralds, druids and early Christian bishops. This association with the concept of authoritative prerogative or boundary ("trespassers will be...."), is also found in Norse and Anglo-Saxon tradition where hazel delineates an area of judgement - whether that be a royal court, a combat area or a battleground. Hazel delineates magical boundaries, to remind one where things begin and end, to clarify and discriminate.

Hazel for Wisdom

It is appropriate that the tree associated with inspiration and wisdom is not a great, impressive ancient tree but a rather medium-sized, friendly, inconspicuous being that provides homely food and everyday practicality.

We tend to see wisdom and inspiration as something special, above the ordinary, as something that has to be striven for but that is rarely reached. If those dizzy heights are achieved then all too soon we shall sink back down for lack of sustaining air, back to the cluttered yard of everyday ignorance. Hazel tells us that this is nonsense. It is merely an excuse not to consider all the options, not to take responsibility, not to use our senses. Wisdom comes from seeing what IS and using what is HERE. Wisdom isn't leaving home to find the riches of realisation in some golden-spired city with ostentatious pavements. Wisdom is observing the energy play, listening to the slight shifts of reality, paying attention, so that when inspiration arises, one is not too busy flustering about to notice.

The Nuts Drop, Plop!

The imagery around the Celtic view of hazel contains complex relationships. We can try to make sense of each vignette as it has come down through the centuries, or the images can be explored separately in the hope that fresh meanings emerge to be of use. The primary motifs are: the hazel-nut; the pool, well or spring; the salmon; the innocent watcher. Some of the associations of the nut have been looked at, now we look at its action. The nut falls off the tree into the pool where it is eaten by the salmon, which thereby gains some aspect of knowledge. One might expect that there would be many examples of people eating hazelnuts to increase their wisdom, but that is not what is found. The tales tell us of druids, already wise men, catching the salmon, cooking the fish and setting an innocent watcher to look after it until ready. A spontaneous, natural, unthought-out, reflex action - sucking a burnt thumb - instantly transfers all the wisdom from fish to human. The innocent watcher becomes the inspired wisdom knower. Is there a teaching here?

If the hazel nut represents the problem ("a hard nut to crack"), then it is dropped whole into the pool. Using modern Jungian associations the pool or well can represent the mind - the deep mind, or the unconsciousness. Whatever it is called, it is that part of us that we rarely pay much attention to except in the dream state. So what, then, does the salmon represent? What is the aspect of our minds that digests the problem enough to fully assimilate it into its own being, as the salmon transforms each nut into another speckled spot on its flank?

Is it really necessary to identify what the salmon represents? The salmon is a powerful spirit in the outer world, as it may also be on the inner. A powerful being who swims half way across the world to return to its spawning grounds each year. A fish with faultless memory. The salmon is thus the spirit of memory, able to return to its own source. It is a powerful fish that swims in salt sea and fresh water with equal facility, a fish that swims against the flow of current. In fact the salmon utilises a special reversed current that flows against and through the normal stream of water. The water seer, Viktor Schauberger, identified this counterflow and it is quite possible that the Celts, too, knew of this. In their artforms many subtle patterns seen in water are used, and it is not unlikely that they also knew of the vortex effect from close observations. The salmon shows tenacious persistence as it climbs and flies through the air to cross weirs and waterfalls on its way upriver. The salmon is a fish that flies, a spirit that can move through many different elements, dimensions and realms.

So the salmon is an indwelling spirit which digests and assimilates the nut. Inspiration is now available but it can't be forced out . All the plans of the druids and Ceridwen etc. come to naught and it is only by innocently watching the process of maturation (cooking), and then reacting appropriately at the natural time. Success comes by watching over the fish: not letting it burn. It is during this careful watching that the inspiration transfer will happen by itself.

One of the three oracles of the Irish seer or "filidh" is the "teinm laida", the illumination of song. Teinm can be directly translated as chewing of the pith, or the breaking open of the pith. This refers to getting to the meat of the hazelnut, the inspiration of poetic imagery. Whenever Fionn put his thumb into his mouth and sang through "teinm laida", it is said that which he did not know would be revealed to him.

In Celtic Irish texts hazelnuts are also poetically linked to the bubbles caused by the nuts themselves falling into the waters of the well of wisdom. Hazelnuts were: *cuill crimond* - the hazels of knowledge; *bolg fils* - the bubbles of wisdom; *bolg imbais* - the bubbles of poetic inspiration; *bolg greine* - the sun bubbles; *imbus greine* - the sun of inspiration. Perhaps significantly, the term *"bolg"* (bubbles) is used in Gaelic names for mushrooms, and the term *"iaochag"* means both mushroom and nut without a kernel.

There has been recent speculation that this convoluted poetic imagery suggests the use of shamanic-type processes to access the wisdom of the spirit worlds, and that certain recurrent motifs indicate the possible use of psychotropic plants, specifically *Amanita muscaria*.

The literary evidence is inconclusive but tantalising. Certainly there are plenty of mushroom images in Celtic art, including figures picking or collecting mushrooms. The latter can be found on tribal coinage, so in all probability it was

regarded as an important or defining activity, standing as it does alongside images of deities and tribal totems.

A second of the oracles of the Irish filidh is the "imbas forosnai". Translated as "manifestation that enlightens" or "kindling of poetic frenzy", it consisted of chewing "red flesh", chanting incantations and spirit offerings and then remaining between three to nine days in total darkness whilst being watched over by others. The red flesh, together with other shamanic initiatory beings like the speckled salmon, the spotted stag, the spotted snake have been seen as kennings for the Fly Agaric mushroom. Hazel itself, and its red nuts, have perhaps less convincingly been added to this list. Yet the obscurity, the fragmentary nature and the dense metaphor of Old Irish make it a veritable Glass Bead Game where it is possible to interconnect the most disparate of images without knowing for certain where metaphor ends and true meaning begins.

Scholastic debate is no match for personal experience and it would be worthwhile to spend some considerable time exploring all the motifs surrounding the hazel and the well from as many different perspectives as possible.

The following two procedures were suggested whilst working with the energy spirit of hazel. Interestingly the form of the techniques emerged only after using a zig-zag stick of beech, which at the time seemed to act as a guide as to how to present the hazel/well imagery in a practical way.

Opposite: This Green Man bears a striking resemblance to the Northwest Coast Indian mask called "Returned from Heaven". Both have the same eyes still fixed on unseen realms and the expression of stunned wonder mixed with confusion and revelation. The same expression as one who has tasted drops from the Cauldron of Inspiration. Old Radnor Church, Powys, Wales.

Bouncing Awareness

This exercise loosens up the normal perspectives with which we view the world. Errors in our understanding are often the reason why solutions to problems fail to be seen. Changing our point of view can allow new answers to emerge, or for the perceived problem to simply disappear.

From where you are, become aware of your surroundings. What you feel, touch, hear.

Be aware that sensations and feelings are flowing into you. They flow inwards and you recognise them within the energy field of your body.

Every new sound, every feeling vibrates your field of energy and your mind turns its attention from one vibration, one sense, to the next.

Be aware of your breath, in and out, expanding your lungs, passing through your throat and nose.

Be aware of your mind following the vibrations of feeling, sound, touch and thought.

Your awareness is a sphere within which you experience your internal world and your external surroundings. Take a minute or so to see this clearly.

Now allow your awareness sphere to change positions. As if it were a rubber ball, allow your awareness sphere to drop towards the earth. Allow it to pass through layers of matter. Allow it to pass down into the earth.

When you have gone down a little way, allow your awareness sphere to bounce back up to its "normal" place here and now.

Repeat this process several times: allow your awareness sphere to travel down into the earth and bounce back up. You will find that you reach different levels, different depths, before you naturally bounce back up.

You may also find periods of time where all motion halts and you get a clearer sense of that level before motion resumes again.

But whether you stop or not, keep on bouncing your awareness sphere down and back.

Until we once more focus on the sensations of here and now and feel the breath coming in and out.......

Roots of Knowing

The energy of any answer, inspiration or illumination exists all around us. We have only to reach out at the appropriate level of awareness and allow the energy to flow into us. This technique holds part of the mind in alertness whilst the rest of the awareness seeks out what it is looking for. The stretching of awareness makes us more attuned to the greater interactions that energy makes.

Sit upright and become aware of the very top of your head.

Frame your intention of knowing (the subject matter, question etc.). Imagine that you are suspended from the very top of your head and relax your body from this point downwards.

Take time to focus on the top of your head. Make sure the attachment is strong. You can visualise it as a fishing line hooked into your skull, a line of light, like the sepals of a hazelnut grasping your skull, or like the calyx of a flower, where your body is the flower.

When you have established an image that feels secure for you, take a moment to dream of a sound that this point of contact at the top of your head makes. It might be a vowel sound or it may be more complicated. It may be a note or some other noise. Trust that your inner mind will come up with the correct sound.

Allow the sound to continue like a mantra at the point where the "suspended line" joins your head. This is important to help keep a portion of your attention focused here as well as elsewhere.

Keep the mantra or sound going easily so it becomes automatic - if you notice that you have stopped the sound whilst being distracted, just easily re-introduce it back into your thoughts. It will be easily possible to keep the sound going whilst moving awareness around.

Having established the sound at the top of the head, your point of awareness in the mind notices the draw of gravity.

Let it pull part of your awareness down towards the earth — dream it like a seed putting down a long, leader root or a stream of water flowing from its source.

Extend your moving awareness further down into the earth. The root or stream of awareness will not spread out much but will focus on the downward pull.

At some point your awareness will come to a halt as if the root has reached bedrock. It will go no deeper - at this level you will find the information you require. Frame your intention once more.

As your roots or streams of awareness slowly spread outwards you will become conscious of other roots or streams around you. You will connect with some of these. Once connection or contact has been made, allow the energy of the answer you seek to flow back up your threads of awareness up into your body.

It may concentrate in certain areas (such as the main chakra points). This is all right. Then continue to allow the energy to travel up to the crown, to your attachment point, to your conscious awareness where the energy can take the shape of thoughts and is able to be understood. It may be a vague change of energy, or verbal thoughts, or pictures, and so on. Assimilation may take time. Understanding may take longer!

Feel the presence of the energy in your mind and allow it to move into your memory centres.

Acknowledge and thank the source of the answer or illumination and gently bring back your extended awareness, back to the bounds of your physical body.
Take a few moments to gently release the head attachment point, and as it were, sink back into your chair.

Make notes of your experiences and record any possible interpretations.

Among the Giants

In the spring of 1997 we were lucky enough to be able to visit some of the redwood groves of Northern California. Most of the forest there is secondary growth - the original trees having been felled years ago. Even these trees are still impressive in height, especially where they cluster around the cliff-like hulks of the rotting remains of an ancient parent tree. A few small areas of woodland, which were mostly privately owned and so protected from indiscriminate felling, consist of primary growth - the original forest that existed before Westerners arrived. These contain the Old Groves of truly giant trees. These sequoia, or coastal redwoods, inhabit the protected valleys of the Coastal Ranges. On a bright morning in late March we headed from the fresh coastal breezes inland. As we climbed through the hills temperature and humidity soared, a reminder that beyond the mountain ranges lay vast areas of desert.

It is not until one is among the trees that the change of scale becomes apparent. Quite suddenly familiar visual cues become misleading. Humans become dwarfs in a giant world. It is very easy to imagine ancient dinosaurs moving between the trees and ferns. Delicate white and pink petalled trillium grew upon the sandy floor of the grove and everywhere streams meandered between the great trunks. Redwood foliage is quite delicate and allows considerable light to filter down to the ground. Even so, one only ever gets a partial view of the giant trees - either their green crowns in the distance, or a close-up of the massive lower trunks with fibrous, ridged bark spiralling around. Even where trees have fallen it is hard to take in the dimensions, for they stretch into the distance like straight roads. This is no place to be in a storm, for the forest floor is littered with fallen branches stuck like spears into the ground. A fall of several hundred feet makes the smallest twig a dangerous projectile. Many trees have blackened and hollowed out bases from the numerous forest fires and lightning strikes they have endured over the centuries.

As we moved further into the Grove there was a deepening sense of quiet stability and communion. There was a feeling that communication, some teaching or message, was being imparted at a non-conscious level. When there was the time and opportunity to return to the experience and record the impressions the following ideas and thoughts were retrieved.

Balancing the Elements

The first impression of teaching from the redwoods contrasted their state of being with that of humanity. The great trees have survived the centuries and millennia by balancing all the elements and by learning to stand still. To them humanity always seems to have the fire element predominant. We are always consuming and moving on. We cannot remain still in our present state of being because the fiery nature in us feels stifled. And so, like a wild-fire on the forest floor we rush by devouring all the dried grass and fern, not realising that a far more nutritious sustenance is all around. Our attention and perceptions hardly register the great beings also sharing our world and from whom we could learn to slow down and see more completely.

So the first lesson of the sequoia is: reconnect with the elements within and around you. A simple ceremony, ritual or meditation to acknowledge their balanced presence will begin to restore harmony. The symbol of the medicine wheel or the Celtic cross can be used, and a representative item for each element placed around you. Or else combine all elements in one focus for visual contemplation. For example, the earth element can be represented by a large bowl filled with earth, sand or pebbles. In this, a smaller bowl could be placed filled with water. A floating candle could be lit to represent the element of fire and incense to indicate air. Take time to absorb the qualities of each element as they appear within you and as they appear in the world. See how they relate to your experiences, emotions and thoughts.

Tiðes of Time

The second teaching of the sequoia is to learn a greater perspective on time and the tides of life. Each expression of life, be it a civilisation or a species, is like a wave on the shore. Life continues, wave after wave. Each one will wax and wane to be replaced by another. New waves will advance and retreat across the ages. We appear to be living at a time of great changes, much of it apparently caused or accelerated by the way humanity has chosen to live. This too, will change, and though we can do little to alter the momentum of the great tides of the Universe, we can choose how we live in the present.

Recognition

How we choose to live may well depend upon our ability to recognise the intelligence around us in this world. Time and technology has been spent looking for other life in the Universe when we haven't learned to interpret the intelligence of the life that is all around us. Only when we have learned the one, will the other become revealed to us. If we cannot see the great life-force of the sequoia, the yew, the oak, we are throwing away diamonds to look for pennies.

One worlð

The sequoias are not American trees - they belong to the Earth. The Amazon forest, the Siberian forest, the yews and oaks, the small spindles and elders all belong to the Earth as a single whole. In the same way, we human beings belong to

the Earth. The presence of each enriches the whole, the absence of any impoverishes all.

Learning to Learn

The message of the redwoods was communicated in their great silence. Many teachings from trees and other spirits are by transferral of gestalts rather than in linear language. Robert A. Monroe describes such communication as a "rote", a mental book or recording complete with emotional and sensory patterns that is transmitted from one mind to another. Rote is an acronym of Related Organised Thought Energy. In his exploration of the subtle universe Monroe soon discovered that communication by rote was the norm among every species except human. If you have a wish to communicate with the spirits of trees then go with a willing quietness. Take time just to be in the presence and receive packets of information for later unravelling and investigation.

To the Heart

In the end the profundity of a communication will not depend on its length or complexity. It is in the degree to which it affects the heart. Ultimately it doesn't make any difference whether it is a spirit-being or the Self speaking, so long as the message provides illumination and clarifies our perception of how things are. Such communications will very often be impossible to relate to others in any meaningful way. In the end we cannot learn revelation, we each must have the direct experience itself.

We hope that this book has given some clues and pointers to those who wish to experience and learn from the Tree Kingdoms, their spirits and teachers. We can best work towards a greater understanding of the interdependence of all life on this planet, and hope that we will always have the presence of the great trees to guide us.

"Let the dawn come.
Let all the people and all the creatures have peace.
Let all things live happily.
We are the children of the sun,
We are the children of time
And we are the travellers in space.
May all the songs awaken,
May all the dancers awaken.
May all the people and all things
Live in peace.
For you are the valleys,
You are the mountains,
You are the trees,
You are the very air you breathe."

(From Don Alejandro Cirilo Oxlaj Peres, quoting the prophecies of the Mia, the Mayan Grandfathers).

Reaðíng Guíðe

Introduction
Anderson, W & Hicks, C (1998) *"Green Man, the Archetype of our Oneness with the Earth"* now reprinted from: Compass Books, Fakenham, England
Maclean, D: *"To Hear the Angels Sing"* Findhorn Press. Scotland
- *"The Findhorn Garden"* (1988) Findhorn Community, Findhorn Press, Scotland

Tree Essences: Magic Mirrors
Barnard, J (Edit) (1994) *"Collected Writings of Edward Bach"* Ashgrove Pub, Bath
Barnard, J & Barnard M: (1988, 1995) *" The Healing Herbs of Edward Bach"* Ashgrove Publishers, Bath, UK
Rudd,C: (1998) *"Flower Essences - an Illustrated Guide"* Element, Shaftesbury UK
Schiff, M: (1994) *"The Memory of Water"* Thorsons Publishers. London
Titchiner,R; Monk, S; Potter, R; Staines,P: (1997) *"New Vibrational Flower Essences of Britain and Ireland"* Waterlily Books. Halesworth, Suffolk, UK

Trees of Possibilities
Adams, G & Whicher, O: (1982) *"The Plant Between Sun and Earth"* Shambhala Pub. Colorado, USA
Coats, C: (1996) *"Living Energies"* Gateway Books, Bath, UK
Pendell, D: (1995) *" Pharmako/poeia"* Mercury House Pub. San Francisco, USA

Spirits, Devas, Fairies or What?
Altman, N: (1995) *"The Deva Handbook"* Destiny Books, Vermont, USA
Bloom, W: (1986) *"Devas, Fairies and Angels"* Gothic Image Pub. Glastonbury UK
Cowan, T: (1996) *"Shamanism as a Spiritual Practice for Daily Life"* The Crossing Press, Freedom CA, USA

DeKorne,J: (1994) " *Psychedelic Shamanism*" Loompanics Pub. WA, USA

Eliade, M: (1964, 1989) *"Shamanism"* Penguin Pub. London

Harner, M: (1980, 1990) *"The Way of the Shaman"* Harper Collins, USA

Hodson, G: (1925) *"Fairies at Work and at Play"* Theosophical Pub. London

Matthews, C: (1995) *"Singing The Soul Back Home"* Element, Shaftesbury, UK

Matthews, C & Matthews, J: (1986) *"The Western Way"* Penguin Pub., London

Monroe, R: (1994) *"Ultimate Journey"* Doubleday, New York, USA

Pogacnik, M: (1995) *"Nature Spirits & Elemental Beings"* Findhorn Press, Scotland.

The Celt, The Shaman and The Tree

Bear, J: (1997) " *Ayahuasca Shamanism: An Interview with Don Agustin Rivas -Vasquez"* Shaman's Drum. No.44, California, USA

Blaen, Dr A: (1995) *"Devon's Sacred Grove"* Bridge House, Crediton, UK

Kindred, G: (1997) *"The Tree Ogham"* self-pub, Matlock, Derbyshire, UK

Matthews, C & Matthews, J: (1994) *"Encyclopaedia of Celtic Wisdom"* Element Pub. Shaftesbury, UK

Matthews, J: (1991) *"Taliesin"* Aquarian Press. London

Naddair, K: (1987) *"Keltic Folk & Faerie Tales"* Century Hutchinson, London

Philpot, J: (1897,1994 ed) *"The Sacred Tree"* Llanerch Pub. Lampeter, Wales

Meeting The Spirits - Methods of Communication - The Sense Fields

Aburrow, Y: (1993) *"The Enchanted Forest"* Capall Bann, Chieveley, UK

Fries, J: (1996) *"Seidways"* Mandrake, Oxford, UK

Grieve, M: (1931, 1994 ed) *"A Modern Herbal"* Tiger Books, London

Heselton, P. (1998) *Magical Guardians* Capall Bann Publishing, Chieveley UK

Kindred, G: (1995) *"The Sacred Tree"* self-pub, Matlock, Derbyshire, UK

Meeting The Spirits - Listening to Silence
Steinbrecher, E: (1982) *"The Inner Guide Meditation"* Aquarian Press, UK

Stewart,R: (1992) *"Earth Light"* Mercury Publ. USA

Stewart,R: (1992) *"Power Within The Land"* Mercury Publ. USA

Tree Teacher Techniques
Goodman, F: (1990) *"Where the Spirits Ride the Wind"* Indiana University Press, USA

Gore, B: (1995) *"Ecstatic Body Postures"* Bear & Co. Santa Fe, USA

Lilly, S & Lilly, S: (1997) *"Crystal Doorways"* Capall Bann Publishing, Chieveley, UK

Rael, J: (1993) *"Being and Vibration"* Council Oak Books, Oklahoma, USA

Rael, J: (1993) *"Tracks of Dancing Light"* Element Pub. Shaftesbury, UK

Yew - The Root of Power
Chetan, A & Brueton, D: (1994) *"The Sacred Yew"* Penguin Pub. London

Hartzell,H: (1991) *"The Yew Tree"* Hulogosi, Oregon USA

Holly - Fire of compassion
Matthews, J: (1990) *"Gawain, Knight of the Goddess"* Aquarian, London

Stone, B: (1959) *"Sir Gawain and The Green Knight"* Penguin, London

FOUR TREES: FOUR SPIRITS

" sound sequences for meditation and trance"

by Nemed

(James Binning, Simon Lilly,
Sue Lilly)

Four pieces of music designed to take you beyond normal consciousness and into attunement with specific spirits of the Tree Kingdoms.

Each side contains two 15 minute sound meditations that use particular note sequences and chants

Side A: 1. Yew   2. Elm
Side B: I. Oak   2. Holly with Ivy

Released through
ANEW MUSIC,
47 High Street, Harborne, Birmingham, B17 9NT
Tel: 0121 428 3138 email: drspear@fabs67.freeserve.co.uk

Tape or CD available from ANEW Music or
Green Man Tree Essences
c/o MCS, PO Box 6 Exminster, Exeter, Devon EX6 8YE
Tel: 01392 832005 email: info@greenmantrees.demon.co.uk

A selection of other Capall Bann titles. Free catalogue available.

Tree: Essence of Healing   by Simon & Sue Lilly

The tree is the epitome of balance and stability. Each tree is a window through which we can experience the seamless wholeness of creation, enabling us to re-integrate and repair those aspects of ourselves that have become isolated and damaged. Through the powerful medium of tree essences we have access to the great healing potential of the Tree Kingdoms. This volume explores the qualities of wholeness that trees and tree essences can bring back to the Human Kingdom. Included is a survey of essences and how they work; different ways of healing with trees; an exploration of trees and their healing qualities. This is a companion volume to "*Tree: Essence, Spirit and Teacher*" and is the second in the "*Tree Seer*" series. ISBN 18163 0816   £14.95

Magical Guardians - Exploring the Spirit and Nature of Trees
by Philip Heselton

This is a book about trees, but a book with a difference, for it acknowledges trees to be wise beings who can teach us much if we approach them in the right way. This book shows how to go about it, revealing the origins of our awakening interest in - and love for - trees. Trees have a spiritual nature, and opening up to this spirit has been a constant feature in human society. Through practical guidance, this book gives hints on how we can make that contact for ourselves. The personalities of the ancient trees - our Magical Guardians - are explored, and the book reveals how we can start to acquire some of their deeper meanings. ISBN 1 86163 057 3   £11.95

The Enchanted Forest - The Magical Lore of Trees   by Yvonne Aburrow

Fascinating & truly unique - a comprehensive guide to the magical, medicinal & craft uses, mythology, folklore, symbolism & weatherlore of trees. There are chapters on trees in myth & legend, tree spirits, trees in ritual magic, trees & alphabets (runes & Ogham) & weather lore. These chapters are followed by a comprehensive 'herbal index' with in-depth coverage of individual trees from acacia to aspen, wayfaring tree to willow. Profusely illustrated. "..*wonderful insight...easy to read...very informative, a lovely enchanting book*". *Touchstone magazine of OBOD* ISBN 1898307 083   £10.95

Healing Stones   by Sue Phillips

There is an increasing interest in crystals, from collectors, magicians and healers, with correspondingly increased pressure on our earth's precious resources. Healing stones sets out a method that works on the same principles as crystal healing, but makes use of stones and pebbles that can be found lying around almost anywhere. Here is a chance to learn what any child knows instinctively - stones are magical. ISBN 186163 034 4   £8.95   **R98**

Crystal Doorways   by Sue & Simon Lilly

Not yet another volume telling you everything you wanted to know about crystals. It focuses on a very particular system of using crystals and colour to bring about changes in your consciousness and an increasing understanding of the energy world around us. Developed as a result of running many courses, 'Crystal Doorways' gives a clear, immediately understandable, system of "energy nets" using small, easily obtainable crystals. These energy nets are simple, usually only requiring small tumbled stones, but they can be extremely powerful. Each net is illustrated and described in full, with what stones to use, where to place them, potential uses and background information. ISBN 1898307 98 9   £11.95

FREE DETAILED CATALOGUE

A detailed illustrated catalogue is available on request, SAE or International Postal Coupon appreciated. **Titles can be ordered direct from Capall Bann, post free in the UK** (cheque or PO with order) or from good bookshops and specialist outlets. Titles currently available include:

Auguries and Omens - The Magical Lore of Birds by Yvonne Aburrow
Caer Sidhe - Celtic Astrology and Astronomy by Michael Bayley
Celtic Lore & Druidic Ritual by Rhiannon Ryall
Earth Magic by Margaret McArthur
Enchanted Forest - The Magical Lore of Trees by Yvonne Aburrow
Familiars - Animal Powers of Britain by Anna Franklin
Healing Book (The) by Chris Thomas
Handbook For Pagan Healers by Liz Joan
Healing Homes by Jennifer Dent
Herbcraft - Shamanic & Ritual Use of Herbs by S Lavender & A Franklin
In Search of Herne the Hunter by Eric Fitch
Magical Guardians - Exploring the Spirit & Nature of Trees by P. Heselton
Magical Lore of Cats by Marion Davies
Magical Lore of Herbs by Marion Davies
Patchwork of Magic by Julia Day
Psychic Self Defence - Real Solutions by Jan Brodie
Sacred Animals by Gordon MacLellan
Sacred Grove - The Mysteries of the Forest by Yvonne Aburrow
Sacred Geometry by Nigel Pennick
Sacred Lore of Horses The by Marion Davies
Secret Places of the Goddess by Philip Heselton
Talking to the Earth by Gordon Maclellan
Taming the Wolf - Full Moon Meditations by Steve Hounsome
VORTEX - The End of History, by Mary Russell

Capall Bann is owned and run by people actively involved in many of the areas in which we publish. Our list is expanding rapidly so do contact us for details on the latest releases.

Capall Bann Publishing, Freshfields, Chieveley, Berks, RG20 8TF